Luxury Player

Luxury Player: My Story

JOE COLE

With Sam Wallace

SEVEN DIALS

First published in Great Britain in 2025 by Seven Dials,
an imprint of The Orion Publishing Group Ltd
Carmelite House, 50 Victoria Embankment
London EC4Y 0DZ

An Hachette UK Company

The authorised representative in the EEA is Hachette Ireland,
8 Castlecourt Centre, Dublin 15, D15 XTP3,
Ireland (email: info@hbgi.ie)

3 5 7 9 10 8 6 4 2

A CIP catalogue record for this book is
available from the British Library.

ISBN (Hardback) 978 1 3996 3734 3
ISBN (Ebook) 978 1 3996 3736 7
ISBN (Audio) 978 1 3996 3737 4

Typeset by CC Book Production
Printed in Great Britain by Clays Ltd, Elcograf S.p.A.

www.orionbooks.co.uk

In memory of George Cole, 1954–2016
(he wouldn't have read it,
but he would have enjoyed the audiobook)

Contents

1

The Best Goal I Ever Scored

In my head, there was music playing. It had been there ever since I started playing football, whenever the pressure was on and, at first, I thought it was odd. I tried to make it stop but the music would come back. A song I had been listening to recently, sometimes just a tune that had snagged in my mind. I used to think that it meant that I was not concentrating, and then I came to realise that the music meant I was concentrating. As I got older as a professional footballer, I came to make my peace with it. The sports psychologists I consulted over the years were generally unconcerned. They told me not to worry about it.

The sun was shining on 29 April 2006, at Stamford Bridge. In my mind, a tune was playing which would have told me all was well with the world, although on that day I would not have needed a great deal of reassurance. This already felt like one of the best afternoons of my life. Now from a vantage point almost twenty years on it seems even more so. Tracking the map of success, trophies, injuries, finals won and lost, opportunities grasped and those missed, perhaps it was a high point. Either way, you have to start somewhere.

I was twenty-four. I played for Chelsea and England. Some had decided I was not the footballer they had expected to emerge from the puppyish promise of the child prodigy they had first identified. Yet here I was, a first choice for my club, and also for my country, despite Sven-Göran Eriksson's original reluctance. Chelsea had begun to feel like the centre of football's world in mid-2006. We had been Premier League champions once already. Now we were about to be crowned Premier League champions again. And exquisitely, here to suffer it all first-hand for the second time in twelve months were Manchester United, the very team who had seemed immovable at the top of English football for so long. The challenge that day was very simple. Beat United and win the league.

A warm spring day and on the pitch I squinted into the sun. I have terrible eyes. I wore contact lenses my entire career, and title celebrations were always a problem because of the volume of champagne being sprayed about. My sensitive eyes would sting like mad if I got champagne in them. The solution should have just been to open my mouth and make sure it went in there instead, although here comes another confession. I hate the taste of champagne. Even the really good stuff. For many years, if I was at a restaurant with my wife Carly it would not be uncommon for a Chelsea fan to send over a glass of champagne. I would make a play of raising it appreciatively in their direction before discreetly handing it over to Carly.

That day in April 2006, during the on-pitch warm-up, I was already thinking about the post-match celebrations. The whole Cole clan was there. Carly, my wife, and my parents Sue and George Cole – my greatest supporters who had followed me all over the world. Also, my brother Nicky and sister Charly and a large collection of friends, cousins, aunts, uncles plus all their assorted wives, girlfriends, husbands, boyfriends, casual acquaintances, lovers. I had invited them all. I had spent thousands of pounds on extra tickets because these are the days you want people to remember. And anyway, you can't take it with you.

But first: concentrate, Joe. The music playing in my mind took over again and I looked around at the stadium, as the pitch was cleared of all the usual pre-match ephemera. Corporate guests ushered off. Cameraman with the mobile camera retreating to the sidelines. Kitman with a great bundle of tracksuit tops. This place had changed. I grew up in Camden Town, north London, and first came to Stamford Bridge as a nine-year-old. I was brought with my friend Ben Burton by his father Rick and now, as a player before games, I would look over to the West Stand where we would sit all those years ago as fans. Only the Chelsea fans of that era will truly be able to recall the discomfort of those uniquely rudimentary concrete seats known as 'the benches'.

I know I should tell you about my great childhood wonder at seeing the green of the pitch for the first time, or being captivated by the noise and the fury of English football. And, trust me, I loved all that. But what I most remember was the fantastic sandwiches that Rick used to bring for us, wrapped up in cellophane for our half-time snack. Yes, I remember the football too, and the smell that hung in the air, that was still there in 2006. The smell of the cigarettes, back in the days when you could still smoke anywhere you liked, and the great gritty fug of London in the April sunshine.

But, anyway, back to the game – that game against United. One game for the Premier League. My third major trophy in the space of two years. Focus the mind, Joe.

I was up against Gary Neville, and – what can I say? – I wanted to win that battle. I played off the left, although I am right-footed, which was where our manager José Mourinho wanted me more often than not. These days it would scarcely raise an eyebrow to ask a creative wide player to cut inside on his stronger foot, although sadly in 2006, English football was still taking its first baby steps into a new era of greater tactical sophistication. When it came to the England team that seemed a problem – obsessed as the nation was at the time with finding a left-footer for the left side. I had spent five years trying to convince three different England managers that I was the man for the job, but by now, with a World Cup in the summer, I seemed finally to have won the argument.

First half. In short, Gary had a decent game. I even felt like he had marginally got the better of me but back in the dressing room I knew we were not going to lose this game. We were already one goal up because William Gallas – Willy – had made a near-post run at a corner and nodded one in for what seemed like about the hundredth time in his career. I would watch him do this again and again in disbelief. He made the same run almost every corner, and there were still some teams who watched him do so dumbstruck, as if he were doing it for the first time. Sometimes I think we give footballers too little credit. And then I watch players fail to stop an opponent who does the same old move week after week and it makes me think – maybe there is something wrong with us.

In the dressing room at half-time, José did not need to say much. Over the last twenty-two months he had at times used the whip with us, and at others the gentle pat on the snout. But everyone knew it. United were not going to score two against us, even with Cristiano Ronaldo and Wayne Rooney on the pitch. Wayne had already smashed my teammate John Terry in a tackle. Wayne was angry and later that afternoon he would break the metatarsal bone that messed up his World Cup – and mine – that summer. The course of English football would turn again in that moment. Much later, after his playing career was over, Wayne would admit that his fury at another Chelsea league title prompted him to wear his long studs that day to try to injure someone. Unfortunately for all of us in the England team, it was himself he injured when those studs reduced his mobility. That's football. A strange game of strategy and high emotion, with all those unintended consequences.

In the next couple of years, serious injuries would take their toll on me too. My life and my career would change for ever, but on this day when I walked out for that second half I was doing what all footballers tend to do. I was not looking much further than the next few minutes. The next touch of the ball, the next dip of the shoulder, or sight of goal. Did I know that something special was coming? I knew that I felt great. I was going to be Chelsea's player of the year, or at least I thought that was the case. I was in a period of form that would last four blissful years. It all felt thrilling, the music playing in my head, my family and my friends in the stand, and somewhere in the stadium that big trophy with the blue and white ribbons already attached.

I had a chance early in the second half. A change of direction, and I bent one at the top corner. Edwin van der Sar, great goalkeeper that he was, flung himself at it and got something on the ball. The size of these top goalkeepers is something else. To beat them with a shot it has to be something hit hard, or hit sharp, or hit early, or with fade, or with curl, or straight as anything. Just something with a bit of magic.

And then, my moment came.

I have watched the goal a thousand times. The first part I feel is testament to my life as a child footballer, raw and uncoached. I played every minute I had spare – which was a lot – all over Camden Town, Kentish Town, Somers Town, in that pocket of north London council estates and concrete pitches caged in with high fences. I played against older boys and bigger boys. I played against skilful boys and dangerous boys. And every moment I was refining the art of what would become my trade. Taking the ball in difficult situations and wriggling out of those difficult situations with nothing but my touch, my instinct and my still fairly undeveloped physicality to help me. I know all footballers say this, but it becomes a kind of muscle memory. That instinct of when to stop, when to turn, when to use one defender's bulk against his teammate. And that is what happened here at Stamford Bridge, although it played out so quickly that I barely even knew I had done it.

I took a position off our striker Didier Drogba for the knock-down and behind me my old West Ham teammate Rio Ferdinand was not tight enough. The same had happened with Rio the season before and I had almost got away from him. At this point Rio was one of the best defenders in the world and he knew me well, and because he knew me well, he knew I was unpredictable. But he did manage to move me away from goal towards a man who would become another Premier League great, Nemanja Vidić. Vidić had just jumped for the ball with Didier. I could sense what was happening in that moment. Ferdinand and Vidić were tired and fed up and they just wanted the other to deal with me. Another United defender, Mikaël Silvestre, was in the vicinity. Three excellent international defenders. But for a moment they hesitated, unsure who took precedence. We had all converged at this moment at the end of a long, tiring season. The difference was I was minutes from winning the league and had a feeling I was going to seize the moment.

Although I cannot remember any of this, the footage reminds me that I backed into Vidić and turned to face Rio and the goal. I used Vidić as leverage to push off. It happened so fast – a series of touches, movements, pivots, that were being dictated from some primal part of my footballing brain. As I turned to face goal, the most critical touch of the ball was coming up next. It was perfect. It took me slightly to the right past Silvestre, and past Ferdinand. At that moment, as if from some kind of revelry of drag-backs and feints, it felt like I came around into full consciousness. And from this point I remember it all clearly. There were three Manchester United defenders behind me, and just Van der Sar coming off his goal-line. Now I was making decisions consciously as one might decide what to have for breakfast or where to park the car. The old wisdom has it that time stands still in these moments before goalscoring. But that's not quite right. You do feel time passing, although you know you have time – and even a little can feel like a lot.

Two options. I'm in the right channel so I can sweep it across him, past his right hand into the left corner. Or I go near post. No space to take it around him. As previously established, Van der Sar was a big bloke. No matter, when I connected I knew it was in. The speed of it, the sharp upward trajectory. All of it felt right. It was unsavable.

Football is about moments – easy to say, but it's true. Chelsea fans remember this moment and when they stop me in the street it is this goal that they mention, my dribble through one of the best defences English football has ever known. It helps that it was also the second in a 3–0 win over Manchester United to win our second Premier League title in two years, on a sunny day at Stamford Bridge. England fans are likely to say the goal I would score fifty-three days later in Cologne against Sweden at the World Cup finals. I played seven hundred-odd games over almost two decades, but it comes down to the moments.

THE BEST GOAL I EVER SCORED

I am sure for Rooney, or Ronaldo or Lionel Messi, there are many more moments that their admirers bring up, but in the end that is what a career can come down to. The bits people really remember.

When you have scored the best goal of your life, it is not necessarily something you know straight away. The first part of it had happened in what I suppose was a bit of a trance. Not even the music in my head playing, just an intensity of concentration that possesses you for a few seconds. A blank section of the tape. Then by the corner flag celebrating I got a bit of the vibe. Willy was shouting in his cool French accent, 'What an effing goooool, Coley!' As for Didier, in moments when he was really impressed by something I had done, Didier would call me 'Zizou'. And he was calling me Zizou in that moment.

A few minutes later we were back in our positions for kick-off and the tune was playing in my head again. I felt calm. I felt great. I would set up the last goal for our Portuguese centre-back Ricardo Carvalho. When I gave him the ball, I remember wondering what Ricky was doing so far up the pitch. My mind drifted back to West Ham, the place where much of my footballing education took place under our youth team coach, the late great Peter Brabrook. He would angrily chastise young centre-halves for any wild run forward in search of glory. He used to call them Buffalo Bill runs. As young players we giggled at his indignation. We were impressed by his passion. We adopted that description for any defender caught marauding out of territory. Here was Ricky, the title secured, granting himself one valedictory Buffalo Bill run.

West Ham was where I was educated. I did not come from a family where football was a passion. I did not play an organised game with refs and shinpads and corner flags until I was about eleven. My dad George never played the game and did not really understand it – he just knew that I loved it. West Ham gave me the kind of grounding that you perhaps could not give a child now. Not only did they train me in how to play the game, they let me hang around the first team dressing room whenever I wanted. In there, I heard all the f-words and the c-words uttered in defeat. I saw the joy and the brotherhood in victory. As I swept up the mud brought in on the studs from the heavy pitches of a previous era, I would listen to men like Steve Lomas and Neil Ruddock talk about the players they had faced. About how they had come off better or come off worse, and I learnt a lot. I studied how Harry Redknapp would communicate with his players. Not always what he said, but how he said it, and I would take note of how inspired it made me feel. I was just there to pick up the muddy shorts and jock-straps. So, God knows what it was doing to those who were actually playing.

Then within a few years, I would be mopping the senior changing room at the training ground at Chadwell Heath one day and Harry's assistant Frank Lampard senior would ask me if I owned a suit. When I said yes, he told me to put it on that Saturday and come to Upton Park at 1.30 p.m. because I was in the first team squad. The memory of my professional debut always stirs something in me. Joy, excitement, and maybe a bit of confusion. Even at seventeen years old I wondered if reporting at 1.30 p.m. was a bit late for a 3 p.m. kick-off. But that was part of the joy of playing for West Ham. They liked to keep it casual.

When you know you are going to win a league title some of the old rules go out of the window. My afternoon against Manchester United ended when I was substituted with ten minutes to go. I came over to the touchlines, in the stadium where I had watched football as a child, and all stood to applaud me. I suppose there are few days quite as good in a career. On the benches behind Mourinho, the staff and players were starting to discreetly pass around beers and quietly ease the corks out of champagne bottles. The thirty-sixth game of another epic season was almost at its end and we just couldn't wait to start the celebrations. The television cameras never picked it up – and if those on the United benches saw it, then they never let on. The Premier League title was back in our hands. United had been beaten again. These are the moments when you feel like raising a glass and toasting your very good fortune.

Not all days were like that. But football gave me a life so far removed from the one in which I was born the son of a single mother living in a council flat in north London in November 1981, that now, in my forties, I felt that I needed to sort it all out in my head and write it down. How did it happen? Why did it happen? As a husband to Carly, who I've shared more than twenty years of my life with, and father of three lovely children, I feel a sense of overwhelming gratitude. Not only for my wife and children but for the parents I had and the life I have lived. The comfort that a life in professional football in the twenty-first century can bestow upon you feels a long way from where it started for me. And then soon after that as a child who was promoted in a weird way – by some elements of the media and also unwittingly by various football people – as a kind of prodigy.

There was something else on my mind too, constantly from my childhood to my early twenties. I also want to tell you about how football – English football – felt different for me. For much of my life it felt like I was in the wrong place, trying to play a different tune. It was there as a schoolboy shoehorned into a coaching system that still favoured big lads winning second balls. It was there at the old Football Association school of excellence at Lilleshall, a wonderful Hogwarts for teenage footballers in Shropshire, which gave me two very happy years. Yet even there they tried to bend me into a certain shape of player and I resisted. It was there at West Ham when we were either fighting for Premier League survival or fighting to get into the top six (you name it, we did it). I felt that way, especially with the England teams of Sven and then later Fabio Capello. I knew something was wrong with the way the team was playing and that we could have been doing it better. I was watching teams like the Barcelona of the late 1990s play a kind of football that seemed to me closer to the truth of how the game should be.

On top of that I was aware that people had a perception of me that was plain wrong. There was a mistrust of what I was and what I represented. It was the usual vague notions. Gives the ball away too easily. Defensively suspect. None of that was right. I worked very hard at my defensive game and under José, let me tell you, that part was non-negotiable. Had I not done it he would not have picked me and, contrary to popular opinion, after some early turbulence he did pick me. By the end, I was so important to José that I would always be in the team when I was fit, and sometimes even when I wasn't. There was also a misunderstanding of what it took to play a kind of game that people enjoyed watching. That you had to take risks at times and be prepared to lose the ball in order to have a chance of creating the moments when you were successful. By the time I had the courage to be able to summon the right words to make my case, it was too late.

That is where the title comes from: luxury player.

I have no wish to be ungrateful. I just think it needs saying: the Premier League I watch now as a pundit is light years ahead of the one I played in during the late 1990s and 2000s. The transformation means that the game feels a friendlier place for players like me. It settled an old argument I was having in my head when I was a young player – the one that said, it didn't have to be the way it was for years. It doesn't always have to be 4-4-2 and a distrust of the creative player – often me, but others too – who wants to take the ball in difficult situations. We have a much better understanding now of how risk interacts with reward. We don't just vilify the attacking player who makes a mistake trying to do something difficult. Although when it comes to mistakes, I made many fewer than you might think. Be prepared for me to quote my pass completion statistics at you.

As a kid I found it easy to play football and hard to concentrate on schoolwork. At Lilleshall, I saved the money I was given for my train tickets home to London and I used it to pay someone to do my homework. But when someone puts a ball in front of me I know exactly what to do. Football was my way of understanding the world and I got to know it intimately from an early age. I can tell a lot about your personality from the way you pass that ball to me – how confident you might be feeling. How strong you are. Even whether it's an act of generosity, or you just want it back immediately when you've got yourself in a better position to shoot. But football is strange. Out there on the pitch the other factors of life don't stop and my mind was always restless. I found little details burrowing into my consciousness when I was playing. I tried to push them to the edges of my thoughts and tell myself to focus on the game but then maybe, like the music in my head, these were the moments that told me I was focusing.

The first time I scored for West Ham, in a League Cup tie away at Birmingham City in November 1999, for a while I could not shift from my mind the droplets of rain that fell from the net as the ball hit it. Or later the way Roy Keane's breathing changed when he was really angry. Or in those early days at Upton Park, the sound of thousands of seats snapping shut as people stood up when I slipped past an opponent and ran at goal. I believe strongly that stadiums sounded different before we all had phones distracting us. The fans were in the moment. There was an immediacy of reaction that feels just so slightly delayed now, or an intensity that has had the edges knocked off.

In the early days at West Ham when I scored I would run into the crowd and I would be engulfed in all these embraces and bodies piling on around me – the supporters in the first few rows, and then my teammates too. I found the experience mesmerising. Then, as the game started again and I tried to focus on my job and the music would be playing in my head, I would find myself wondering – what are all those people doing now? Did they spill their drinks? Did they lose a bag in the chaos? Were they talking about that moment that had felt so intense? And then I would chastise myself for letting my mind wander and force myself to think about the game. The sound I really loved was when I did a piece of skill that I knew only a few players could do. I would say the reaction is universal, whatever the stadium and wherever that stadium is. The sound hangs in the air deliciously for just a fraction of a second. Somewhere between a gasp of surprise and a purr of approval. I lived for that moment of validation. I suppose I also knew that there were many players who went their whole careers and never heard that sound for them.

I won three Premier League titles, I played in a Champions League final, I played at three World Cups. Don't forget West Ham's legendary Intertoto Cup triumph of 1999. I was there for most of the great moments of the 2000s at Chelsea, and for a few of them, like that day in April 2006, it was me at the centre of it. I won a lot. Maybe I didn't win enough for some people. But it was a wonderful time. A beautiful life and, yes, the money was great, although in the end it was about the football. The only thing I knew how to do. I can tell you how I got there, which was not as straightforward as some people assume, and about all the characters along the way. About what it is like out there on the grass. With the ball at your toes and Rio or Carles Puyol on your shoulder and all those faces in the crowd turned towards you in expectation. I want to tell you about all of it. We will have to go back to the Camden Town of the 1990s, cradle of Britpop, home to its stars and, from my childhood perspective, still full of rough pubs populated by dangerous characters. We will stop off at my dad George's market stalls in Kentish Town and Burnt Oak. To Harry's West Ham where Paolo Di Canio might want to fight you at half-time or kiss you on both cheeks. We will have to visit the various dysfunctional England camps of Kevin Keegan, Sven, Steve McClaren and Fabio – aka Fabs, Postman Pat, The Man Who Banned Butter. And of course, the Chelsea of the mysterious Roman Abramovich and his revolution in English football.

I can't promise to make sense of it all. The older I get the more it all seems like a bit of a miracle that it came together. But here it is: the life and times of a luxury player.

2

If Verón Gets Number 10,
Joe Won't Sign

No one tells you that on the day you make the biggest transfer of your career you should buy a nice suit for the occasion. Or get your hair cut. Football is like that – people just assume you know and if you don't, well, that's your bad luck. The day I signed for Chelsea I showed up with my dad George at Stamford Bridge. I was in a pair of tracksuit bottoms, a T-shirt and some trainers. George was in what he always wore: one of his colourful Ralph Lauren shirts – a real one, not one from Camden Market – a pair of jeans and some loafers. Dad always wore good shoes. I'll give him that.

We were walking across the car park when we caught sight of the other big Chelsea signing that day, Juan Sebastián Verón. He had an entourage. All of them in suits and sunglasses, looking like a presidential bodyguard, or an Italian football team turning up for a big final. Verón himself looked like you might expect an expensive footballer to look, or a really top-notch hitman. One glance at him and you'd think, yes, that's an £80 million footballer. In those days no one was worth that much although Manchester United had spent the 2003 equivalent of it on him two summers earlier.

On the other hand, I looked like I might have been turning

up to deep-clean the carpets in the club shop. I winced. I should have worn a suit.

I was twenty-one that summer, the captain of relegated West Ham. Not just relegated to the division now known as the Championship, but skint too. Roman Abramovich's spending did not just save Chelsea from financial oblivion that summer, it saved West Ham too. First the chairman Terry Brown sold my teammate Glen Johnson to the new Chelsea owner and then, in August, he sold me. Terry was an accountant from east London who had built a decent business buying up sites that he rented out for caravan holidays. When a Russian oligarch who counted his fortune in billions bought into football, Terry knew the game was up for his generation of club chairmen. You could have the best summer in history for selling caravan pitches and you were not going to compete with that. West Ham had debts and a wage bill it could not afford to pay without big player sales.

This was my first transfer, although there had been what amounted to an auction of my talents around the age of twelve or thirteen when I was invited to play for every club in London. One week I might be in Arsenal's kit, the next in Tottenham's. As a favour to a scout my dad had known in HMP Wormwood Scrubs, Ronnie Joyce, I even ended up playing a game for Millwall, although it has taken me this long to admit that to West Ham fans. Word got beyond London. I played for Everton. I turned out for Manchester United at a tournament at Keele University wearing that classic retro Newton Heath green and gold-style away kit from the early 1990s.

Dad was quite clear with all these clubs. He said that I would go where I was happiest and that money had nothing to do with it, although of course money was always mentioned. Clubs would size us up – two parents and three kids in a

Camden Town council flat – and assume Dad could be bought. But he was adamant that money was not a consideration. My dad could make money one way or another to support his family. That wasn't my job. He just said to me I should go where I felt comfortable. I love him for many, many reasons and they include the way he protected me when others might have seen me as an asset.

In May 1994, when I was twelve, my mum picked up the phone in our flat in Donnington Court on the Clarence Way estate on Castlehaven Road, and said, 'George, there's a man with a Scots accent who wants to talk to you.' I suppose I should not be surprised that Alex Ferguson had called our home phone number. If you were a talented schoolboy footballer in those days you could change your name by deed poll and go into witness protection and Ferguson would probably still turn up at the safehouse with a signed shirt and tickets for Old Trafford. I guess that was one reason why he was so good at his job. Even George Cole, who was unimpressed by football and football people, and frankly didn't know who many of them were, seemed to straighten his back and pay attention. Fergie knew about my game for United at Keele University. He wanted me to sign for United and he had a cunning plan. He had found out that I was a Chelsea fan – nothing he could do about that – but United did have a game coming up against Chelsea later that month. That game happened to be the FA Cup final. He could not get me the Chelsea mascot gig, but he could make it happen that I lead the Manchester United team out. How would I like to try that? Very much, was the answer. Chelsea had not been in a cup final since 1970. Every Chelsea fan had waited a long time for this moment. Tickets for Wembley were scarce. When we discussed it as a family, Dad asked me if, ultimately, I wanted to sign for Manchester

United. No, I said, I did not. Well in that case, Dad said, I don't think we can accept this offer. Dad found someone, a mate of his in the wholesale fruit trade, who had a ticket to sell and was prepared to take me. I saw the final, although not wearing a United kit – which turned out to be a blessing.

As I grew up, week after week, Mum and Dad had been besieged by scouts giving them their business cards on the touchline of my games for Sunday teams around Camden and Islington in north London. At Chelsea during that period of my life I could be ball-boy at Stamford Bridge any Saturday I fancied, and I could bring my mate Jason Richardson and he could too. They would give us tracksuits and never ask for them back. There would be a few quid thrust into my hand for the Tube home and packets of biscuits too. Mind you, that was a very different Chelsea to the one owned by a Russian billionaire that I would walk into ten years later. In those days at Chelsea one of the challenges for a ball-boy retrieving the ball was the disability cars parked on the track around the pitch at the Shed End. If the ball got lodged under there the game would stop and the whole stadium would wait impatiently as you scrambled around under the car trying to hook it out with your foot.

By the summer of 2003, I had been a Premier League footballer for more than four years and captain of a West Ham team that had hurtled up the Premier League and then plummeted back down. I had been the main man in a failing team, which might not be every young footballer's childhood ambition but meant that I had accumulated some valuable experience. I had played for England seven times including sixteen minutes at the 2002 World Cup finals the previous summer. During my time as a first team player at West Ham I had played a lot, and yet the game itself seemed unsure of me. Later that season

Sven-Göran Eriksson would send me back from the England seniors to the Under-21s. I had been the boy wonder of English football, and although that meant I was occasionally cherished it could also be a double-edged sword. Prodigy status means that a kind of debt is established. I felt it at times. You get the place on the pedestal, but you also get the indignation when events don't quite play out as hoped. It's all part of the dance.

Ferguson wanted me again in that summer of 2003. He had sold David Beckham, missed out on Ronaldinho and he would end up that summer signing Eric Djemba-Djemba, Kléberson, David Bellion and a teenager called Cristiano Ronaldo. Not all bad. United told me to wait and then wait some more because they were trying to sell Verón. Arsenal had first refusal on me and my fellow West Ham youth team graduate Michael Carrick, and Arsène Wenger decided against us both. At that point in English football, the Premier League was a tussle between United and Arsenal. If you were an ambitious footballer, and you were good enough, then you went to one or the other. Then at the last moment, with Chelsea on the brink of financial collapse, the club was bought by a Russian with an aversion to speaking in public and the whole English game changed.

The day before I met Verón in the car park at Stamford Bridge, I almost never signed that contract. I would have been happy to sign it, but George Cole walked out of the negotiations with Chelsea at the very last moment. And to understand why you need to know a bit about George. He was born in 1954, the youngest of fifteen siblings in a poor Irish Catholic family in Kentish Town, north London. In the first few minutes of his life, his mum, Beatrice Cole née Murphy, who, it's fair to say, did not have an easy time, was told that her baby would not survive. The priest was called in for an emergency baptism. When he asked for the child's name, my grandmother was so exhausted that she just gave her husband's – George. George Cole junior survived but by then Beatrice was struggling. The experience of George's older siblings had been different. Beatrice had been younger then but the challenges of her life, the serial pregnancies, the poverty, had taken their toll. Dad said family life was chaotic. He was parented, in the main, by his older sisters Pammy and Carol, who he loved dearly. Or he just had to parent himself.

George reached adulthood unable to read or write. He spent a fair bit of time in young offender institutions and later in prison. He had to get out on the streets of north London and make a living from a very early age and, in this Dickensian street urchin lifestyle of his, George developed some unusual skills. The man could find his way home from anywhere thanks to a phenomenal sense of direction, even though he could not read road signs. His work on market stalls meant he was an absolute authority on fruit – what kind of apple that was, when that pear was in season. He developed some other skills too, not all of them the sort that you can do a government-sponsored apprenticeship in, but we will come to that later. Most of all he had an instinct for reading people – when they were kind-hearted, and when they were not. When they were crossing him or when they were on his side. He could be generous to the point of putting himself at a huge disadvantage. He could also be brutal to those he considered a threat. Most of all he could not stand authority figures, especially police officers. We think it came from his treatment by the prison officers in the institutions in which he served time as a kid, and it's fair to say it got him in a few scrapes.

Yet as we put the finishing touches to that Chelsea contract in August 2003, George Cole's instincts were well and truly engaged. The club's CEO of the time was Trevor Birch, a clever man who has had a long career in the game. He had run the club for Ken Bates, the previous owner, negotiated the take-over by Abramovich and was overseeing the transfer window. I had spoken to the Chelsea manager of the time, Claudio Ranieri, the night before and he had said it so often that he saw me as the number 10 I had asked if that meant I could have the number 10 shirt. Of course, Claudio said, and so I told Dad, who never forgot anything. I don't know how Dad noticed it on the contract given his struggles with the written word, but he asked Trevor if it was right that the club wanted me to wear the number 20. 'Yes,' said Trevor. 'Unfortunately, although Claudio had said Joe could wear number ten, Verón had just signed his deal and he had asked for number 10.' Trevor assumed that wouldn't be a problem.

'Come on, Joe,' Dad said, standing up. 'We're leaving. These are not people of their word.'

I had seen him in this mood before. Trevor tried to explain that Verón was one of the most famous midfielders in the world, although I could have told him that wouldn't cut any ice with George Cole. Dad wouldn't know Juan Sebastián Verón from Eva Perón. Dad said he didn't give an f-word who was getting number 10. The club could not go back on their word. He walked out. My agent David Geiss and I were left sitting there speechless.

I am very different to my dad in that respect. I've been told by the various psychologists I've spoken to over the years that I fit the template of a classic people pleaser. I don't like upsetting anyone and maybe that has been to my disadvantage at times. I would've worn the number 20 shirt for Chelsea if it had avoided an awkward silence with Trevor. Although by this time I knew we couldn't back down. I found George in the corridor outside staring straight ahead.

Trevor came back to us about ten minutes later. He had spoken to Verón's agent and it turned out Seba was prepared to wear number 20. Number 10 was all mine. I looked at my dad who regarded his negotiating position as completely normal. His view was you don't go back on your word and this subsequent outcome was the vindication for his stance. Sometimes I did wonder if he was wired right.

Seba turned out to be a lovely bloke. We sat next to each other at our press conference and I whispered to him before it started that I was sorry about the issue over the shirt number.

'It wasn't me,' I said, 'it was my dad.'

Which made me sound even more like a little kid. However, Seba was such a gentleman about it. With me sat next to him, it looked like bring-your-child-to-work day. None of the reporters asked me a question. They were all directed at Chelsea's number 20, who had been Ferguson's big signing two years earlier and had not performed at United as they had hoped. Verón was asked who he was most excited about playing alongside at Chelsea and, picking up on the fact they were all ignoring me he said, 'Joe'. I could see all the journalists thinking, *really?* Not Marcel Desailly or Emmanuel Petit? On Seba went, telling them that I was the best young player in the country, and much more like a typical Latin American footballer than a British player and I watched them all scribbling it down in their notepads, my confidence growing. I must be a good player, I thought. At the end we got up to leave and Seba caught my eye and winked. He whispered in perfect English, 'You owe me £50 for that bulls—.' I thought, I like this bloke.

In every newspaper and on all the phone-ins one thing was agreed: Chelsea were now the richest club in the world. On the training ground it felt like Chelsea were a few years behind

even West Ham. We trained way out in the west London suburbs, just to the north of Heathrow airport and right under
the flight path, at the notorious Harlington sports ground.
Abramovich will have been surprised to learn the club he had
bought did not even own Harlington outright. We shared it
with the university, Imperial College London, and some of the
most expensive footballers in the world were obliged to get out
of the dressing rooms in time for student hockey teams to get
changed in the afternoon. I arrived at Harlington as Chelsea
entered a new era, when the notion of high performance, elite
environment and sports science were still somewhat foreign
concepts to a club like this. But I loved the contrast. To the
outside world we were a team of stars assembled at great
expense from around Europe. Take a look beyond the gates and
you would see not everything matched the new Chelsea brand.
When Verón was driven into Harlington, he would have been
waved through the gate by the man known to all as Busy Al.
That was Alan Barratt, the friendly security guard, who was
in his seventies and unlikely to stop any intruder. Busy Al was
a Chelsea fan who used to work for British Airways and took
care of the gate as a kind of retirement hobby. Verón might
well have been driven in by John Ham – Hamsy – a masseur,
who only did the massaging in his spare time. The rest of the
time Hamsy drove a black cab and he would also be commis-
sioned at times by the club to ferry players around in it. That
did lead to some confusion for new signings who did not yet
know about Hamsy's dual role. They would ask for a massage
and look up from the table in some surprise to find their taxi
driver looming over them.

Although it was basic, I have to say that I enjoyed Harlington. The building itself felt like a cross between a village cricket
club pavilion and a tatty council leisure centre. At one end

was a fully stocked bar with sticky pub tables. The kitman would come around after training, chucking towels and kit into a Tesco shopping trolley that he had co-opted for the job. Meanwhile we were trying to win the Champions League. You had to wonder what the great Argentinian striker Hernán Crespo, most recently of Inter Milan, made of it all. The club was changing so fast that very soon we would move twenty-five miles around the M25 motorway to Cobham where a vast multimillion-pound state-of-the-art complex would be built in the discreetly expensive Surrey commuter village of Stoke d'Abernon. Searching for homes we were told to base ourselves in that area. In the meantime, new signings had the option of living in one of the two hotels at Stamford Bridge – at that time also in need of some refurbishment.

At Harlington, there was no games room or breakout area. We made our own entertainment, as young footballers were obliged to do in the days before Instagram or TikTok could while away the hours for restless young minds. This required some degree of creativity. We would put the masseur Billy McCulloch in the kitman's Tesco trolley after training and see which of us could push him hard enough to get Bill all the way down the dressing room corridor through the double doors at the end. When it snowed we would snaffle the keys to Bill's car and spend some time constructing a snowman in the driver's seat. Some of them were actually pretty good.

No one ever really got to know Roman, the man behind it all. He would appear in the dressing room after games, and then disappear as if in a puff of smoke. He came into English football as suddenly as he left in the summer of 2022, sanctioned by the British government after Russia's invasion of Ukraine. I only heard him speak a few times. One occasion was after we won the Champions League quarter-final second leg at Highbury. Later in my Chelsea career he would call me into his office and calmly listen to me tell him that I was fed up with José Mourinho and wanted to leave. And then he told me why I shouldn't leave – and, in fact, couldn't. Needless to say, I didn't leave. All of this amounted to a revolution in English football. That summer Chelsea spent around £115 million in fees alone – unprecedented back then – on eleven players (I was among the cheapest at a mere £6.6 million). Chelsea seemed to have signed me as a bit of a long-term project. In midfield they had brought in established stars like Verón, and the more defensive-minded Claude Makélélé and Geremi from Real Madrid. Damien Duff, a couple of years older than me, was already a big Premier League player who arrived from Blackburn Rovers. From Serie A came even bigger stars such as Crespo and the Romanian goalscorer Adrian Mutu. Already there were the great French World Cup winners Desailly and Petit, as well as the Danish winger Jesper Grønkjær. We even signed the captain of Russia, Alexey Smertin, and loaned him out immediately because there wasn't any room in the squad.

I only found out years later from Dad that as soon as Chelsea concluded the deal for me, they told him and David, my agent, that they wanted to send me on loan to CSKA Moscow. You can imagine my father's splenetic response to that. No effing way. But Dad was smart. He knew if he told me in the moment it would crush my confidence so he simply told the club never to mention it again. Yet he was under no illusion that I was going to have my work cut out getting into this Chelsea team.

It was the same for Frank Lampard, my old West Ham teammate who had joined a very different Chelsea two years earlier. So too for John Terry, a schoolboy prodigy from east London I'd known for years and would occasionally bump into in the nightclubs of Romford in Essex, during my West Ham career. I say nightclubs in the plural – there is only really one in Romford. Wayne Bridge, Southampton's best young player, signed for Chelsea the same summer as me and we would become best friends. None of us knew for sure whether we would be able to jump on the train of the Chelsea revolution or would find ourselves deposited at one of the figurative stations along the way. I was determined it would not be me left behind.

Even then I knew that there was a general uncertainty about me. Was I a midfielder? Was I a winger? Was I quick enough? Was I strong enough? These were the kind of stock questions you would get in those days in an English game that was all about certain archetypes of player, and certain qualities that were prized above all. The answer to all four questions from some quarters would have been: no. But that did not mean that I was not a very good player. I had played defensive midfield for West Ham in our last desperate days to avoid relegation and I could certainly do it there. I was aggressive rather than physical and, in my view, aggression always trumped strength when it was deployed properly. Although I could play centre midfield, I was probably not a central midfielder in the conventional sense. You would have found enough people who said I was not a typical winger either. Wingers were supposed to be speedy on-the-outside, get-to-the-byline merchants playing on the side of their strong foot. I was not that. I was not the quickest of players but I could read the game as well as anyone and my touch and vision were good enough to give me a head start. I could dribble. I could pick a pass. I could assist. I could score goals. In my best days at Chelsea I would get into double figures for goals. I was a number 10. I was a wide attacker. I was a wide attacker who did his defensive work. In 2003, I was lots of positions that did not yet exist in the English game.

In charge of it all was Claudio Ranieri, the Italian manager who Roman Abramovich had inherited from the previous regime. Given the great contrast between Chelsea's new-found wealth and the club's less than auspicious past it was fitting that I first met Claudio in a service station somewhere off the M40 motorway. I liked him immediately. He seemed to like me and told me in his broken English that I would be his key to open the doors of Premier League defences. Claudio looked like a man who was being hurried. The club he was in charge of had changed overnight and everything was now running through him. That was an advantage in terms of the players he could sign, but it was uncomfortable for him too.

As a squad we were hungry for success. This might make you snigger but there was a definite vibe too that we were anti-establishment. Yes, us – the handsomely paid footballers employed by a Russian billionaire. But we were footballers and none of that mattered. In our minds, Manchester United and Arsenal had dominated English football for the last ten years and they signed the best players. Everyone else had to play second fiddle. Now there was a new contender on the scene and one that was regarded as something of a brash upstart. We liked it that way. There was a seriousness about us, even when we were launching ourselves chest first, water slide-style, into the massive puddles that would accumulate on the pitches at Harlington. Even when we would play intense games of headers and volleys before training, much to the chagrin of Claudio's ultra-serious fitness trainer Roberto Sassi. He would express dismay at multimillion-pound footballers attempting overhead kicks before they had done their stretching. Even when we were carefully arranging pebbles into the eyes, nose and mouth of the snowman sitting in the driver's seat of Bill's BMW. Make no mistake: we wanted this.

At the same time, it was chaos. There were just too many players, and too many players who thought they should be starting games. Frank saw off Verón after a few months to partner Makélélé in central midfield. I got the sense that I had been bought as understudy for Verón who played at the point of the midfield diamond at first. But then even he could not get into the team. Verón was brilliant in training. His passing was so good he lent you the ball rather than gave it – because you knew at some point you would probably have to give it back to him. He had won the league in Italy and played number 10 for Argentina. Verón could drop a shoulder and glide past you off either foot. A joy to watch. But in the Premier League it was a different story. The league is not for everyone. There is a relentlessness to it that perhaps he had not experienced anywhere else. The game here never lets you rest – it tugs at your sleeve, snaps at your ankles. When you think you have it under control it surprises you. To succeed in the Premier League you needed something like Frank's mindset: utterly focused and ultra-competitive for every minute of every game, every week of the season. Verón has all sorts of ability but he didn't have that.

I had to go up a level. All around me were players who had been the best at their clubs elsewhere. While Verón was quiet and modest there was Mutu, who was brash and bold. But I recognised his type of character from the streets of Camden Town. A bit of a chancer, borne up on his self-belief and I liked him too. He would wear big fur coats and refer to himself by what he said was his rapper name. He would later tell me, in a more candid moment, how he had come from a life in Romania where he had very little and now suddenly he had all this money. He made mistakes, no doubt about that, but you can't take for granted that everyone has the same support network that I had in my family when fame kicked in. It's a problem lots of people would like to have but for some it's still just that – a problem. Mutu, before his fall from grace, once called me over when we were aboard a team flight. He said to me, 'Joe, I think I should wear the number ten shirt and I'm going to show you why.' He had a DVD of his best goals and he insisted that I watch them with him. I suppose my ego was a bit bruised at first by his directness. But watching him watching himself, rapt as he gazed at the screen, I realised that he was just a kid like me who loved the game.

I didn't give him the number 10 shirt, though.

I had come from a club where the fans loved me, and no one really expected anything much other than the usual. I had the manager's ear at West Ham and the late Glenn Roeder, a lovely man, would consult me on most things. Now I was towards the back of a queue of international superstars trying to catch the manager's eye. That was my challenge at the Chelsea of 2003. A wonderful place to be – all at once a club that felt like it was thrusting into the future while looking back into its past. How did I do? I did make that Chelsea team. There were twenty-five starts and another twenty-five off the bench in the first season. By the end of the season, I was starting pretty much all the big games for a manager who changed his line-up so often that the newspapers christened him 'The Tinkerman'. Some, like Frank, John, Eiður Guðjohnsen, Makélélé, Duff, Bridgey and Willy would thrive at Chelsea. Others, players as good as Verón, Crespo and Mutu, would not stay around for the ride. We did not win the Premier League in that first season, but we came close. Our best night was that quarter-final second leg at Highbury when, finally, a

Chelsea team beat Arsenal for the first time in five years and knocked them out of the Champions League.

The old away dressing room at Highbury in the West Stand had windows that opened out over the street. And as we flooded back in, jubilant after Bridgey's winning goal, the Arsenal fans must have been able to hear our shouts of delight and the music booming as we celebrated. I have to say I lived for those moments. It is wonderful to celebrate with your fans out on the pitch. The elation in the supporters rebounds to the players and generates an energy of its own. But in the dressing room there are no television cameras. You can shut the door and revel in the moment with your teammates and all the members of staff. You can let go of your emotions, swear at the top of your voice, dance like a maniac, chug a bottle of beer wearing just your underpants and, thankfully, no one other than those in the room has to see it.

That night Roman came in as usual with his crew. You could see in his face that even this guy – poker-faced and inscrutable at the best of times – was, in the football parlance, absolutely buzzing. So were we and it wasn't just about the glory of the semi-finals. We players had each secured a £50,000 last-four bonus. Mutu turned down the music and shouted, 'DOUBLE BONUS!' All the lads looked at Roman. Someone started making that noise crowds do, until we all joined in, a low ooooooohhhh that builds and builds to something. 'DOUBLE BONUS!' shouted Roman in agreement. The room went wild. Mutu turned the music down again and shouted, 'DOUBLE DOUBLE!' We turned back to Roman but his guys were already bundling him out of the room before he promised to drop another million pounds.

I know what some of you are thinking. Greedy footballers.

Billionaires throwing cash around. You might even be thinking, this lot didn't actually win the 2004 semi-final against Monaco. And you would be right on that point. But all I can do is bear testament to the moment. That was how it went down and, at Chelsea, it was about to get wilder. We never got paid the double bonus, though. Turns out that changing a bonus schedule mid-season is completely against the rules.

3

I'll Always Be Your Dad

I knew something was up when, as a ten-year-old visiting some of Mum's family in Hertfordshire, my dad asked me if I wanted to go for a walk in the countryside. George Cole never really wanted to walk anywhere if he could help it. In Camden Town he owned a minicab company which he oversaw as well as doing some of the cabbing himself. Walking was not his thing. His primary objective that day was for us to be on our own. On that walk, George told me four things. First, that he was my dad. Second, that he loved me and always would be my dad. Third, he told me that he was not my biological dad. Fourth, he said that if I ever wanted to meet my biological dad then that would be fine. George would organise it, and it would not change anything about the relationship that the two of us had. My dad George, as I would learn, had met my mum Susan when I was a baby. He had loved me as his own from the start. In case I haven't been clear, I am my father's son – and my father is George Cole.

There is the small matter of my biological father, although I consider it just that – a small matter of biology. When I learnt the story of how my mum ended up on her own I had no desire to meet my biological father and I never have since. I am well aware that he surfaced pretty soon after I emerged onto the scene as a professional footballer. I know that he was approached by newspapers and some of what he said to a reporter ended up getting published. Although whether he knew that it was going to find its way into print, I do not know. That is as much as I know because I never read it. My biological dad was this phantom presence who existed briefly at the edges of our lives when he would pass comment on me in the newspapers more and more often. It did get to the point that George went to meet him with Mum on one occasion to say: this has to stop. They met somewhere off Baker Street in a pub, the setting for most serious meetings involving my dad George. Mum brought along Jimmy Hampson, a West Ham scout, to keep an eye on George and make sure things did not get out of hand. That was it.

When I was still very young, George and Susan had applied for my dad – George – formally to adopt me. It went through eventually although my biological father never responded to the legal process. You might say this paperwork was the first big transfer of my life. I had been Joseph John Rooks and, with a few strokes of a pen, I became Joseph John Cole.

I am aware that my biological father has a range of children with a variety of mothers. I have never asked anyone to do a headcount and nor, respectfully, am I interested in exploring that part of my life. On one occasion a black cab driver pulled over when I was strolling near my house in west London, and I expected to be asked for an autograph. He told me we had the same biological father, and that he also had no contact with him. Another man came up to me once in a pub in Essex to tell me the same. On both occasions it came as a shock. In my life you can pop out for a pint of milk and come back with another sibling. Both times, I politely explained that I was not really up for extending my family. I wished them all the best and explained I did not want to be rude, but my life was and is mine to shape. I had my parents and my brother Nicky and sister Charly, the children George and Susan had together. Then came Carly and my own children, Ruby, Harry and Max. I cannot control what others do but I can control the way I deal with their actions. It is the shared life and experiences that make a family. My abiding memory of the man in the pub who claimed to be my half-brother was that he was taller than me and had a better head of hair. Both of which were slightly annoying given the alleged coincidence of our parentage.

My dad George was a ducker and a diver. He had an instinct for earning money. He used the c-word a lot – as if he had accumulated a surplus of them, like the Ralph Lauren polo shirts that mysteriously appeared in big teetering piles of cardboard boxes at Donnington Court and stayed there until Mum insisted he get rid of them. He was an excellent trampolinist. He had his issues with alcohol and cocaine. Those addictions sometimes took him away from us on nihilistic benders although he always came back to us. When we lost him it took the air from my lungs like a punch to the ribcage. I had grown up to believe that such a big man could never be felled.

I cannot really tell the story of my childhood without telling the story of George and Susan. Like a lot of footballers, I grew up in a rough neighbourhood and many of my peers fell by the wayside. Very few had two parents at home, and many saw one or the other succumb to drugs or booze. I, on the other hand, had two parents who had a lifeforce that propelled us forward as a family, through the good times and the setbacks. What I knew above all was that when I pushed the key into the front door of Donnington Court, I was stepping into a loving, safe home with food on the table and two parents who loved each other. It's the best gift you can give a child.

That's the serious bit over with now. Let me take you forward for a moment into the 1990s. I must have been around fourteen when I knocked on the door of a big house in Primrose Hill, which lies just beyond Camden Town, north of Regent's Park and west of the great railway tracks that run out of King's Cross. This was the home of Noel Gallagher, the creative genius of Oasis and one of my two childhood heroes. The other being another creative genius, Paul Gascoigne. Given that we played football every day for hours, roaming all over the neighbourhood – although not every part – we found out where Noel lived. I had read that he liked football and so I reasoned that he would like nothing better than to put his Manchester City shirt on and join us. To our disappointment instead of Noel it was Meg Mathews, Noel's then wife, who answered the door and she was not happy. Understandably, she told this group of teenage lads to do one. When she closed the door we did what all irritating teenagers do – we knocked again. There was a wait and then it was opened by the man himself. I was speechless. Noel was from a background like ours and he knew how to deal with us. 'Sorry lads,' he said, 'I can't play football today. I'm off on tour and I've got to get ready.' We nodded solemnly. These days we would have posed for a selfie. No such concept existed back then so you'll have to take my word for it. There was a pause and I announced to my friends, as they still remind me to this day, 'Lads, it's Noel Gallagher.'

When we first moved to the Clarence Way estate the local kids tested me, as they did all newcomers. I came home one day having run the gauntlet and both Mum and Dad could tell something was wrong. Mum's instinct would be to sit me down with a cup of tea. Dad knew that I had to grasp the nettle. He took me back to the group of boys who had threatened me and said if they didn't like me then why didn't they fight me there and then. I could feel the rising panic, but I also knew that with my dad there nothing bad would happen. Dad asked them again: do any of you want to fight him? No one stepped forward. Quite a nerve-wracking experience but surprisingly effective. No one messed with me again.

Dad's childhood had seen him moved from school to school until he left full-time education at the age of thirteen, although full-time would be a stretch to describe his schooldays. He was so difficult in class that the teachers just tried to find something to occupy him. One such pastime that they discovered kept him out of trouble was trampolining. It was a source of some amusement to us all that he remained an enthusiast for the sport his whole life and a stickler for the right terms for the different tumbles, somersaults, pikes and the rest. He was not the slightest bit interested in football. Dad would often tell me that the television had to go off in the evening before the end of a game and I would respond that I should get special dispensation because the club in question was my team, Chelsea. Because Dad couldn't read and didn't know a thing about football, so long as the team in question were in blue I was usually able to persuade him.

When he came back from work across the estate, the local kids would flock around him. He would pull his hand out of his pocket full of whatever change was there and chuck it in the air, prompting a delighted scramble for the coins. When we went on our first foreign holiday we bumped into an old prison friend of his at Waterloo Station. Once we had got to Spain he finally told my mum that he had given the guy half our holiday cash. Dad would just explain that his mate needed it more than us. 'Don't worry,' he would say, 'I'll find a way to get some more.' At the flat in Donnington Court we would occasionally put up fellow ex-prison inmates who Dad was trying to help get back on their feet.

The first thing I did when I signed my first professional contract aged seventeen was buy Donnington Court for Mum and Dad on Camden Council's right-to-buy scheme for residents of its social housing. We did not stay there for much longer but even now I could never see myself selling it. The memories are much too powerful of the fun, the love and the sheer adventure that presented itself to an optimistic boy in north London, in the 1980s and '90s. There was so much sport on offer on the concrete and green spaces of our estate. We played football until it went dark and then on summer evenings, I would bring out my miniature snooker table – purchased from the Argos catalogue – for some al fresco late-night frames. It was our own Crucible Theatre, the baize lit by the light thrown from the kitchen window. I grew up in London's inner city but it strikes me now, when I sometimes return to the places of my childhood, just how much there was to do.

I occasionally get on my bike now on a quiet afternoon and find myself heading from my home in the west of London, back to explore those streets of Camden. They have changed. Sometimes for the better and sometimes for the worse, but all the things I needed as a child are still there. Outside my parents' council flat is the small expanse of concrete between two sets of garages that was the first place we would stage football matches that would draw in children from all over the estate. But from there I can map out all the scraps of ground, or places we would play football. We played on what was then a patch of tarmac on Castlehaven Community Park, then strewn with broken glass and sometimes the needles of the addicts who lived nearby. Or Talacre Gardens, the small park in Kentish Town, or even further into town. Market Road pitches in Islington. Coram's Fields, by Great Ormond Street children's hospital, and just a short walk from Chancery Lane. By there you are heading into the heart of London. Looking back now, it is a strange place for a footballer to emerge given the lack of conventional football facilities. Yet there was always somewhere to play if you made the effort to find it. And, crucially, there were always people to play against. Later in my career people would talk about me being a street footballer, a phrase that is used widely to encapsulate so many qualities. I suppose I did play on the streets and my street football education was testament to the availability of the games and the quality of the opposition I encountered.

My parents did not have very much spare cash but what they did have Dad spent on me and Nicky and Charly. I would go through many beautiful leather Mitre Delta footballs, pairs of Adidas World Cup trainers and my shoe of choice, the Reebok Classic. There were always replacements apart from the two periods in my childhood when Dad was in prison and money was much tighter. Then Mum explained that I had to settle for the dreaded Mercurys, trainers for which I had such a strong dislike they mostly stayed in my schoolbag. The agreement with Mum was that I wore the Mercurys when playing football and for the rest of the time I could be in my Reeboks. Whenever I encountered a game going on somewhere on the way home the Mercurys would come out, weighing about a kilo on each foot, and I would play. I would put the Reeboks back on for the walk home.

Seeking out a game gave me and my friends a strong sense of independence. I was a child accustomed to being outside all day, albeit with the great security of coming back to a loving home whenever I needed. My dad's two prison absences were occurrences not unusual in our community, and as a family we coped with it. At times it could feel upsetting, but it was not the hammer blow some might imagine. There was a resilience that came with the life we knew and a confidence in its rules of survival.

How my life has changed. Within the space of a generation I recognise that the kind of childhood I had must feel completely alien to my children. For that reason there is something that compels me to hang on to the spirit of it. Most of all it gave me experiences and the older I get the more I realise those experiences in turn gave me the confidence to do the things that I achieved as a professional footballer. I don't wish to pretend it was all easy. Or that it was all what one might wish for in the life of your child. Yet I feel very grateful for it.

Donnington Court was six storeys, just one wing of a big social housing project. Among my earliest memories is being asked by a neighbour to climb two storeys up the outside of the block, and in through a window, because his mother, who lived there, had locked herself in and he had no key. At the time that felt like a perfectly normal request to me. Although if a neighbour asked one of my children to do the same now I would be, to say the least, unhappy about it. When I dropped in through the window his mother was there – she was just flat out on the floor on a heroin high. It was the first time I had ever seen anyone like that.

I would have an insight into the lives of the boys I played football with and against, as our free time took us across Camden, back and forth, in search of a game. Another boy, also talented, and later himself signed by the youth academy of a Premier League club, invited me into his flat when we were passing. It was a warm day and we were hungry and thirsty.

I will always recall his embarrassment when he opened the fridge and it was empty. His mother was in the other room, eyes shut and obviously out of her mind on drugs. We never discussed it, or even acknowledged it. We just moved on. I had always presumed, as a child does, that his life was like mine. Now I could see he was struggling and that there was a look of malnourishment about him. He seemed perpetually hungry. I wanted to help him. I would tell Mum these stories and she would tell me to bring him and his brother round to the flat whenever the opportunity arose so she could give them dinner.

What was never obvious to me at the time was that these hours of football were preparing me for something. I did not know what that would be yet, and my dad who had no interest in football was none the wiser either. After a good day on the market stall he would often indulge me with a new Mitre Delta because he could see that made me happy. But he was not preparing me for anything or urging me to practise harder or dragging me out at all hours to work on my weaker foot. For a long time, it did not become clear to us that my development as a footballer was outstripping that of my peers. Frankly, we had no idea. Mum recalls summer evenings when Dad took us to the pub and I would insist that she watched me attempt to break my keepie-uppie record. For all her love for me and her deep well of patience, they are, she says, some of the most boring evenings of her life. By the age of nine I could comfortably do nine hundred keepie-uppies. For a young mum on a rare night out with her husband, watching that must have taken up a fair chunk of the date.

When I was fourteen years old Mum and Dad had to come to collect me from Kentish Town police station where I had spent the afternoon pacing the cell, like an old jailbird – albeit a very anxious one who just wanted his mum. Mum made Dad wait outside in the car knowing full well that to bring him in was likely to invite a dispute of some kind. I had been caught by the officers of the Metropolitan Police driving a car around Somers Town despite having neither licence, the requisite number of years to hold one nor any real grasp of how a car worked. The brown Honda was parked by the housing scheme we knew as 'the red, yellow and blue towers', three twenty-storey tower blocks – Dalehead, Oxenholme and Gillfoot.

Somers Town is nestled between the railway stations of Euston and King's Cross. A few streets over to the west is Regent's Park. We were a stroll from Bloomsbury and Marylebone. In the 1990s, Noel and Meg were in Primrose Hill, just over the tracks. His fellow titans of Britpop were getting their breaks all over Camden Town's pubs and live venues. The Appleton sisters, Nicole and Natalie, who would go on to make a big impact in 1990s British music with the band All Saints, lived for a while upstairs from our flat in Donnington Court. Somers Town, meanwhile, was still as rough as it had always been, and getting rougher.

I was there because the tower blocks had a good football pitch. The pitch was interesting to us because it was an unusual design, with two goals for each team to defend and we played three players on each side. We had our own intense game with our own rules. But we were not just there for the football. We were also there for a group of girls who sat near enough for us to notice them pretending not to watch our game. We had been handed the keys to the brown Honda by Sean – not his real name – who knew our crew and would also persuade some of my friends to store, in their homes, the cannabis resin that he sold around the estate. He was an adult, albeit still a teenager, and we were very much children. So, let me be clear, this was wrong on his part. There were, nevertheless, rewards to be had for that level of collaboration with Sean. Some of my friends earnt themselves trainers, or the new Nokia phone of the day. Sean would occasionally oblige us with a lift around the neighbourhood, or further afield. That might involve a trip into the West End to the teenage emporium of the 1990s, Trocadero, at Piccadilly Circus.

That day, Sean came over to us and asked whether we would like to drive a car to which he had access, and handed over the keys. We soon had it going. All over the towers there must have been net curtains twitching, and among those watching will have been people who knew us. Jason, Paul Ellis, Ossie – my three best friends then, as they are now – took it easier when it was their go. Just a little drive up and down the access road that ran from the small car park by the Gillfoot tower down to the start of Barnby Street behind the Royal Mail depot. When it was my turn, I got carried away. With my mates in the car, I pulled a left onto Eversholt Street, then across the traffic onto Aldenham Street and, finally, a left onto Chalton Street where South Camden Community School stood, opposite what was then the Eastnor Castle pub. Much of it has gone now – the pub no longer exists, and the school is on its third name change. But the memory of that summer day never goes away. Me, triumphantly turning the car back around, only to see a police car facing me from the other end of Chalton Street. In my mind's eye, I stared them down, gunning the engine, gripping the gear stick. In reality we all ran for it, and not for the last time I was left cursing my lack of pace.

Having arrested me, the police just wanted to know whose car it was. On my estate, and the others around it, the one thing you could not be was a grass. I know that culture can be destructive when serious crimes are committed. I know how it frustrates police who want to effect proper change. But I also knew that however afraid I was of the police, there was no way I could give up Sean's name. The police officers' anger was palpable. Still, to me that was preferable to being a grass. By the time we got to Kentish Town police station I think they had probably decided that they were just going to punish me with a few hours in the cells. While I was there, Sean came to the station and put his hand up for obtaining the car. That was important in our world. I would have guessed that within about ten minutes of that Honda rolling erratically out of the estate with me at the wheel, someone would have tipped off my dad. Those were the days before mobile phones although word travelled only a fraction more slowly around Camden. Neither Mum nor Dad said much in the car. Meanwhile, I was snuffling through the tears about how sorry I was and asking whether I would still be able to go to Lilleshall. Dad just asked me for the exact details of what happened. Whatever conversation he might have had with Sean, and whatever deal was struck – that was not to be disclosed by him.

Growing up, we celebrated the small wins, and there were many of those. I was fifteen by the time of the famous Prince's Trust holiday which all my friends, now in their forties, still claim was the best holiday any of them ever went on. By then my life was being much more strictly marshalled by West Ham which meant I could not go. Although I have to say, it counts as one of my great regrets. The Prince's Trust, now The King's Trust, is the charity established by King Charles III when he was the Prince of Wales, to help young people from disadvantaged communities develop and try to change their lives through skills and training and experiences. It is admirable stuff, and just the sort of thing that our area needed. When the trust visited Somers Town in the late 1990s to see what could be done there was considerable excitement among the locals – but one major obstacle. How to fulfil the criteria that would persuade them to spend some money on us? Football seemed to be the answer, but Somers Town did not even have a proper local club. The boys that played football did so for various teams around Camden, Islington or further afield. I played for England schoolboys by then and was so far out of the picture with local sides that West Ham did not even want me playing for my borough representative team.

Metin Hasan, the dad of my friend Ossie, was eager that the opportunity did not pass us by. He was a great enthusiast for football and the community. He had a casual football team for Ossie and his mates like me but we never trained. So that week of The Prince's Trust turning up, any boy who could play had a knock on the door and was told to show up for our training session. We acted like we had been doing so twice a week for years. I was asked to come over wearing my England tracksuit and was introduced as the team's best player who had gone on to greater things. Metin, a Cypriot immigrant, said there was a big tournament in Cyprus. The Prince's Trust agreed to meet the costs. There was no tournament in Cyprus. But Metin knew that many of the kids who played football in the area, and a good few who did not, had never had a holiday in their lives – much less one abroad. With the grant, he managed to give a load of kids, who hardly got out of north London, a holiday that many of those who went still talk about now. As my mates love to recall, they did play one game against the hotel's waiters and it all kicked off over a disputed penalty. Did the Prince's Trust people know there was no team and no tournament and went along with it anyway? Who cares? I would argue it was among the best money they ever spent.

If I am to focus on all the possibilities that I felt growing up, then I also cannot forget the fears we held. It all leads me back to one event that dominated the community for a while at least. The murder of the fifteen-year-old Richard Everitt in Somers Town in August 1994, just a few yards from Euston Station, was a national news story. He was killed by a single stab wound delivered by a member, never identified, of a gang who had chased Richard and two friends. The death of an innocent teenager – a gentle boy, described as 'stolid' – was always likely to attract media attention. What made this murder and the trial that followed in November 1995 so dangerous was the race of the two parties. Richard was white. The gang that killed him were of British Bangladeshi heritage. It was presented in some of the newspapers at the time as a racist killing. The circumstances and the aftermath of it were much more complicated. The murder of Richard, who I did not know personally, loomed very large in my teenage years. I would continue to roam free but my mum, in particular, was more concerned about where I was and what I was doing. I became conscious of a need to be vigilant when I was out and also that certain streets were no-go areas. These are my childhood memories. But I have also gone back to those who were there at the time to check those memories, and to make sure that they were not just the irrational fears of childhood. I don't believe that they were.

Richard was just three years older than me when he died. He liked football. He attended what was then the South Camden Community School, on Chalton Street. That in itself was unusual. The school then had such a bad reputation that neither I nor any of my peers, when we moved up to senior school in Year 7, were sent to South Camden by our parents. I went to Haverstock School, by Chalk Farm Underground station in Camden. Then in Year 8, when Mum became worried about me falling under the wrong influence, to St Aloysius' College in Highgate. St Aloysius was a north London Catholic boys' school where discipline was taken seriously. My football ability meant they accepted me. By the time I reached Year 10 in the second half of 1996, I was sent to Lilleshall and my schooling continued at the local comprehensive there.

Richard had not been a member of a gang and his parents had been so concerned about him being subjected to bullying at his school that they had visited the school in person in the months before his death. He was, quite simply, in the wrong place at the wrong time as the feuds, grudges and divisions of teenage boys fractured and ran out of control. At the trial at the Old Bailey, only one person was convicted of murder, Badrul Miah, then twenty. The judge, Mrs Justice Steel, accepted Miah did not commit the act. He was convicted on the basis of joint enterprise, and that he knew the gang member who did so had a knife and was prepared to use it. Another man, Showkat Akbar, nineteen at the time, was convicted of violent disorder for taking part in the case in the prelude to the killing. He was cleared of conspiracy to murder. A third man was cleared altogether. The person who did kill Richard was never identified or convicted. It was accepted at the time that some who had been there on that night quickly left the country in the aftermath. The Met faced a huge problem of fear and non-co-operation from the local community, until eventually they gathered enough evidence from witnesses prepared to testify. For a short time at least, the area was on the brink. There was the prospect of escalation and of Richard's murder being used by the far right as a call to arms.

The racial differences and the tensions that existed in the area at the time became a key feature of the reporting. 'Killed for being white' was one headline in the *Daily Star*. There was much more of that. This is as uncomfortable a subject now as it was then. Yet I feel it is impossible to ignore when taking account of my life and the lives of my friends, which were carefree at times, less so at others. We knew there were places we could not go, and my friend Jason fell foul of that on one occasion. He was hit with a bike chain by a gang.

One border we observed was the Hampstead Road that ran down from Mornington Crescent Tube station, over the lines out of Euston Station. The three towers where we picked up the car were situated next to the Hampstead Road and on the other side of that road was the Bangladeshi community centre on the junction with Robert Street. It seems crazy now but we never crossed that road. If we wanted to play football in Regent's Park we took the longer, indirect route down Hampstead Road on our side of it to the Euston Road and then into the park via that southern entrance. I tried to avoid the streets where I felt unsafe and the South Camden youth club which was attached to the school and where many of the feuds played out in the build-up to Richard's death.

In putting my thoughts in order on what was going on in Somers Town in the 1990s, I have to say I have read the work of the late Dr Rosemary Harris, an anthropologist who studied the phenomenon of tensions between teenage gangs in the Somers Town community before Richard's death. That she was there even before it happened probably tells you just how serious that issue had become. Dr Harris's studies meant she was at the centre of it. Indeed, she had encountered Richard's parents when they came to his school to complain about his treatment in the months before he was killed. Reading the pages of her study I find it hard to fathom the reality of life for many kids in Somers Town in that era. I am grateful that football kept me away from so much of it. 'Bad as it is,' Dr Harris wrote of the violence, 'it is the reactions to it that constitute the major problem.' Somers Town was a rough place.

She witnessed fights between white boys and fights between Bangladeshi boys but none of them ever attracted the same attention, nor did they divide the community, as much as the fights between boys in different gangs divided by race. Richard's death cast a shadow over my childhood, indeed over all our childhoods. His family have had to live with it for evermore. It is important to remember Richard, and the destructive feuds that led to his murder, to assemble a proper picture of what life was like in Somers Town in the 1990s.

I asked my mum recently what my dad made of my own day in the police cells, given that he never really said much to me afterwards. She said that he was just proud that I had held it together and taken responsibility while not blaming anyone. He was not angry with me, she said, she knew that the silliness we boys had got up to that day was par for the course in our neighbourhood. Besides, if that was the most serious trouble I was likely to be involved in, Dad could live with that. He had certainly seen much worse.

4

Enter, José

You know when a manager isn't coping. It's the little things that betray his mood. In Monaco that night in April 2004, something was eating away at Claudio Ranieri. On the bench, he would look behind him as if the answer was there among his staff and players. He wore the expression of a man repeatedly searching the same spot for his lost wallet – as if he could will it to be there. We were in the Champions League semifinal, playing the first leg in Monte Carlo, and chucking it all in the bin. First, we went 1–0 down, then 2–1 and then 3–1. This little French club only had ten players on the pitch for most of the second half. It was to be one of the most infamous defeats in the history of Chelsea.

Maybe Ranieri knew that what was also going in the bin was his chance to manage Chelsea in this new era. He was so close to the big one – a Champions League final. When we were in the dressing room at Highbury, the windows opening onto the streets of Islington where I had once played as a kid, someone had come in to tell us that Monaco had knocked out Real Madrid. Monaco! They had beaten the Real of Ronaldo, Zinedine Zidane, Roberto Carlos and Raúl. We had cheered. Oh, the hubris. As the first leg unfolded, I wondered if maybe we would have been better off playing Real. We had fallen

49

off a cliff after the Arsenal win. And this after we had been flying earlier in the season. We had beaten Manchester United at home and Liverpool at Anfield – and more importantly in those wins we had been the better team. I had some big wins at West Ham but often with the Hammers it was not just a case of riding our luck – more like getting into the passenger seat and letting luck chauffeur you there. After the Arsenal quarter-final we won only two of our last eight games and the second of those was on the last day of the Premier League season, when it was all over anyway. The 2004 Champions League was the one that got away. As a young footballer you think: I'll be back. I'll win it next year. But the promise of redemption that next year offers – that runs out eventually.

Pressure does strange things to a manager. In Monaco, Claudio brought on the striker Jimmy Floyd Hasselbaink in right midfield and the big German centre-back Robert Huth came on at right-back. Verón was sitting next to me on the bench and, as the catastrophe unfolded, I reasoned it was either me or him coming on, but it could surely not be Seba. He had not played for Chelsea since 30 November 2003, bar half an hour against Middlesbrough three games and ten days ago. Seba didn't even have his socks and shin pads on. He was in his sliders, and he was as surprised as me when Claudio told him – you're coming on at half-time. Seba wasn't fit. We all knew that. After that game he only played another ten minutes all season. But Claudio wasn't thinking straight by then.

Training under Claudio had featured a bit more tactical work than West Ham. I wouldn't say it was enjoyable, but it was more structured than I had experienced before. Yet even so I was left thinking – is this it? It did not seem like the height of sophistication and certainly it was a long way behind what we see now with inverted full-backs, asymmetrical formations or the pinning back of full-backs. We set up in 4-4-2, sometimes a diamond shape in midfield. Every other side in the Premier League did the same. We were solid at the back and we broke with pace. What was new, I suppose, was the rotation of players in and out of the side. This was a forward-thinking concept. It anticipated the changes in the game that were coming. The problem was that the media didn't understand it and assumed that Claudio didn't really know his best team – and they could think of no worse crime for a manager. From Claudio's perspective, he made the mistake of never really explaining it to us, the players. We had been brought up in a culture where the best team played and we felt the sting of rejection keenly. Claudio was managing a huge squad in those days and he was trying to keep players happy and fresh. A bit more explanation of the strategy would have helped, but that's football for you. We like to keep so much of it shrouded in mystery.

I played the second leg against Monaco at home and we were brilliant. The caution we had fatally showed in that first leg was gone. Jesper scored, then Frank scored and it was just a great time to be alive. Every tackle was being won, every pass found its man. The crowd were into it and I felt it was just a matter of time before the third, fourth and fifth goals would arrive. At least that is what I told myself when I missed a couple of chances. At 2–0 I played in Jimmy and was certain he would bury it. When he didn't, and their full-back Hugo Ibarra went down the other end and scored, we still thought we would win it. At half-time, I expected Claudio to calm us down. They were 4–3 ahead on aggregate. In those days away goals still counted double in the event of a draw. The next goal was crucial. But we went out and tried to play at the same frantic pace. That was the naivety of the early Chelsea. I doubt

ENTER, JOSÉ

Manchester United would have done the same in those circumstances because they had learnt what you needed to do – as
well as what to avoid – in the Champions League. Yet we went
out and did the same, conceded again, to Fernando Morientes,
and suddenly we needed three goals to rescue it. Our bubble
was burst. I looked around at teammates who had seemed
invincible forty-five minutes earlier and they just looked shot.

Roman came into the dressing room afterwards, as he
usually did, but this time it felt different. We all knew that
Claudio was cooked. We had missed our opportunity in the
first leg when we should have gone out and taken the tie to
Monaco. It was as if Claudio was still managing the Chelsea
from before the summer of 2003. A club that was not quite
sure of itself and certainly didn't have the players to go on the
attack away from home in Europe. When the pressure is on
to win, human nature means you can often go the other way
and play it safe, as Claudio had tried to do in Monaco. That
wasn't the required mindset any more. Chelsea were ready for
a new manager.

You will know the early José Mourinho story, so I don't
need to recap his days with Bobby Robson at Porto and then
Barcelona, or how it all took off so rapidly for him in his
management career. How he won the UEFA Cup in 2003 and
then the Champions League a year later with Porto. What you
need to know is what football was like then. Claudio's training
was more structured than it had been at West Ham, with an
emphasis on defending, but there was not much more to it
than that. It changed so much over the course of my career.
In fact, I can say with confidence that the last manager I
worked under in my final season as a player, Neill Collins, a
Scottish coach younger than me, at the Tampa Bay Rowdies
in the second tier of professional football in the US, was more

advanced in terms of tactics and preparation than Claudio. In less than two decades, the game has changed in ways you would scarcely believe. A coach like Neill is expected to give so much more to his players. That development wasn't just confined to Neill. It has happened all across the game to a generation of coaches. In 2004, José was a leap beyond anything I had ever seen. Which is not to say that big changes have not happened since then. What he was doing in 2004 will not be what he or other top coaches are doing now. But it was like a lightning bolt for me and my teammates. Even though it wouldn't have taken that much greater detail and sophistication to impress us, José gave us lots.

I did not play a single minute of Euro 2004. I left Portugal frustrated. England had a great midfield of David Beckham, Paul Scholes, Steven Gerrard and Frank Lampard in those days. I didn't expect to start but I certainly expected minutes off the bench. I was restless and ready to go. Either way I told the club I would not be taking the full break allocated to those who had been at the Euros. I would be there on the first day of full-season training. In truth I was curious to see what the hottest managerial property in Europe was like in his first training session under the Heathrow flight-path. Many of the others – including Frank and John Terry – were still on holiday. They started calling me around lunchtime to ask what it had been like.

First of all, I was knackered. Flat out on my bed in a room of a Heathrow hotel that had been booked for the players for a lunchtime snooze between double sessions. Earlier that day, when I stepped out of the temporary cabins we changed in, the first thing I noticed was something I had never seen at a training ground before: ballboys. I asked one of them what was going on. He looked like he had won a competition. In some ways you could say he had. He was a Chelsea fan, a teenager, who had spotted an advert to work at the training ground. He and his fellow ballboys would supply a steady stream of balls into the small-sided games we were playing. That meant there was no break in play. And that was the essence of José's training method. We didn't know it then, but this was the periodisation model that is commonplace now, more than twenty years on. You train by playing football. There were possession rondos – a posh phrase for piggy in the middle – and three against three games, four against four, five against five. Short, sharp, exhausting and designed to practise certain patterns of play. All timed to the second, on the stopwatch that José wore round his neck. Drinks breaks? Timed too. Then onto the next pitch that had already been set up for the next exercise. No standing around, no idle chit-chat, no pinging balls at the kitman's head twenty yards away. My mind was working constantly, my body was aching. But I loved it.

In pre-season at West Ham we had gone on long runs through Epping Forest, all of us trying to stay up with Frank Lampard senior, super-fit in his running spikes and having trained all summer. Now, instead of puffing away behind him, somewhere in the middle of the pack, I had the ball at my feet. 'How much running?' JT asked on the phone that lunchtime. He was incredulous when I told him it was all with the ball. Lamps called a few minutes later. 'No running?' He'd already heard. 'No running,' I said. Well, none of that kind anyway. Now we all know the famous quotation attributed sometimes to José, sometimes to others, that a pianist doesn't practise by running around the piano. But you have to understand how unusual that was at the time. English football was coming out of a long darkness. The years of the Charles Hughes method, the old-school FA ideologue who had pioneered the long-ball game principles, were still all around me. That was before we came to the boot camp-style training methods. Everywhere I had been before then, at West Ham, at Lilleshall, even the first year at Chelsea, had to some extent tried to separate the physical challenge of football from the football itself. Crazy, really. All those long pre-season runs that footballers have been doing for generations, along beaches, up stadium terraces, through forests. None of it ever worked. The research we have now shows that. Certainly, none of it ever suited me. My game wasn't about my physicality. My strength was in my touch, and my ability to see the game in ways others couldn't. Running long distances in a straight line, up hill and down dale, always felt like a waste of time to me. Here was the proof.

After three days of this brave new world, I went to see José. I wanted to know where I stood. José was direct. He said to me he could have signed Deco, the Porto midfielder who had won the Champions League with him. 'But,' he said from the other side of his desk, 'I have got you, Joe. I could have Deco, but I want you.' He had watched me closely and he pulled out a sheet of paper with my stats on it. I said that more often than not I had played on the right side of a four in midfield. He said he already knew that. I said I played defensive midfield at times for West Ham in my final season. José said he knew that too. Then he said: you know, Joe, you're not a midfielder. I recognised in that moment what he meant. I had long thought it myself but it was the first time anyone of any position of authority in football had said that to me. I had spent my life ostensibly playing in a midfield but the term 'midfielder' felt like an inadequate description of what I did best. José saw me as I saw myself. An attacking player – not a forward as such – but versatile. He said he would play me sometimes as a number 10, but principally coming from a starting position on the wing and just as capable of doing defensive work. In possession Chelsea would be a 4-3-3, and he did not see me as a contender for the midfield three, only the attacking three. I had never played wide left or wide right of a front three – but José knew that too. 'You are going to learn that role,' he said to me. And I knew that I would. He explained that transitions, the moments after which a team wins possession, would be important. He was impressed I had come back early to training when my England teammates were still away, but he also warned me that there would be competition for places. 'I will help you become a better player,' he said, 'if you trust me.'

José was very clear. 'I am going to play you on the left or the right,' he outlined. 'I need more penetration from you. The team is going to play in a certain way.' Then, as an example, he used the Brazilian Derlei, who had played for him at Porto. Derlei, José said, did not have the quality I had but he had an obsession with scoring goals. That was something I could learn from. Derlei, José pointed out, had played in a Champions League final. 'You haven't, Joe. You need to be better on transition and you need to score more goals.' I certainly knew where I stood with him. Well, at least I did at that moment.

José had an aura. Even in our squad that meant no one took him on. As we built up to a full squad in pre-season, I could feel myself getting fitter while mentally it was exhausting. He was challenging us intellectually – and, yes, I know that people might snort at that. Thick footballers and all that. But when you are working at your physical limits and having to make decisions that are different to the usual instinctive way you have played since you were a child, it can be hard at first. Hard but also revelatory. José was obsessed with his players pressing at the right time. These days most managers are the same but to me, and to many others, it was new. If you pressed at the wrong time, and you got passed around, then you got told at the next timed drinks break. As you were gulping down water, José would be in your ear. 'When the ball goes in here, you go here,' he would say. 'Now do it again.' There might be two of us pressing four others, holding our shape until a bad pass was made and that was our trigger.

I had thought that making the first team meant that I was established as a footballer. Now I realised there was so much more to learn. Young pros need to realise that too. It's hard. It should be hard. But José was a good teacher and it started to stick. I found myself thinking about this new playbook all the time – even when I was wandering around the flat that Carly and I were living in in the little Surrey commuter town of Esher. Wait for the trigger. Go hard on the transition. If Carly dropped a magazine or a piece of cutlery, I was ready to tackle it. I felt tuned up and alive.

We had a pre-season tour in the United States and already you could feel the vibe changing. We stayed in none other than the Beverly Hills Hotel. You have to bear in mind that a standard West Ham pre-season – this was my first pre-season at Chelsea – would have peaked with a stay at Nigel Mansell's hotel in Devon. Now I was sitting in the lobby watching someone go by who looked just like Jennifer Aniston. Wait a minute. That is Jennifer Aniston! There were parties everywhere in Beverly Hills. We were getting invitations all over the place from friends of friends and all the general hangers-on, but it was early to bed and double sessions under José. By the end of it we were bursting to get out. We spotted a gap in the schedule. It was a free morning that would allow for a lie-in. The organising was done by the English–Irish group of players plus honorary Icelandic member Eiður Guðjohnsen. Word went around. 10 p.m. Out through the kitchens. Transport would be waiting. Tell no one. Destroy this message. We discreetly reached out to the different friendship cliques in the team. Did the French/Francophone lads fancy it? *Non*, came the word from Makélélé and his new mate Didier Drogba. Did the Portuguese/Brazilian lads fancy it? *Não, estamos apenas relaxando*.

Half the thrill was the covert slipping out. We got to the club elated. It was everything you'd expect of a club in Los Angeles. Absurd choice of drinks. Dancers. Music. Sparklers in drinks. As we scoped it out, we noticed a table of blokes in the corner. Wait a minute. Is that . . .? That's Makélélé and the French lads! And – over there – on the other side of the dance floor. The Portuguese lads! The cheeky buggers had been coming all along. We all crept back in at 4 a.m. and were in time for breakfast at 9 a.m. Did José ever know? I think he knew everything. He let us have that one.

José soon realised we were coming to the boil in terms of fitness and the system he wanted us to play. We had played Roma in a friendly in Pittsburgh and ripped through them. You could see the Roma players looking at each other wondering: aren't we supposed to be the conditioned ones? I was also quickly aware that I had some serious competition. When Arjen Robben signed, I was blown away. I had seen skilful players with a good touch. I would respectfully count myself among them. I had seen absolute speedsters, who could blow past a full-back when they hit top speed, like my teammate Damien Duff, aka Duffa. A fine player. But Robben seemed to be a combination of my skillset and Duffa's pace. And it was hard enough getting in the team ahead of Duffa. Robben was the single most talented footballer I played with. Until, that is,

I met Eden Hazard. The other big change was Petr Čech. Not just because this Czech goalkeeper from Rennes was so good, so young and so bloody big, but because he went straight into the first team ahead of a Chelsea institution. Carlo Cudicini was one of the best goalkeepers in the league, never mind Chelsea. The fans loved him. I had supposed at the time that the 21-year-old Petr was going to give Carlo some competition. Then José flipped the famous flipchart for the team against Manchester United on the first day of the season and Čech was starting. Carlo was devastated. As for José, he wasn't waiting around. The team was changing, and he never looked back. In that moment, Carlo went from number 1 to number 2 and José was set on his course. Čech went on to become the greatest goalkeeper in Chelsea's history. Another lesson in how fast football moves.

There was another name missing from that first team for the game against United. It was mine. I wasn't even on the bench. John, Frank, Bridgey and Eiður all started. Scott Parker, who had signed for us in January, was on the bench and came on as a substitute. I was distraught. I jumped up from my seat in the stand and celebrated when Eiður scored the only goal of the game. Inside I felt terrible. We were all desperate to be part of this new thing with José and I couldn't even get on the bench. I knew I had to swallow whatever bleak thoughts I had and put a supportive face on for the team. That's rule number 1 for me when any player gets left out. Get through the matchday and sort it out later. You learn a lot about someone's character from how they behave in that situation. I went to see José the following Monday and asked what I needed to do to change his mind about me. Always a more sensible question to a manager who hasn't picked you, although there would be times with José when I was less polite.

ENTER, JOSÉ

'Don't worry,' he said, 'your chance will come.' So I made sure I took it. Next Saturday, Birmingham City away, on as a substitute on 63 minutes and my first goal of the Mourinho era five minutes later. We won the match 1–0. Three days later I started against Crystal Palace at Selhurst Park and was man of the match in a 2–0 win. Four days after that I started in a 2–1 win over Southampton. It was my misplaced pass – yes, a bad one – after literally ten seconds, that fell to James Beattie. From 35 yards out, on the run, Beattie had a lash at it and scored the goal of his life. Which I considered very fortunate for him and very unfortunate for me. I had scored a winner against Birmingham, I had won man of the match at Palace and we had won our first four games. But all anyone wanted to talk about was that silly pass to Beattie. I felt like I should be elated but something told me that this was going to be the way: Joe's lost the ball again. Every midfielder in England that weekend lost the ball at some point. In my case the lucky recipient of my bad pass had a Bobby Charlton moment. What are the bloody chances?

I had still not won Sven's trust with England, three years in. I was worried that perception of a player who took risks and lost the ball would slip over into my life as a player at Chelsea. I could feel that gathering. Maybe I should have been more strategic about it. Courted a few journalists. Hired a PR person. Written an autobiography. But I felt that would look weak. And anyway, I was of the belief that people would see my performances, which would soon convince José, and then judge me accordingly. It might surprise you to know that football is not really like that. You get judged early and it can be hard to lose that reputation if it goes the wrong way. The focus tends to be on moments not the whole 90-plus minutes. Even now people say it to me. My response is, how many times did you watch me play?

I was in that Chelsea team for all the big games in José's first season. I scored the winner both home and away against Liverpool in the Premier League. I started the League Cup final. I started home and away in the Champions League against Barcelona, Bayern Munich and Liverpool. You don't start games for José if he doesn't think you can pass the ball accurately, or do your work defensively. I was the Premier League player of the month in March. I know that sounds a bit lame, player of the month, when John and Frank won the big individual end of season awards. They deserved it, but in a title-winning side I was not too far behind. I wanted people to love me. I admit it. The fans had loved me at West Ham. The Chelsea fans seemed to feel the same. I thought winning trophies would end the argument and they are a good card to play, but it never quite seemed to be enough. Everyone needs to feel vindication for their work and footballers are no different. First, from your manager, then from your team-mates and then from the fans of your club. It is those fans who watch you the most – sometimes every single game of the season. They may not know your injury problems, or the politics of the club, but they see the performance and they judge accordingly.

Playing for José was a bit like joining a cult. In a good way of course – if indeed there are any good cults out there. You want to please the leader, and he has a certain way of doing things to make you want to please him. For instance, in José's case he would tell me all the things I could not do, in order to make me want to do them even more. Yes, I know it was a pretty simple psychological trick. Look, I'm not here to tell you that footballers are the world's most intellectually complex creatures. We want to be in the team every week and be praised for our efforts. That's about it, and José knew that only too well. He would pounce on the slightest defensive lapse, and when I say lapse it would be that one-in-a-million hit from Beattie after my errant pass, or the slightest misjudgement, the merest hesitation. It wasn't like I was standing around oblivious to the game, watching the pigeons roosting on the East Stand roof. It might be the briefest moment. But José wanted me ready for every covering run in every moment.

All of this leads to the famous occasion on 3 October 2004 when we beat Liverpool 1–0 at Stamford Bridge and I scored the winning goal. It marked the start of the rivalry between José and Rafael Benítez, the Spanish coach Liverpool had appointed the same summer. Their careers had been fairly similar – quite rapid rises, domestic league titles in their respective leagues and Benítez had gone on to win the UEFA Cup with Valencia. They didn't hate one another from the start. In fact, they would have a friendly chat before games in the early days, although that was about to change. Our rivalry with Liverpool was pretty epic and it started with that game in October 2004.

I felt pleased with myself. Scored the winner for Chelsea. Went out for a few drinks that Saturday night. Only in the morning, when the Sunday papers came out, in those innocent pre-social media days, did people start calling me about José's comments. I had started the game as a substitute but come on in the first half when Didier got injured. The goal had come just after the hour, a nice flick from Frank's free-kick. Asked about me later, José surprised the reporters. He wasn't happy with me. He said that he had ten players when he needed eleven. José said that I had 'two faces – attacking and defensive'. Without recounting every word he said, I can summarise it thus: José hammered me. 'They [the media] wanted to put Joe Cole on the moon,' José said, 'and I was thinking if that was what they wanted I would have to kick him.'

When I first heard about it, I remember thinking, that's a bit weird. But I didn't realise how this would fan the flames. José was just doing what he does best. Picking fights. Talking in the kind of extreme terms that mean no one can ignore what he is saying. He did it to me in private too. He barely ever criticised Frank, John, Čech and Didier. I know why. These were the spine of his team. As long as he had them onside he would be fine. I was never part of that inner circle. They would announce the man of the match awards over the public address system at Stamford Bridge before the end of the game and whoever got it was given a big cheer. Once I got in the team regularly, I started winning them. Then I was told that José got annoyed with that too. Who knows if that was true? But I did miss out on a lot of free business class flights – which was the prize. What I do believe is that José spotted that the English media had not made their mind up about me, and that I was not yet a fixture in the England team. He used that to harass me into becoming the player he wanted me to be. Looking back I appreciate what José did for me. He taught me that the game was about winning, not just about playing well. You might say he found the snarling dog in me and once he found it he would like to provoke it. I can see that now. I just didn't like it at the time.

That public denouncement of me was nothing compared to what José would say to me in private. Once he came up to me on the Monday after a Saturday game, while we did our stretches on a nice bright day at Cobham with the sun shining and the sound of birdsong in the trees. He told me I would never ever effing well play for him again if I ever repeated whatever it was I had done in Saturday's game. I stood there wondering what that thing was when the thought occurred to me: it doesn't actually matter. He's doing this for a reason. He's testing me. Besides, I was enjoying it too much, because by the end José was playing me all the time. And Chelsea still felt like the centre of the world.

5

Dad's Going Away

I'm back in the flat in Donnington Court – in my childhood and without my dad. He is about a mile away from us in Camden Town but he's not coming home tonight or any other night soon.

Dad was at HMP Pentonville, a notorious prison near King's Cross where violence and overcrowding were common. Dad was always sanguine about doing time. It had been part of his life since he was a teenager and he would always assure us he was fine. As for Mum – she got us through. She could cope with anything. At night I would watch her rearrange her ornaments on the windowsill at the front of the flat on the ground floor. In the absence of a burglar alarm, they were there as an early warning system if anyone tried to break in. It was always a possibility. Everyone would know my dad was not there, including those who might just be nasty enough to take advantage. They would know that George Cole always had money, and that some of it would be in the house. Years earlier when I was much younger, I had believed that my dad was a helicopter pilot. Unfortunately, the reality was that the secret helicopter base we occasionally went to visit him at was a prison and my mum gave me the pilot story to protect me from the much harder truth. I was so young that it all washed over me. When he would go to prison for a second time later in my childhood I lived through the whole process, from his arrest to the trial. Then I would feel it all much more keenly.

I do not offer any defence of my dad's crimes. He went away the first time for stealing a till from a post office. In his younger days my dad was rated as a 'hoister'. He was strong enough to lean over a counter and hoist a cash till in one arm and then run with it, like a rugby ball. I am tempted to say that in both our chosen professions, father and son suffered from a lack of pace. Dad always said he was offered much more violent, serious jobs by the criminal network that existed around us in Camden Town. He declined on the basis, he said, that he did not wish to threaten innocent bank clerks. He said he would never point a gun at someone. Now, I accept that it is a fairly low bar when it comes to most people's career choices. All I can say is that in the circles in which he moved it meant something.

When Dad came out of prison after that first spell, he worked hard. Those felt like golden years for us as a family. He worked the market stalls and anyone who has ever run one knows what hard graft that can be. He started with one outside the butcher's on Queen's Crescent in Kentish Town. There was also a bit of illegal fly-pitching around Waterloo Station and the South Bank. As a kid I would go with him sometimes. He and a couple of others would back the van into the spot they had selected and sell whatever they had from the open doors. Two lookouts to watch for the police and Dad would sell as quickly as he could. I learnt to whistle, shrill and loud, if I saw the vigilant officers of the Met. As soon as he heard it, the gear was shoved back in, his mates slammed the doors shut and we were away in less than a minute. Whether you had been selling for a couple of hours or twenty minutes, what you had got by then were your takings for the day. You did not push your luck by going back the same day.

The Ralph Lauren shirts were another venture. For a while it seemed that everyone on the estate was wearing Ralph Lauren. The postman, the milkman, the man who owned the corner shop, even the teachers in the schools. They were clearly being offered some very competitive deals by their pupils. We learnt to distinguish between the fakes – which were very good – and the bona fide Ralphs. It all came down to studying the tiny emblem of the polo player astride his horse and the position of his hammer, or the horse's tail. Legend has it that a consignment of Ralph Lauren clothes that went missing in Camden Town once featured on the BBC's *Crimewatch* show although no one has ever been able to confirm that. Either way, *Crimewatch* was a very popular programme on our estate. For many in the area it represented their best chance of seeing someone they knew on television.

My football career, in terms of organised games, had started inauspiciously. First on the street and then for a team called Tarmac, named literally after the rough surface we played upon, in what is now Castlehaven Community Park. Dad didn't know anyone in football. Mum, originally from Lisson Green Estate, which is further west, had a friend who knew about a team that played on Paddington Recreation Ground – Paddington Rec – a park in west London between Kilburn and the expensive mansion houses of Maida Vale. It was where Sir Roger Bannister trained for his four-minute mile when he was a young doctor at St Mary's Hospital and where Sir Bradley Wiggins would later ride his bike as a kid. Both have a heritage plaque on the old cricket pavilion at Paddington Rec. And a knighthood. If anyone fancies giving me one or the other – or both – I won't say no.

I scored a lot of goals on Paddington Rec, even though my team, Paddington, were the worst in the league. I couldn't pass to my teammates because they were all useless. Sorry lads, but we all knew that to be true. We would lose 9–3 and I would come away with a hat-trick. We didn't even have a kit – just bibs over our T-shirts. No scout from the professional clubs ever watched Paddington. Then, when I signed for Chapel Boys who played on Coram's Fields, just a brisk jog from the British Museum, that was heaven. We wore the AC Milan kit and the scouts flocked to my dad's car. Arsenal, Spurs, West Ham, Chelsea, Millwall. All these business cards pressed into Dad's hand, which I would study on the way home running my fingers over the embossed club badges.

My mum's dad, John Holloway – I called him Poppa – had been a Queens Park Rangers fan, but we never went to Loftus Road. When I was a hyperactive three-year-old he would walk me from Lisson Grove through Hyde Park to Buckingham Palace to see if the Queen was in – or so he told me. He was trying to help my mum by wearing me out. Even then I could walk all the way myself. I was so active as a child that I would run all the way up Hamilton Terrace, one of London's most expensive streets, to my nursery at the top end. It wasn't until Mum had Nicky and then Charly that she realised it wasn't normal for a small child to run everywhere, all the time.

Later it was those trips to Stamford Bridge with my friend Ben Burton, taken by his dad Rick, that lit the fuse. The Burtons lived in the nice part of our area, Seymour Buildings. Rick had his own lighting rigging business for film sets, which on our estate was a source of wonder. Bear in mind that if you lived round our way and had a market stall, you'd made it. If you drove a black cab you were practically aristocracy. Rick's kindness to me, as well as his excellent sandwiches, established my lifelong love for Chelsea and paved the way for the seven years I played there. I still work every now and then as an ambassador for the club. There is even a postscript. Chelsea signed Ben as well. He is the club's head of operations, which means he's in charge of all the catering hospitality at the club, right up to the premium boxes where the owners sit. He's been there since I was a player at Chelsea, and before you ask – no, I didn't get him the job. He got there by his own hard graft and talent. So, just remember when you take your kids to a game it's not just the football that could inspire them to make a career in the game. It might be the football, but it also might be the high-quality homemade sandwiches.

After that aforementioned spell in prison, my dad's fortunes took a turn for the better when he got a market pitch in Burnt Oak. A tiny smudge on the map of the sprawling outer north London suburbs, but a lucrative one for someone prepared to work hard. Saturdays were the big day. Mum would also help out on the stall on Saturdays, to keep costs down, as well as a couple of day-boys. Initially I would stay with my mum's parents, John and Pat, until I was old enough to join Mum and Dad. I was desperate to be part of the family business. I have glorious memories of those days. I had my own market trader's fingerless gloves and money belt. Mum and Dad would entrust me with the coins to get the teas from the café across the road. Dad would give me the melons to sell – basically anything I did not have to weigh or that required any mental arithmetic – and he even promised me a bonus if I sold every last melon. As the day wore on, he would ramp it up. 'Are you going to sell them all, boy?'

I was determined to do so. Mum and Dad would play tricks

on me. They would persuade a customer to steal some of whatever I was selling. I was sent into a panic as they pretended to grab the thief – and then, finally, they would let me in on it. Then Dad would secretly give a customer the money to buy the last few off me and I would come over to him triumphant, my pallet empty and my reward claimed. At the end of the day we would pack up and pile back into that empty van that smelt of produce. Me and the day-boys would jump in the back, no seatbelts, skidding around the dark empty chamber as we made our way back into the city. We would challenge each other to guess where in London we might be and then peer through a small hole in the van's side to confirm it. Nowadays I do not take my kids anywhere in the car without strapping them in like astronauts. We used to roll around in the back of that van like loose apples.

Dad was good at earning money and then terrible at keeping hold of it. There was an accepted rule that in a cash business, like a market stall, your casual workers took the money for their lunch out of the takings, and perhaps a little more. Dad would turn a blind eye to it. Mum felt differently. She made it a better-run operation. Yet for all his generosity, Dad had a knack for knowing what kind of day we'd had. His estimate of the takings was always very close to the final figure. My dad's issue was that he could lose his temper when he found himself confronting someone he considered to be a bully. It was that temper which would bring a temporary halt to our happy hand-to-mouth existence. I was twelve when he went to prison for the second time in my life. I can still recall the wider family gathered at my grandmother Pat's flat. I remember the telephone. A chunky plastic 1980s design which, with push buttons instead of a dial, seemed modern then. We were all waiting for it to ring with word from court.

That morning my dad had gone for his sentencing with a bag packed for prison. He had said goodbye to me and told me to be a good boy. When the news came the adults were celebrating. Just eighteen months. They had feared it would be much longer – perhaps even four years. I knew that this was good news, but it didn't feel like that. My dad was not coming home. Not that evening and not for a while. I didn't feel like celebrating.

Later that evening a cousin would take me to football training, something my dad would ordinarily have done. In the gym, I sat waiting for my team's turn and our coach John came over and asked me if I was okay. He had been an excellent footballer himself, and had won an England Under-18 cap. He did often show us the one cap he had won, that the Football Association had given him, and to us young lads it felt magical. Like a holy relic. It was just that one act of kindness from John, who knew what had happened to my dad, that set me off. The pressure of the day had built up, especially when the adults around me had been relieved about the outcome. All I could think was that my dad was going away and I wouldn't see him. It was the only time I cried publicly during my dad's sentence. I will never forget it.

Dad had got himself in trouble. At our pitch in Burnt Oak he had taken a dislike to the binmen who came to clear the high street. He found them overbearing and rude, and the foreman among them the worst of all. That was how the tension began but it erupted when the foreman threatened one of the day-boys, a cousin of mine, at the stall. That tipped Dad over the edge. He pursued the bin lorry, hauled himself into the cab and attacked. In the fight that followed, Dad pulled the knife he used at the stall and cut his adversary on the face. It was not a bad wound, but I am not going to defend what he did. It

71

happened and he paid the price. I don't think he ever expected the binman to go to the police. That was a first for Dad.

Dad had built up a lot of goodwill among the people who lived on our estate and our wider family. He was the person they went to when they needed help – whether that was for money or influence – often to get themselves out of trouble. When I was a child one of my many cousins had become addicted to heroin. He had lost it to the extent that when I said hello to him on the bus, my cousin, out of his mind, exploded at me. He didn't know who I was, and I was terrified of him. Dad took him, at the request of my dad's sister, to a rehab centre in Spain and stayed there with him. Dad brought me back a Barcelona shirt with 'ROMARIO' on the back, which became my most prized possession. I don't know how Dad had managed that as he had no clue about any of Barcelona's team and neither could he read.

There was a whole private hierarchy of power and influence that existed on our estate, away from the police and the courts. It involved those in the criminal world and others who were not. If one of my cousins had got on the wrong side of a local gangster, then it might just as likely be my dad he would come to for help as his own father. Dad was regarded as someone who might just be able to broker some kind of peace. That was never a given, though. Those conversations were stressful for my dad. He would be dealing with people who were volatile and could often be vindictive.

When he went to prison, people stepped in to help us and I will always be grateful for that. I was taken to training at West Ham by cousins while my dad was away. I can only think that people were repaying favours. Dad had started putting money aside when it became clear to him that he was going to get a prison sentence. Still, every night Mum laid out the ornaments on the windowsill just to be safe. By then she had the three of us: me, my brother Nicky and my sister Charly. He started in Pentonville. I was young but not so young that I did not realise it was a terrible place. Mum would tell us to shout up to him when we went past the prison on our way back from football on the Market Road pitches. Tipped off by her, he would tell us when he next visited that he had heard us. Later he would be transferred to Highpoint prison in Suffolk. I will always remember the appropriately named Hard Times Café where families of the inmates could get a bite to eat and have a cry. If you ever find yourself there – and I sincerely don't wish that on any of you – I can highly recommend the milkshakes.

It was also in prison that Dad was briefly Jewish. He noticed that the Jewish inmates' kosher food was of a much higher quality than the slop he was getting so he told the prison authorities that he was Jewish and would henceforth be attending all prayers and mealtimes. He said that Cole was not his original family name but an Anglicised version of what had come before. He had, it is fair to say, done his homework. Somehow his persistence paid off. The rabbi who attended the prison was kind to him and said something along the lines of, look, George, we know you're not Jewish but as long as you behave yourself, we would be happy to have you. My dad was obviously fun to be around. It was a source of great amusement to us in later years when, watching TV or hearing something on the radio, he would, unprompted, recount accurately – or so he claimed – some teaching or piece of history from the Torah. He was actually listening to the rabbi, it turned out. As ever with my dad's life there was a final twist. Years later he bumped into the rabbi in question, who recognised him. If ever proof was needed that the Almighty notices a holy man's acts of kindness, it turned out that the rabbi was a Chelsea fan. Dad and the rabbi became friends again. Once I signed for Chelsea, the rabbi would call him for all the player gossip and Dad would get him tickets for games. My accountant Malcolm Webber went to synagogue every Saturday and he would ruefully point out that, in spite of that, he never got as much of his rabbi's time as my dad did.

My dad never found prison hard. It had been a part of his existence from such a young age that he could adapt to life inside better than most. He said that he watched it break some people. His approach was never to look at the time left on his sentence in its entirety. Instead he would break it into shorter periods of time and only ever look back at what he had done. Years later when I got the worst injury of my career – the injury that changed my life for ever – in 2009, I would do the same with my rehabilitation. There was always something useful I could learn from Dad.

By the time he came out, it was obvious to Mum and Dad – even given their lack of knowledge about football – that I had a future in the game. Mum was straight with Dad. There could be no more brawls, prison time or Ralph Lauren shirts sold out the back of a van. He had spent his life looking for opportunities to make money outside of the usual routes. He didn't have much option. Dad was never going to get accepted on the Marks and Spencer graduate trainee scheme. He accepted he had to change and that change would be so big that eventually we would leave Donnington Court and the Clarence Way estate for good. The whole family moved first to Romford in Essex, near to West Ham's training ground, as I went from schoolboy footballer to professional. The life of hand-to-mouth, of ornaments moved to the windowsill, of making ends meet, was coming to an end. That's the dream, I suppose. Young footballer makes it in the pro game and gets his family a new life. But I think often it is more complicated than that. I am immensely grateful for the opportunities I was given, and the way the game made me wealthy. I am glad Dad never went back to prison, and that Mum had all the things her hard work deserved. I am also conscious that they sacrificed the only world they had ever really known to follow me into a new one. Camden was a tough old place at times but it was their place.

One small corner of the world closed to them – and the rest of it opened up. I made sure that Mum and Dad watched me wherever I played. They travelled the world, to Japan and South Korea and the Middle East and the United States. Dad had barely left north London before then. After we left, he would sometimes go back to Somers Town and Queen's Crescent. On a couple of occasions, he might drive there in the Ferrari that I foolishly bought in the days when I thought being a footballer meant owning a car like that. Maybe he was just trying to make a point – none too subtly either – but I often wonder if he missed the days on the market stall or the Del Boy existence of trying to make a few quid here and there.

By the time he was out of prison, I was working my way through the stages to qualify for Lilleshall. Without wishing to blow my own trumpet, the undergraduate selection process for Cambridge University has fewer obstacles thrown in the way of applicants – and a lot more places on offer. Every year the Football Association went looking for a cohort of the sixteen most promising fourteen-year-old boys in the country to live full-time at their base in Shropshire for school years 10 and 11. You lived there, did your GCSEs at the local comprehensive and played football with the best players in the country. The system was so successful the French Football Federation copied it in establishing its Clairefontaine centre outside Paris as well as all its other regional centres. The FA's

Lilleshall no longer exists. It is the clubs that run development football programmes now.

The Lilleshall trial process started when you were in Year 9. I had seen England Under-15s play on Sky Sports and I wanted a slice of that. I really wanted it. I wanted it so much that I stopped all the flirting with other clubs and signed with West Ham because having an affiliated professional club was one of the requirements Lilleshall made. The first trial was for the best boys in the south-east of England, which primarily meant London, at the old FA base in Bisham Abbey in Buckinghamshire. I was confident because I had seen most of the opposition playing in London inter-borough football for Camden and Islington. My mate Paul Ellis from Somers Town, an excellent schoolboy centre-half who was with QPR at that time, came too. The old boys from the FA would grade us on different parts of our game and at the end they would let you know how you scored. I had got seven As and three Bs and I was immediately desperate to know what everyone else had got. Someone told me that another London lad, DJ Campbell, who went on to have a decent pro career, had got eight As and two Bs. I was crushed. As someone who had never given much thought to his academic career, I thought this must be what it's like doing your A levels.

The next set of trials were at Loughborough University with all the kids from up north, who to me were an unknown quantity. I quickly realised that the best players were either Londoners, Mancunians or Scousers. The level had gone up again. I didn't think I was necessarily the best any more, although others said I was. There was always someone who could do one thing better than me – quicker, or stronger. The lads I had gone with from West Ham didn't make it to the final round of thirty-two at Lilleshall for those sixteen golden tickets. There was a difference with Lilleshall in that they were not picking sixteen boys to win games there and then. If they had been doing so they would have selected the most physically developed. They were taking the sixteen they thought had the potential to be developed into the best players.

Mum had never been apart from me. From her year on her own when I was born, to meeting George and the two children, Nicky and Charly, that had followed. We had been through so much together and the idea of me living somewhere else for two years was very hard for her. Any mum would be the same. At one point, Mum just told me quietly that she didn't want me to go. She showed me how much she loved me by letting me. My daughter Ruby wanted to do the same many years later and she boards at school – or flexi-boards, as they say. That is because I cannot bear not to see her a couple of days a week. I know myself how hard the separation can be on a parent.

I checked the post every day. When that letter arrived, to tell me I was among the sixteen best players of my age in the country, the effect it had on my confidence was huge. I had always rated my ability. With the ball at the feet, I could skin anyone on the estate. Every big club wanted me. But this felt different. I felt like it was officially sanctioned by the kind of establishment figure you didn't see around the Clarence Way estate. A man in an FA suit down the road at Lancaster Gate had sat at his desk and typed it on some headed FA notepaper. Joseph Cole, of Donnington Court, Castlehaven Road, London NW1, was off to Lilleshall.

They invited all the families for an induction day, which was an eye-opener for me as well as George and Susan. For a start I noticed how well behaved all the boys were. Some of the parents were asking questions about chemistry GCSE or French exams. Two serious men from the FA reassured all the parents that they were not just going to make good footballers of us, they were going to make us into responsible young men. We were going to be taught to make our own beds and do our homework. I must confess, my mind wandered. Once I had been reassured that I would be playing football every day I felt I knew all I needed to know. Mum and Dad might have felt a bit out of their depth at first. I was put in a room with two goalkeepers, Rhys Evans and Stephen Hodgson. Great lads. Steve's dad was a police officer, which was a bit different to my dad. For the first time I was mixing with people from outside the estate. It was good for me. And Mum and Dad made friends too. They would come to see me on Sundays and after a while would drive up to Shropshire on a Saturday night to have dinner with some of the other parents. Nicky and Charly came along too, of course, and there were other siblings to play with. My family followed me playing games in Finland, France and the United States. It made Mum's job easier in convincing my dad that the ducking and diving had to finish. The parents they were meeting at Lilleshall didn't do that sort of thing. For all of us boys and our families too, Lilleshall was a huge part of our lives. That didn't mean we all made it as footballers. But we all took something from it. At the very least it was the friendships we built. I am still in a WhatsApp group with my Lilleshall teammates. Some are teachers; some work for the players' union, the Professional Footballers' Association; some work in player development at academies. The likes of Danny Webber and Leon Mike, who were at Manchester United and Manchester City, had good football careers. So did David Noble, from Stevenage, who played for Arsenal and was a talented boy. Our captain Ronnie Wright, from Preston North End, was always the smartest. He is now a clinical scientist in genetics.

Our lives were ruled, from the FA side, by a Yorkshireman

named Keith Blunt. If ever a name could conjure up an accurate picture of an individual then Keith Blunt was that name and Keith Blunt was that person. Mr Blunt was as tough as he sounded and he was hard on me. 'Flash Londoner,' he would say, 'here he is, Joe Cole, with all his flicks and tricks.' I couldn't stand him at first. I had been used to doing whatever I liked – free tracksuits at the clubs trying to sign me, a few quid here and there, the run of the place at West Ham. Suddenly I had this big gruff northerner telling me where I was going wrong. But I like to think I have some of my dad's ability to read people. After a while I began to understand what Mr Blunt was up to. He was trying to teach me that the game was hard, and also that at the very top level of football, all my feints and shimmies needed to be reinforced by something else. I needed to know how the pieces of a football match fitted together. What positions to occupy and what others might do. Where the space was on the pitch and where it was not. Already, at this age, I did not agree with the prevailing philosophy of 4-4-2. In those years the direct football that had been the FA's ideology for so long was still very much in effect.

At Lilleshall we all had designated jobs, as we would do as regular apprentices when we left at the age of sixteen and joined the clubs to which we were affiliated. Mr Blunt used to say that Don Revie had told the Leeds United apprentices that you could tell a player by the way he did his jobs. Did I agree with that? I am not sure I did wholeheartedly, but I also never forgot it. I must admit at Lilleshall I was a bit of a tearaway. Once when I had been more than a little slapdash with my job and hoped Mr Blunt wouldn't notice, he stopped all of us going into dinner. Mr Blunt shouted above everyone's heads: 'Joe Cole, flash Londoner, thinks he's too big to do his job.' I was sent back in to do it properly. The rest of the lads were furious with me. He was right, though. He wasn't asking a lot. Twenty minutes to clear up the changing room and mop the floor. I've mopped a lot of changing room floors at Lilleshall and at West Ham since then.

By the end of my time at Lilleshall, I had learnt from Mr Blunt. I had grown to like him and came to realise that he cared about me. He would later come to watch me play when I was a professional. I also think that he learnt a bit from me too. Our Lilleshall England team had played 4-4-2 for as long as anyone could remember. It had been that way when Michael Owen had been there, and Andy Cole, but in me they saw something different. They started playing a 3-4-1-2, with me as a number 10 behind the two strikers. That was a big change for Lilleshall and for Mr Blunt. Looking back, I admire them for doing that. For so long English football had been about forcing square pegs into round holes – in fact they'd force you into that round hole whatever shape you were, peg or not. It was a small concession to what I was as a footballer.

Just to complicate things further, Lilleshall did not constitute the official England schoolboys' team as it was then. As a squad we were the FA's school of excellence. In those days the coveted England Under-15s team was still selected by the English Schools' Football Association – the ESFA. It's much simpler now, the FA picks every junior team from the clubs' academy sides. In my year, just six of us from Lilleshall were selected by the ESFA and I was among them. Finally, I was destined to be live on Sky Sports, playing in the England kit, on this occasion against Wales in Cardiff. The night before, as our final preparation, we were told to gather downstairs in our hotel and all stood around the piano while someone struggled through the chords of 'God Save the Queen'. We had to practise singing it.

LUXURY PLAYER

The ESFA had forgotten to get my shirt done. I had been assigned number 13 and so my shirt was sent off to a sports shop in Cardiff the day before for the number to be printed. Except the shop did the '13' in red instead of the blue that had been requested. This caused quite a panic among the coaches who I guess were just at the beginning of a new era for educationalists in football – one in which they were trying to make sure children were not made to feel different or awkward. They were so serious that before the conversation began, I was worried someone in my family had died. I sat down and was asked: 'Joe, is it okay if you play for England with a red number?'

I said it was no problem at all, as long as I played for England.

There was a coachload coming from Camden to watch me play. How did it go? Well, at one point in the first half I got the ball in a tight space, drifted past one player, a stepover broke their lines and I thought: let me just have a go on this with my left foot. I didn't catch it quite as I had hoped but it flew. Bottom left corner of the goal. I knew where my family were in the stadium and I ran straight towards them. FA or not, rules or otherwise, I celebrated that one like a wild man.

I thought, I like this feeling.

6

Chelsea vs the World

José Mourinho would present his pre-match video clips to us on a big screen, next to the projector in a cabin at Harlington, talking us through it with his laser pointer. He would sit relaxed among his players, deep in his seat, with his legs stretched out as if he were watching a movie at home. I thought he chose to sit among us to show that we were together as a team and coaches, considering the details of our next challenge. Then if he had something more serious to say he would turn off the projector, rise slowly out of his chair, walk up to the screen and turn to face us. There was a certain theatre to all this. Serious face. A pause before he spoke. This time he seemed more serious than ever. We had lost the first leg of the Champions League last 16 tie to Barcelona at the Nou Camp 2–1. Didier Drogba had been sent off – a soft red card. In a rather eventful aftermath, José had accused the Swedish referee Anders Frisk of having a private half-time conversation with the Barcelona manager Frank Rijkaard. Frisk had quit refereeing, citing the threats he said he received. In response the head of UEFA's referees, Volker Roth, then called José 'the enemy of football' after the aggravation between José and the Barcelona fans.

And that wasn't all. We had already won our first trophy of

the season by then, the League Cup. We had beaten Liverpool in the final in Cardiff four days after Barcelona – during which José had courted more criticism by telling the Liverpool fans to be quiet. Our fans loved it. We were top of the Premier League. Around us there was, admittedly, chaos. UEFA hated us. As a team, we felt like the outsiders no one wanted to succeed. None of us knew what José was going to do next. He had been quiet on the flight home from Spain. We didn't know what he was thinking.

In the TV room, José looked around the faces staring up at him. 'Your first big test as a team,' he said. 'And you failed it. You went to the Nou Camp and you hid. Cowards. You went missing. No effing bravery.'

He turned to Petr Čech first and José did something he had not done since the giant keeper had joined the club. He tore him apart. Then he did the same to John Terry. 'You gave me nothing,' José said. 'You puff your chest out in the Premier League but Samuel Eto'o ran you ragged.'

'Frank Lampard? Xavi and Deco destroyed you.'

Bloody hell, I thought. He's doing twenty seconds on everyone. Wait until he gets to me. I'm usually his favourite target. They'll be scraping me off the floor. It was like a room of condemned men awaiting their turn. Willy Gallas got off reasonably lightly. He had been the best of a bad lot according to José. 'Didier Drogba, you cost us,' José said. 'You didn't hold the ball up.' These were his favourites. The core of his team. José was swearing in perfect English. Effing shit. You've got no balls. Sometimes accompanied by a sneer. Sometimes a look of bewilderment at how these players who he knew so well could have let him down so badly. I don't know what happened by the time he got to me and Duffa. Maybe he had just run out of steam. Maybe he just felt he had made his point.

But he critiqued us as a two-for-one. He said we had played okay. We had worked hard. He left it at that. I felt like a blind-folded man in front of a firing squad, spared by a late pardon. I was sure José was going to remember a bad moment I had in the first few minutes involving Giovanni van Bronckhorst, but it must have slipped his mind. The room was silent. No one even cleared their throat. José walked out, closing the door gently behind him.

This was March 2005. One bad half against West Bromwich Albion at the end of October and I had lost my place in the team. José had substituted me at half-time and I just couldn't get back into the side, at least in the Premier League, through November. It was not hard to see why. Duffa and Arjen Robben were red-hot. Robben was the Premier League player of the month. Duffa couldn't have been far behind. At that point Robben was the best player I had ever played with in my life and I didn't feel there was a way around him. For the first time I couldn't see a way back, which was in part my imma-turity. I had never been in this situation before and I couldn't stand being left out of the side. I blamed José. I shouldn't have done. It wound me up when Mateja Kežman would come on ahead of me. I didn't want to admit that he could offer something different. I heard Steve McClaren wanted me at Middlesbrough. There was even a shout I could go back to West Ham. I didn't tell my agent to discourage them. By the end of December I was beginning to wonder if my next game for Chelsea might be my last. Yet it was all about to change so quickly that in six months' time I would wonder why on earth I had ever worried.

I had not been on the bench for the whole of December until the 28th when I came on as a late substitute at Fratton Park and scored in the last minute. Four days later I came on and scored the winner at Anfield. That is one of the great grounds to score at, although there were sadly not that many goals when I did sign for Liverpool. On that day for Chelsea I scored in front of the Kop and ran the length of the pitch to the Chelsea supporters at the Anfield Road end. Away goals are the best goals. Somewhere in the stadium you can hear the distant noise of your own supporters celebrating, like the music from an earphone that has fallen on the floor. As you run towards it there is a quiet all around you. Frustration, anger, a bit of impotent rage. You grow to love it.

We were all in thrall to José. In pre-season he had introduced us to ice baths. For most of us it was the first time. He told us to get in and no one blinked: straight in, no questions asked, gritted teeth through the initial agony. He told us to wear recovery tights, these strange itchy garments – so we put them on. It wasn't all bad. He demanded a chef on the team coach whose job was essentially to put M&S ready meals in a microwave as we sped towards whatever airport. At West Ham it had been fish and chips. That season was relentless. You fought your way into the team and you tried to stay there. One bad game and you could be out. Those who couldn't stay the pace were just left behind. My friend Wayne Bridge went down after a challenge from Alan Shearer, in an FA Cup tie we lost to Newcastle United in February three days before the first Barcelona leg. When I got to Bridgey, his ankle was pointing the wrong way. I clearly remember his anguish and also my own dawning realisation, there on the pitch at St James' Park, that a life in football can change in a moment. Bridgey would still go on to have a great career but at the time he was England's second-choice left-back. He didn't play again until October. These days we go skiing together. I have even staggered up and down a mountain trying to keep up with him. He remains one of the strongest blokes I know. A monster in the gym. Six-pack still in effect. He is a great friend.

Landing in Barcelona for the game was a thrill. I had played many times at all the great grounds of English football but the Nou Camp was something different. I loved Barcelona. I loved the idea of Barcelona. I had treasured my Romario shirt as a kid and watched Barcelona on the telly. They had always given me an idea of how football might be far away from the hyper-physical game the youth teams of the English clubs played. First, though, we had to get through the airport. These were the days before private terminals and private arrivals and departures. The Barcelona fans had turned up to greet José at the terminal and we had to walk past them. He got what would become the usual jibe – 'the interpreter' – as he had been in part in the days of Sir Bobby Robson. When we got a hostile airport reception I always used to wonder whether people had booked a day off work to do it. It seemed such a waste of annual leave.

The first time you train on the Nou Camp, as we did the evening before the game, you get a sense of why Barcelona have become famous for playing the kind of football they do. The pitch is vast and it is immaculate. The ball moves so fast and true across its surface. I know that Roman Abramovich eventually fell out with José, in part, because he wanted us to play like Barcelona. The first problem with that, I would say, is the size of the pitch at Stamford Bridge. It's so much smaller. If you want to make nine hundred completed passes a game, to find the space and make the pitch feel too big for your opposition, the first thing you need – and this may sound obvious – is a big pitch.

We knew this game was a major test. We hadn't lost many that season and conceded very few goals but we were out of the FA Cup and a response was required. We were sitting down to dinner at our hotel after training when the televisions in the room started showing José's press conference live from the Nou Camp. Normally Sky Sports is on somewhere in the background and we keep one eye on the injury news. Suddenly on the telly, José asked the reporters if they want to know his team for the game. I could feel the lads tense up. We were trying to play it cool, but this was something new. When you go into a team meeting you are prepared. You are ready for the bad news. You might even have a good sense of which way it was going. But this was completely random. I was halfway through my pasta. I was not ready for this. I didn't have my poker face on. I thought: if he doesn't pick me I could end up chucking my food at the curtains. But the team was coming whether we liked it or not. José rattled off the names. When he said mine there was a huge sense of relief. Then an acute sense of awkwardness settled over the room. People tried to change the subject. Anything but address the fact that the bloke eating his salad next to you might have just been dropped live on television.

I loved the whole experience of the Nou Camp. The smell, the colours, even the sound felt different. Off the tunnel there was a small chapel where the players could go to ask for divine intervention, or whatever else they needed. I knew that I had to do the defensive part of my job. This was a key part of my game. I did not let my runner go. I knew that if I did I would get stick, principally because of the reputation that followed me around. As I lined up by the chapel in the Nou Camp tunnel these were the things on my mind. Track the full-back. Be sensible with the ball. Don't give people the grounds to make those lazy criticisms. I challenge anyone to watch me in that era and say I didn't do my defensive job.

With one small exception.

It was a moment of Ronaldinho genius the like of which I had never seen before. Early in the game he got the ball with his back to goal, rolled his studs over it and backed into Paulo Ferreira. Suddenly Van Bronckhorst made a run off me. What a stupid run, I thought. No point. No chance is he going to get the ball there. Then came the magic. Ronaldinho did a number of things I had never seen done on a football pitch and then zipped a ball across that beautiful surface to Van Bronckhorst who was now in exactly the right position to receive it. As for me, I was nowhere near it. I might as well have been watching at home on the telly. Suddenly, I found myself praying to the little crucifix in the Nou Camp chapel. Please don't score. Please. We would be 1–0 down and it would all be my fault. Van Bronckhorst stroked in a cross that was begging to be knocked in but – Praise the Lord! – no one was there. In my peripheral vision, I could see José on the touchline. He was raging. His arms were flapping up and down. He was shouting something. For my own sanity I decided not to look over at him. I got the message. I wasn't leaving Van Bronckhorst on his own again.

What a game it was. In Ronaldinho, we were in the presence of a footballer who could do things I didn't think possible. We hung in there. A bit of counterattack. Lots of defending. Make them play in front of us. But beyond that we were passive. Pinned back. Duffa and I swapped flanks and all we could do was defend until suddenly he went down the right. He got in and I came into the box from the left. Duffa crossed it on the money and I thought: bloody hell, I'm going to score at the Nou Camp. This is really happening. I'm going to score. I was already thinking about what I might do when it went in. I would be watching this goal on YouTube for the rest of my life.

Then, just as the moment came, Barcelona's Brazilian defender Juliano Belletti dived in desperately and stuck it in instead. It would have been much better for both of us if he had just let me do it. No one knows who to celebrate with when it's an own goal. The camera shot immediately lands on the nearest attacking player. And you have this pleased expression, but definitely not that thrilled-goalscorer look. You can't take the credit. It's a whole different celebration dynamic. We were shocked to be ahead. It wasn't going to last. After Didier's red card, we worked hard but eventually they hunted us down and we lost 2–1. They were a very good team.

Before the second leg, it would be fair to say that José's pre-match demolition of the team had an effect. For me it was par for the course. I was criticised regularly in public by José and Sven and the English media had picked up the scent. One dodgy pass to James Beattie and I knew I was in for it. For that reason, it was easier for me to take. After that day in the TV room I noticed some of the lads had the sort of faces that you see when you tell your kids off. It was a new experience for them. After his chat José stood back and watched how we responded. Either way, he had called it right. That first thirty minutes against Barcelona at Stamford Bridge might be the finest thirty minutes of football played in the history of Chelsea. The whole ground was alight that night. We got the feeling that Barcelona had turned up with a swagger. They thought they had won the tie. They didn't know what was going to hit them. We had already played well enough against them with ten men for sixty minutes in the Nou Camp when the referee had given them everything.

The home dressing room was full that night. Everyone who wasn't playing was there. I know how disappointed Scott Parker would have been to be left out but he was there. You don't forget that in your teammates. Everyone knew that something special was going to happen. José wanted aggression and pressing. He got it. Frank won possession for the first goal – a classic transition attack that went from Mateja Kežman to Eiður Guðjohnsen who scored. Frank scored the second on the rebound from my shot. We were 3–0 up on the night before Barcelona had even seen our end of the pitch. I didn't think much of Pierluigi Collina's refereeing either. We had to adjust in those days to a completely different style of referees in the Champions League from the Premier League and in this case there was another penalty we didn't agree with. Ronaldinho put that one away, but it was his second goal that night which everyone still talks about.

We were up against the best player in the world. Bear in mind I had spent a fortune on tickets for friends and family, and I was pretty sure most of them were there to watch Ronaldinho rather than me. He was at his peak and the goal he scored on 38 minutes silenced the stadium in a way I had never experienced before. On the pitch my first thought was: how has he done that? Could someone please rewind it? Because I don't get it. John Terry will always say simply: we had him covered. John is right. Two of the world's best defenders were in front of Ronaldinho, in JT and Ricky Carvalho. Frank Lampard behind him. Ronaldinho couldn't go backwards. He couldn't go forwards. He couldn't even shift it out from under his feet for the shot. He would have been tackled. Drag it back? Tackled. And so he did this thing. A wiggle of the hips, a feint with his foot. Then his right leg drawn back, although not a proper backlift. More a pulse of the muscles from that powerful core of his, down that strong leg and he struck it with what seemed like the force gathered in his big toe. I was right behind it. I gasped.

That brilliant toe-poke goal should have been a hammer blow. We were leading 3–2 on the night, 4–4 on aggregate and going out on away goals. We couldn't keep up the pace we had set in the first thirty minutes. We had to drop off and find another way. We were good at set-pieces. Kežman grabbed their centre-half at a corner and John scored our fourth. The place erupted. I dropped to my knees at the final whistle, but then out of the corner of my eye I could see a familiar figure in his grey coat, and he was heading straight for me. My first thought was: effing hell, what have I done? But this was different. José grabbed me and – this is the only way to describe it – he paraded me around the pitch. He was shouting at the fans. They couldn't hear him, but I could.

'Joe Cole!' José was shouting my name. 'Joe Cole! We won because of him!'

Or at least words to that effect. I have to admit this meant a lot to me. In those days José had me on a bit of string. I craved his approval and when I got it, I felt fantastic. Then there were the times when he dragged me back down and there would be more of those too. In the dressing room afterwards, Scott Parker came over to me and said, 'Joe, we won because of you.' I can't tell you how generous that was of Scottie. He was a great player for us. Always ready to come into games and serve the team. We had got into Barcelona and disrupted their rhythm. But it was more than that. There was quality, tenacity, a sense of togetherness. We were a real team. From that moment I knew we would win the Premier League.

That turned out to be the simpler of the tasks. I scored the winner against West Brom a week after we eliminated Barcelona and by the time we came up against Bayern Munich in the next round we had won twice more in the league. UEFA had also gone after José. He was banned from the touchline for the two legs for the Bayern tie which immediately gave him another reason to tell us the world was against us. If the Barcelona tie had been marked by his speech in the TV room, the Bayern tie was about his appearance in the home dressing room at Stamford Bridge in defiance of the UEFA ban. I don't know how he got in. He just seemed to materialise in front of our eyes. Then they famously took him away in a kit skip. By then the UEFA officials in the corridor outside had got wind of what was going on and were banging on the door. José took a bit of persuasion to get in the kit skip. I think he must have felt a bit claustrophobic. His last words before the lid went on were something like, 'Lads – don't mention this to your agents or anyone else.' I remember thinking: someone will definitely mention this.

Bayern folded that night. We worked out early on that Lúcio, their Brazilian defender, couldn't handle Didier. Frank got two great goals. I think Bayern were embarrassed and we saw that in the second leg at the old Olympic Stadium in Munich. We came around the corner in the tunnel and they were right in our faces. I'm not sure what their pretext was – we were a bit late – but it was a proper ambush. All their biggest lads: Michael Ballack, Oliver Kahn, Lúcio. John Terry, as his way, was straight in without missing a beat. He was very good at that. Totally unflustered. Nose to nose with their main antagonists, staring them down, the referee trying to get in between. I was some-where at the back bouncing up and down to get a view of all the commotion while our big boys ploughed forward. No one was going to bully us. In fact, it lit us up.

Another great game. At 1–1 I was on the ball and was trying to draw a foul to slow things down when I saw Didier at the back post. It's funny how even in games you remember those details. Didier was on his own with Lúcio so I thought, let's see how Lúcio fancies it this time. I floated one in and Didier flung Lúcio aside again to get our second. Bayern scored two late goals and won it 3–2 on the night but it wasn't enough to win the tie. Most memorable was our half-time team-talk. José was still banned and now UEFA were hyper-vigilant about him being spirited into the dressing room. The decision was made that we couldn't risk it again. The Olympic Stadium was full of history, but also falling apart. Even the plaster on the walls in the away dressing room had holes in it. Before the game I saw our coach Mick McGiven going around the room, with the tape we used to strap our shin pads on, covering the holes. The levels of paranoia had escalated by then and we were convinced that UEFA was spying on us. I could see why at half-time. Someone had set up a conference phone speaker in the centre of the room which seemed the height of technological sophistication at the time. Suddenly José's voice crackled out of the speakers and he gave us a remote half-time team-talk. The whole room was silent, listening to the man UEFA couldn't ban. At one point, José – or José's disembodied voice – got stuck into Ricky Carvalho, who was one of his regular targets for criticism. José was doing his usual thing: 'Ricky! Don't effing lose concentration!' I glanced over at Ricky and he was looking directly at the speaker nodding silently in acquiescence as if José was in the room. That was the hold that José had over us.

The Premier League and the Champions League in the palm of our hands – but could we get over the line? At this stage of a season, you can feel drained. You feel like you've heard every team-talk before. This is when you see the genius of the great managers. They find something new to say. They find a way to connect with their players. The greatest compliment I can give José at that time was that he would give team-talks and I felt like he was talking to me directly, and addressing my worries and anxieties. But, of course, he wasn't. He was talking to twenty-five players. He just knew us so well that it felt that way. We played Fulham in late April and we were poor. It was 1–1 at half-time and we were playing dismally. Instead of tearing a strip off us, José did the opposite. He said, 'I know you're tired. I know it's hard. I know you have nothing left. But I love what you have done for me this season. Just one more half of football for yourself and for your families.' The contrast with the Barcelona second leg pre-match couldn't have been greater. I didn't play well but I scored a good goal in that first half. I was so knackered that when he subbed me it was one of the only times in my career I was relieved to see my number go up.

We won the league in our next game, away at Bolton Wanderers. It was the end of a fifty-year wait for the club's second league championship. It was a monumental day for our fans who had been through so much uncertainty, especially in the 1980s when the club came close to losing Stamford Bridge and might even have disappeared. We wanted nothing more than to celebrate with them. They gathered around our coach outside the stadium and I couldn't resist climbing out of the sunroof with a bottle of champagne. As usual I wasn't drinking the champagne but it was going all over the roof of the coach which was getting ever more slippery. Suddenly I lost my footing and for a moment I could envisage myself plunging over the edge onto the Bolton car park. My Champions League dreams over, and the victim of one of the most infamous football injuries of all time. Luckily, I had nimble feet in those days. I regained my balance and composure and returned to my seat.

An hour or so later I was back at our hotel playing *FIFA* with John Terry. I remember saying to him: did we really just win the league? It felt like we should have been out celebrating but there was no time to do so. We were halfway through a Champions League semi-final with Liverpool and the second leg at Anfield was three days away. José allowed us one beer on the lawn of the hotel, and then we were sent to bed. Maybe José knew that if he had let us go back to London we would have been out all night celebrating. I have always believed it would have been better to have won the league after the second leg at Anfield. I think there was an emotional release that day at Bolton which didn't help us. Then we had to stuff it all back inside and prepare for Liverpool. We were a better team than them – thirty-seven points ahead in the league. They had some wonderful players, not least Steven Gerrard. Stevie is an exceptional footballer. He is a friend and a team-mate who I admire greatly. He carried a lot on his back in his career. He wasn't the only one in that team. Jamie Carragher, Sami Hyypiä, Xabi Alonso, Didi Hamann. Good players. But we were a better team and we missed our chance to cash in.

José changed our team that night. I had been playing on the right all season and had a good understanding with Paulo Ferreira behind me. José switched me to the left and dropped Duffa who had a bit of an injury. He picked Tiago on the right to press Djimi Traoré at full-back. There was a logic to it because Traoré was not great on the ball. My feeling was: we've beaten Liverpool three times already this season. Why are we worrying about them? Willy Gallas was behind me at full-back which made it two right-footed players on the left side. On the right Paulo would receive the ball on his back foot and his body would open up naturally. He always had a ball he could play inside to me if he needed to. These patterns of play are important. They become second nature. But we disrupted our own rhythm with the changes. They scored early on and we never got it back. You have to hand it to the Liverpool fans – it was intense in that stadium. That didn't affect us as players. We had seen it all before. But the referee was melting and giving Liverpool every decision including that goal from Luis García that never even crossed the line. That's football. Ultimately, we had no one to blame but ourselves. I didn't play well that night. I was watching from the bench by the time Eiður missed the chance for what would have been the equaliser – and the decisive away goal winner. If someone as cool as him in front of goal couldn't bury that, it told you everything you needed to know. We could have played all week and not scored.

I got the hook for UEFA drug testing after the match which had one advantage. They give you beer to help you to pee. I said, 'I'll take four please.' I needed to get drunk. I downed them sitting in my kit while I waited for nature to take its course. By the time I got back to the dressing room it was empty. There is something very poignant about a dressing room after a big defeat. All the blood, sweat and tears have been expended for nought. Discarded tape all over the floor, the smell of the turf. A sense of the previous occupants' gloom. A room vacated as swiftly as possible. Maybe I was imagining it as I stood alone under the shower. Once the dopamine fades and the buzz of the sponsor's lager recedes, you can feel pretty crap.

We had won the league and hadn't even lifted the trophy, but it already felt like we had lost something. José gathered the lads together. 'This has been a great season,' he told us. 'We are going to collect that Premier League trophy and celebrate with our fans.' He was right, of course. There was just one home game of the three left, against Charlton Athletic, and that was when we would receive the trophy. We had been partying for the last three days, which isn't the normal preparation. But we were at ease with the world. We were upstairs in our lounge before going down to change when someone asked the question. What price is Maka to score today? Our great French defensive midfielder Claude Makélélé – Maka - had not scored all season. That wasn't unusual – goals weren't part of his job. Maka told me once that he had started his career at Celta Vigo as a speedy winger. I said, 'Maka, I don't believe you.' As a squad we did like a bet and in the days before the FA banned any kind of gambling by the game's participants we would have had a bet on anything we could. No apps in those days, just the cash in our pocket. I don't know who organised it. Was it me? Sorry, I just can't remember. Everyone who fancied betting on Maka scoring handed over the cash they had on them. About seven hundred quid all told and we sent the kitman out to one of the bookies around Stamford Bridge to put it all on Maka to score. I think we had forgotten about it ten minutes later.

We played beautifully that day. We still wanted to win. Then we got the penalty and a ripple went through the team. Maka! Our wager! It was probably worth more to Frank on his goal bonus to take the penalty himself but quickly the ball was in Maka's hands and you can see from the footage how much we loved the mischief of it all. We are footballers. Simple creatures. It doesn't take much to get us excited. Maka then took what could only be described as the World's Worst Penalty followed by the World's Worst Penalty Rebound Attempt. It was like he was trying not to score. He somehow managed to hit the penalty into the ground. Then three players converged on the ball and he scuffed it into the goal. You can see the joy and elation on our faces and the delight of the crowd.

When the final whistle went the emotion hit me in a way that it never had before. I am a bit of a crier. I was a weeping wreck at the birth of each of my three children. On the pitch at Stamford Bridge, I remember thinking this might be a bit much.

I think a few tears are permissible if you've won the World Cup, but someone wins the Premier League every year. So I dropped to the ground and hid my face while I got it together. It's nothing but pure joy winning a Premier League. All your favourite people are in one place at the same time. Family, teammates, friends and the Chelsea fans who have watched us all season, as well as the trophy. Everyone together.

Did we ever cash in that bet? I believe common sense prevailed. Someone may have said, lads, I'm not sure that's a good idea. Someone else might have said, there might be a rule against that. That was one lucky bookie.

7

Famous at Sixteen

I was sixteen years old when I was featured on the front page of a national newspaper and that first time remains one of the weirdest experiences of my life. A reporter from the tabloid the *Sunday People* approached my parents at a game I was playing for England Under-16s. Mum and Dad spent most of the conversation trying to get away from him and at no time were they aware that anything they said was going to be published. I had a decent relationship with the media throughout my career – all things considered. On the football pages they had their suspicions about my defensive instincts, which I disagreed with in the strongest possible terms. Certain columnists seemed to dislike me for reasons I couldn't quite understand. Lots worried constantly whether I was fulfilling my potential. But by and large it was fine. This occasion, however, was not.

When the piece was published in March 1998, I was only sixteen years and four months old. I was in my second year at Lilleshall and would not be able to sign my first professional deal until I was seventeen – which was that November. I was relatively well known within football, and West Ham fans who paid attention to the matchday programme will have read about the success of our youth team. But I was not a public figure in any way and I certainly wasn't ready to be on the front page of a national newspaper. These were very different days in terms of footballers' relationship with the media. The newspapers – the print media – ruled the roost. The days of social media and the digital age in publishing were still a long way off. People tell me now that the Sunday newspapers in particular were then in a ferocious battle for readers. They certainly took no prisoners when it came to me. £5,000 A WEEK AND HE IS JUST 16 was the headline on the front page of the *Sunday People* that Sunday morning. And underneath: AMAZING DEAL FOR SOCCER APPRENTICE. I accept that there is always an interest in footballers, and perhaps even footballers too young to sign professional deals, but commanding the front page of a national newspaper seemed – even to my young mind – completely disproportionate.

There was one major problem with the story. I wasn't on £5,000 a week. It was made up. A lie. There was no way George Cole would ever have discussed money with a reporter. In fact, when he wouldn't leave my parents alone, George had ended the conversation by telling the reporter to eff off. Where the claim about my salary had come from, I had no idea, but the effect was instantaneous. Everyone believed it to be true. The next week at my school in Shropshire a teacher cracked a joke. 'Lend us a fiver, Joe.' Made with good intentions, I'm sure, and I have only happy memories of the school. But I felt suddenly self-conscious. I felt that the story made me different and had marked me out. I guess now, a newspaper front page like that would prompt an intervention by a school. But this was a different time and none of the teachers asked me what I thought about it, or whether I was comfortable with it. Instead, it was my friends at Lilleshall who could see it was a problem and they enquired cautiously about how I felt which did help me.

I would sign a lucrative contract at the age of seventeen. It was nothing compared to the vast sums the best seventeen-year-old footballers can command now on their first pro deals. It was not £5,000 a week. The deal I would sign on the pitch at half-time of a West Ham home game against Chelsea on the eighth of November, my seventeenth birthday, was worth £1,000 a week.

It was a lot of money and, as I progressed in the first team, I would earn much more at West Ham. I felt I earnt that with my performances. What that front page in the *Sunday People* did was subtly change perceptions of me. A mood that I was spoilt, overpaid and had too much too soon. It wasn't explicit but I felt it was there. The truth was that I could have earnt many multiples of that if my parents and I had manipulated the interest in me from every big club in England. I signed for West Ham because I liked the club, and I thought it would be the best chance to become a first team player. The money was incidental. I didn't have any notion what I might spend it on.

Lilleshall had gradually been teaching me how football worked, even if I did not always agree with their theories. I sat my GCSEs in my second year at Lilleshall, in May 1998, and got two C-grades, two Ds, two Es and the rest, I think we can agree to forget about. The Cs were in English and history, both subjects which I have come to enjoy much more as I have got older. I appreciate the school trying to broaden the horizons of an estate kid from Camden. On the Clarence Way estate, school was generally regarded as somewhere the kids went while their parents were at work rather than an academic opportunity. I am very proud of my own children's efforts at school. They work so hard on homework and projects. It is a very different approach to my own school years.

Around the time my GCSE history coursework was due, I discovered the internet. By this stage it was no longer possible to use the money I had been given for my train fare home to bribe others to do my homework. My project on the Second World War was overdue. The headmaster of Lilleshall, Mr Pickering, gave me permission to use the computer in his office which was the only one at Lilleshall with an internet connection. As I was researching the Battle of Britain, I began to wonder what else might be available on this remarkable new resource. Not long after I was looking at pictures of some of the more well-known glamour models of the era. This was an astonishing discovery for a teenage boy who spent all his time at an all-boys' school deep in the countryside. I clicked some more. I wondered whether I should share this with my team-mates. Very soon the likes of Danny Webber, Craig Pead and others were crowded around the computer in Mr Pickering's study while I introduced them to the wonders of the world-wide web. Then we heard Mr Pickering coming through the adjoining office and heading our way. There was another way out of the office and, as sharp young athletes, my teammates were through the door and away in seconds. Unfortunately, I had still not mastered the details of web browsers and as I clicked in a panic trying to shut the thing down, I succeeded only in zooming in on the item on the screen. By the time Mr Pickering had come to check on what all the commotion was about, I had on my screen an enlarged picture of a very large pair of naked breasts. I accepted my punishment. It was a gate run, the standard tariff, which involved a run all the way down to the gates at the end of the long driveway, three miles in all. Nothing I couldn't handle but quite spooky nonetheless after dark, so I didn't hang around.

Mr Pickering was a kind man who cared for the boys sent to him from all over the country. He knew I was a Chelsea fan and when Chelsea reached the FA Cup final in 1997, at the end of my first year at Lilleshall, he called me into his office that very Saturday morning. He said that he had two tickets and I could pick someone to go with me. All I needed to do was hurry up and get my Lilleshall FA tracksuit on. There was a car waiting outside to take us. It was one of the best surprises of my life. Three years after I had watched Chelsea lose to Manchester United – having turned down the United mascot gig – I sat in the Wembley Royal Box with Craig Pead and watched Chelsea win the FA Cup. We even got a glimpse of Helen Chamberlain, the star presenter of *Soccer AM*, who we all watched on Sky Sports every Saturday at Lilleshall. We all had a crush on her.

Lilleshall was good for me in many different ways. It protected me from growing up in an environment that was becoming ever more hazardous for a teenage boy as I found out to my cost on one of my trips home to Donnington Court in the school holidays. I had been seeing a girl who lived in one of the three tower blocks in Somers Town where the stolen car journey had begun. We were inside the stairwell of the Gillfoot tower one afternoon, canoodling, when a local man walked in. I knew him. In fact, I turned to say hello to him as he walked behind us. I knew him to be volatile and I probably said hello as a way of reassuring myself. I then turned away from him, which meant his first punch was in the back of my head. I had no chance. He had walked past me and then attacked. Before I knew it, he was raining punches all over me, as I turned away from my date and faced him. It happened so quickly I had no time to react at all. I had fought before. At school those kinds of confrontations would even be arranged, like prize fights, and in Camden you had to be able to look after yourself. But this was totally different. He was a man and I was a boy. I was overwhelmed very quickly and another punch knocked me off my feet and sent me tumbling down the flight of stairs to the door.

I went back to that landing in the course of researching this book and as soon as I walked through that door at the base of the tower block I felt the fear and the powerlessness of that moment. The girl in question had wisely run away by the time I got to my feet. He started coming down the stairs towards me and at that point it was a bit like one of those horror films. Those moments when the victim knows they need to get the door open and get out. I wrenched at the door, flung it open and ran out across the estate and away. I ran to my friend Ossie's flat which was the nearest place I knew. He said I was so badly beaten and bleeding that his parents didn't recognise me at first. In many respects I had been lucky. I had been beaten up pretty mercilessly and fallen down a flight of stairs. There was no serious damage. When they took me back to my parents, I could see the fear in my mum's eyes. Not just for what had happened to me but what she knew would happen now. Dad took one look at me. He asked me if I was okay. Then he asked me: 'Who?' As I told him, I saw Mum shake her head. Mum knew there was no point trying to stop Dad. He went into another room and got a knife. Then he walked out of the flat and didn't come back until the morning.

I know what my dad would have done had he found the man he was looking for. I am glad he didn't find him. Moments of violence can have far-reaching consequences in the community we lived in. We found out soon after that my attacker had realised who he had assaulted and the severity of the likely repercussions. He swiftly left north London. Word reached us that he had thought the girl in question was in a relationship with a friend of his. My guess is that he was out of his mind on drugs when he attacked me. I am fortunate that it had not been worse. Years later when I was established as a Premier League footballer I was driving through Camden and saw him. It was quite a poignant moment. The intervening years had not been kind to him. He looked broken. I felt a rush of rage. For a moment I thought about pulling over and attacking him in the same way he had attacked me. But it really isn't in my nature. I had so much to be thankful for, and this man had nothing.

I left Lilleshall in the summer of 1998, desperate to get on with my football career. I had been rising up the hierarchy of junior teams at West Ham when I came back to the club in the school holidays away from Lilleshall. Every day I walked from Donnington Court to Kentish Town West and got the Overground train to Stratford, then changed for the Tube to Chadwell Heath and walked the rest of the way to the training ground. I would just turn up whether my team was training or not. It would never have occurred to me not to do so. West Ham in the 1990s was the perfect place for that kind of informality. I had the run of Chadwell Heath. I might train with the Under-19s, or the reserves, and sometimes the first team manager Harry Redknapp, who already knew about me, would say he needed me to work with someone from the first team. I might be crossing balls for our striker Paul Kitson to practise finishing. There always someone who was prepared to pull me into a game or a session. I assumed it was normal but the reality was that I was getting this unique football education at such a pivotal age.

That summer after leaving Lilleshall, I went on holiday with my parents to Turkey – with my friend Ossie in tow as well – and broke three of my toes. A nightmare. Unbeknown to my parents, Ossie and I had hired mopeds despite being too young to do so. That was the mindset of the Camden estates. Mopeds were very popular and I would later buy one with my first professional wages. I had a lot to learn about disconnecting the recklessness of the world I grew up in with the demands of being a Premier League footballer. In Marmaris, I crashed into the back of a tourist coach. I was in agony. I told Mum and Dad I had done it jumping off a wall. They took me to hospital and then rang West Ham. We flew back and I was sent straight to a private hospital in Loughton in Essex. I was distraught. They operated the next day. I won't forget the doctor, Tom McCallif, who treated me because I felt like my career was in his hands and what good hands they turned out to be. I missed pre-season. The three broken metatarsals had pins inserted in them but what I didn't know – because I couldn't see, and Dr McCallif and my parents wisely chose not to tell me – was that the pins stuck out of the ends of my toes. When the moment came Dr McCallif told me that the bone had set well. Then he produced a pair of pliers and said, Joe, this won't take a minute. He pulled out the pins there and then. It was over so quickly even my famous squeamishness didn't have time to kick in. There was a bit of blood and that was it.

I had wasted three months. I was officially an apprentice on £45 a week until my seventeenth birthday in November when I could sign the pro contract. I had been playing for the Under-19s ahead of schedule. That was the team for second-year apprentices as well as older players who had been offered a professional deal of some kind. I was still sixteen. But when I recovered from my broken toes I was brought back to the Under-17s for a while. A few weeks later, Tony Carr, the club's famous head of youth development, who had overseen the careers of Rio Ferdinand and Frank Lampard, and many more before them, called me into his office around the time of my seventeenth birthday. Tony told me that I was miles off the first team.

For the first time I disagreed with Tony. I said that I thought I was close. By then, I was playing for the reserves on a Tuesday night. I was playing for the Under-19s again. Tony listened to me but stuck to his guns. Over the years I have wondered if he was doing it to provoke a reaction. I like to think that I would have put the hard work in either way. Tony said that I was perceived to be coasting. So, I dug in and trained harder. When I was ten years old I believed that unless I played football every day I wouldn't become a professional. I have no idea where that had come from but it lodged in my mind and dictated my life. Now on the brink of my seventeenth birthday, I went back to that mindset. I pushed myself. I would take a ball around the back of Chadwell Heath, where there was a wall, and get back to what I used to do on the estate. Right foot, left foot, against the wall. Sometimes the coaches would come with me and how lucky I was. Paul Heffer, Peter Brabrook, Jimmy Frith as well as Tony himself. They all gave me their time. I would practise for hours. What Tony had said to me stung. Perhaps I needed it. I felt my body getting stronger. I was back to my best in the youth team and I was getting frustrated because I wanted to be with the first team. Sometimes I expected too much from my teammates. I was impatient.

As an apprentice under the old regime, one that could be traced back through the years of Bobby Moore and Trevor Brooking, I had a football education that included the famous apprentice jobs of yesteryear. We would train in the morning, eat our lunch and then we would clean the boots of the first team players and parts of the training ground. I became very handy with a mop in those months. Both in the first team dressing room at Chadwell Heath and then the first team dressing room at Upton Park on Saturday afternoons, after we had played our youth team game in the morning. The strange thing about this is that there was not really any structured coaching. We just sort of muddled through. What I learnt at West Ham was from proximity to the first team and I got that through my apprentice jobs.

I had watched many games at West Ham over the years but now, as I felt my first team debut was coming close, I tried to watch the team from as many different parts of the old stadium as I could. I sat behind the benches so I could hear Harry and Frank Lampard senior speaking to the players. I sat high up in the main stand. I even sat among the lunatics in the Bobby Moore stand. When a big goal went in there was this feeling of a pulse running through the place and you got the sensation that Upton Park was bouncing up and down on its foundations. I am sure that a structural engineer would take issue with that analysis but it felt that way. Then afterwards, I would make my way down to the home dressing room where I would sit with my broom waiting to be summoned. A few years earlier, Harry had let me and my friend from Camden, Paul Ellis, wander in and out. Now it was part of my responsibilities. Win, lose or draw the door would be shut and I would sit as close as possible so I could listen to Harry grilling people. There was often a lot of shouting. I could hear him effing away at the likes of John Moncur or Steve Lomas or Ian Bishop. Already at that time I would imagine myself in there and how I might respond to a similar tirade from Harry. Soon after the shouting stopped, Harry would come out and slam the door behind him. Then Frank Lampard senior would come out and slam the door behind him. They would go into the manager's office. Then the coach Roger Cross or the kitman Eddie Gillam would pop out to tell me I could go in.

I loved those afternoons, especially when the team had won. Neil Ruddock might be singing along to some Frank Sinatra. Or there might be eighties music playing and some of the players would be dancing. There were mugs of tea but no booze because Harry didn't like booze around the dressing room. This was a very masculine environment on the face of it. But beneath the surface there was a lot more to it than simple bravado. There was fear, anxiety, relief and lots of wisdom if you were prepared to listen. I would be taking it all in as I swept up the mud brought in by their boots from the old pitches, which had a much greater soil content than the modern surfaces. Strappings would be all over the place. Discarded briefs and towels I had to deposit in the kit bin. I would listen to the players talk about the game I had just watched. They might discuss how quick Ryan Giggs was or what it was Nicky Butt had said to one of them. Looking back, all this was valuable to me. The first team players, who were to become my teammates, were kind. They would ask how my youth team had got on that morning. Sometimes they would ask me what I thought of their game. I had to wait for every player to leave and then get the mop out and clean the floor one last time.

Cleaning the dressing room prepared me for making my debut. When I finally joined the first team as a player I had some notion of what it might all be like. I had a feeling for what it would look like in its worst moments, when the team was beaten. The anger, and the testosterone, and all the egos and the arguments. I was an interested bystander before I was a participant. Even now I'm sure people all over the world watch the Premier League on telly and notice that it looks a certain way. A little sanitised – the perfect kits and perfect pitches and perfect hair. But in the privacy of the dressing room you will still see the eternal conflict that exists in professional football. The anger and the exhilaration that comes with trying to win football matches. I am glad I was exposed to that from such a young age. I only did it for six months at the start of that 1998–99 season. I stopped cleaning the home dressing room at Upton Park once I was picked in the first team squad in January, but I still had to clean the dressing rooms every day at the training ground even after that. I also had to clean the boots of the older professionals I had been assigned at the start of the season. Which meant that I cleaned the boots of Shaka Hislop, my teammate and the first-choice goalkeeper, as well as those of Chris Coyne who was captain of the reserves. Even though I was in the first team and Chris wasn't, it was never a problem. He was a nice Aussie guy and just made a joke about it. The rules were the rules.

Over Christmas 1998, Harry asked me to come in every day but I would have turned up even if he hadn't. I had Christmas Day off and that was it. I was performing well in training. The dressing room floor was also sparkling. I had the mop in my hand when Frank Lampard senior asked me on New Year's Day 1999 whether I owned a suit, and then to put it on and report to Upton Park at 1.30 p.m. the following day for the FA Cup tie against Swansea City. My fellow apprentice Bertie Brayley was cleaning the other dressing room at the time. Yet I didn't even tell Bertie, himself a really talented footballer. I wanted Mum and Dad to be the first to know. I got on the train home from Stratford that evening. I remember looking around at the people on the train in the days before everyone had their heads in their phones. I felt that I had this remarkable secret inside of me: I might be playing in the FA Cup on Saturday!

I had been in the dressing room, first to arrive, for hours

before 1.30 p.m. on Saturday 2 January 1999. I read the programme over and again. My name was on the back. Gradually the place filled up with the famous players of the West Ham first team. I had trained with them, picked up their pants and towels and listened to their conversations and now I was about to become their teammate. It's nothing that remarkable in football. Life moves fast and people just accept that the kid with the broom is now one of them. But when it's your turn to make the jump, it does feel incredible. Harry never wrote a team down and pinned it to the wall. He would just come into the dressing room and name it on the Saturday afternoon, including substitutes, and then leave. Often the aggrieved parties would follow him angrily out of the door and we would hear the shouting and recriminations down the corridor. This day, I was on the bench.

I had played at Upton Park before but never when it was packed and the floodlights were on by full-time. This winter day came with the classic West Ham assault on the senses. The aroma of fried onions and cigarette smoke. There was mist too. For all the aforementioned, a freshness in the air and the keen sense of anticipation. Needless to say, spoiling this happy scene with twenty-five minutes left to play was a Swansea goal. The reality was that West Ham found themselves behind to lower league opposition and heading out of the FA Cup in front of a home crowd. Harry was calculating. He knew that sending on a kid, especially one who was well known to the better-informed fans, might lift the stadium. At the very least he knew they wouldn't boo me. It's different today where you can watch academy games online and get to know all the promising youngsters coming through. But even in that pre-digital era, I felt people knew who I was – Lilleshall, England Under-15s, that front page of the *Sunday People* newspaper. I had been billed as the best kid in the country. The vibe among the fans would usually have been: let's see if the kid can entertain us. Now I knew there was the added expectation that I could do something to get us back in this game.

I stood next to Harry on the touchline. He put his arm around me and by this point the whole stadium could see I was coming on. The response will live with me for ever. It set the tone for the relationship I have with the West Ham fans. There was a ripple of excitement and goodwill. There were no coaches standing around me with tactical folders. I didn't know who I was marking at corners. Or whether I was taking the attacking corners we won. I wasn't even sure if there would be extra-time if we equalised. My mission was beautifully simple. Harry said casually, 'Go and make something happen, son.' The break in play came, and at last the moment had arrived. I stepped onto the pitch and could at last call myself a professional footballer.

When you are on the pitch you are treated as an equal. Whether you have played seven hundred games or it is your first, there is no mollycoddling. The best you will get from your teammates might be some mild encouragement. 'Come on, son,' someone said. 'You're good enough.' I felt all eyes on me. My first few touches were good. I had the opportunity to play in Ian Wright but declined it. These decisions are made in a millisecond. If you don't make that pass the instant you see it, you don't make it at all. Wrighty was a huge figure to me. Around Camden he was a god to the Arsenal fans. By now his career was winding down but he had been unlucky not to have gone to the World Cup the previous summer. He used to call me 'the kid'. If I dropped a shoulder and glided past a senior teammate in training I would hear his booming laugh. 'Oi,' he would shout at my opponent, 'he's rinsed you again.'

This time, on the pitch at Upton Park he was not happy. He shouted, 'I made the run. Effing pass the ball.'

This is how quickly it changes. On the pitch as a first team player you are now subject to all the same demands. I would live or die by my decisions. Forwards always want you to try to pass to them but they are not the ones who are going to get booed when the ball goes out of play. By the last few minutes we were throwing everything at Swansea. In my head the music was playing. I was thinking sharply. We won a corner and as per our pre-match plan I had no idea where I was supposed to be. The ball nearly dropped for me. It was just out of reach but loose and in that second I just thought, please, let it fall to a West Ham player. It did. It would be Julian Dicks's last goal for the club. The crowd erupted. There was joy. We had saved our FA Cup lives. From my own point of view I was just delighted that my debut had not ended in defeat.

Afterwards, I was still too young to have a drink in the players' bar. They couldn't serve me because the club knew only too well how old I was. I also had not yet passed my driving test so I went home sat in the back of my parents' car, with Nicky and Charly. Mum made dinner back at the flat in Donnington Court. Then Ossie, Paul Ellis and Jason came over. I set the VHS recorder for *Match of the Day* and we went out across the streets that we knew so well. We were heading for The Verge in Camden Town and then on to the Forum nightclub in Kentish Town. These were then two very suitably down-at-heel establishments which defined our teenage years until we realised my wages and fame would gain us entry to more upmarket places in the West End. The Forum was the kind of club that attracted people of all means and all ages. It was by no means cool. I might well run into one of my aunties and all her mates on the dancefloor. The DJ's setlist might best be described as wedding music. Word had gone around Camden that I had played my first game for West Ham and people were kind and generous in their praise. They mostly said that they had never doubted I would get there.

8

Negotiations with Roman

Roman Abramovich was a rare presence in the lives of his Chelsea players. We would see him briefly after games. He gathered us together once in 2010, after we lost in the Champions League to Inter Milan, by then managed by José Mourinho, to ask us pointedly whether we were top players, or just players on top salaries. That was the only time in seven years I saw him speak to us as a collective squad. It was also the only time I saw him angry. I went to see him once, memorably – for me rather than him, I should add – to tell him I was leaving Chelsea. Fifteen minutes later I left his office fully on board with staying at the club. I don't suppose it was the most difficult negotiation he ever faced. Other than that we had some brief impromptu conversations over the years. He was a man who felt quite comfortable walking into a room and saying nothing at all. Maybe he just liked to see how people reacted. I can't say that's my style. Roman didn't waste words. He didn't bother with small talk. He only engaged if he was genuinely interested. I once found myself explaining to him in detail what a particular piece of equipment in one of the medical rooms was for when he wandered in there one day when I was rehabilitating from an injury. He spoke decent English. His questions were specific. I realised about twenty seconds in that he was not shooting the breeze; he wanted to know. And once he was satisfied he understood what the device was for – he was off.

I do often wonder where in the world Roman is now. I would like to think that one day I can talk to him about what happened, and how his life went from a young man, orphaned as a child, selling rubber ducks on the streets of Moscow, to being one of the best-known billionaires on the planet. And then to what it is now – whatever it is now. Although I doubt that I will ever meet again the man whose fortune funded the rise of Chelsea and the best years of my career. I was fascinated by him when I was at Chelsea. He was far too remote from us to have the kind of conversation I would like to have. He was the boss. He would suddenly appear in the building at Cobham, the new training ground in Surrey we moved to from Harlington in 2005, and then we might not see him for weeks. There was never any doubt who was in charge. You could feel it, in the times when a manager was struggling – José, Luiz Felipe Scolari – that this would not be tolerated for very long.

I went to see Roman because I wanted to leave. And I wanted to leave because in that moment I'd had more than enough of José. I have tried many times over recent years to pinpoint this moment. My strong belief is that it was in the 2005–06 season when we won the Premier League title for a second time and I was at the peak of my powers. Come the end of the season, I would be the club's player of the year – or at least that was what I was told until I was then informed that there had been a change in the result. I would be a starter for England at the World Cup finals that summer. I would even sign a new contract towards the end of the season, which I would see out to its conclusion in the summer of 2010. I really wanted another Chelsea contract then too, but it was never offered. By the next season, 2006–07, when I underwent the first major surgery of my career, I would be a fundamental part of José's team. So much so that the issue was that I was playing when I was not ready to do so. Even before my scheduled return date from a problem, José would be asking me whether I was ready. Like all managers, he wanted his best players on the field, even if they were not always 100 per cent fit. He brought me off the bench for a Champions League quarter-final against Valencia in April 2007 when I couldn't be sure that my ankle, which had undergone major surgery, was ready for the demands made of it.

But all that was to come. In the summer of 2005, I was twenty-three years old and had already seen off Juan Sebastián Verón, Emmanuel Petit, Geremi and Jesper Grønkjær in the battle to be part of this José team. Yet as the season went on, I felt that José's criticisms of me got harsher and harsher. If it was José's way of lighting my fire, my view was that I just didn't feel I needed it. The additional problem was that it fed into a general mood that I was lazy, wasteful, defensively suspect or – as I kept hearing from various quarters – not a complete player. I was never sure what that complete player was supposed to be, I just knew I was playing as well as anyone. Sven-Göran Eriksson, the England manager who it took so long to make an impression on, seemed to buy into this mood of scepticism about me. For England, I felt I had to be the best player on the pitch so that I would not be substituted by Sven. When I was not the best player, there always seemed to be an alternative. Every time I had a really good game, even the praise would have a sting to it. There would always be this suggestion that I had turned the corner. That I had finally grown up. But I was by then an experienced pro. Instead, it all contributed to this sense that I was immature, the eternal child prodigy who just wanted to mess around with the ball.

My pass completion for this season alone was 91 per cent. I would never claim to be perfect, but the defensive part of my game was crucial. I took pride in that, as much as anything else I did. In the other direction, creative players sometimes have to take risks, you have to wager something to gain something – but I never took a gamble that was not calculated. I never shirked the defending that came with it. It would have been beneficial for my attacking game to do so. To take up those positions that Pep Guardiola permits his wide attacking players to assume – high up the pitch, and wide, with no thought of coming back. We used to call those the cheat position.

José's position on me in that season, 2005–06, was at its most volatile – in public and in private. No one aside from John Terry and Frank Lampard played more than me in that season either. When we beat Anderlecht in the Champions League in late November he said I was – his words – 'a total player'. Against Portsmouth a few days later there was more of the same. I scored away in a win at Arsenal in December. I scored the winning goal on 28 December, away at Manchester City.

Three days later against Birmingham City at Stamford Bridge, José went berserk at me. I glanced over at him on the touchline. He was mimicking wasteful drag-backs and silly flicks and all this was directed at me. José said of me afterwards: 'One more match from Joe like that – for himself and the public – and he's out.' The Monday after that game I was warming down on the training pitch and José came over to me, his finger wagging. Effing this, effing that. Bullshit performance. He went on – 'Joe, if you ever do that again you will never play for me again.' I was trying to recall what it was that had made him so upset.

We had won 2–0. At one point I had gone through on goal and then tried to square it to Hernán Crespo. He hadn't read that the pass was coming and when that happens, as it sometimes does, it always looks bad. I just did not think that the response on this scale was warranted. The strange thing was, I was used to it by then. I felt it was normal. The rest of the lads around me just watched in silence. No one could understand the relationship. There wasn't any point trying to argue.

If it wasn't me that José was demolishing in front of the squad then it tended to be Ricardo Carvalho, who, for all the stick he took, can lay claim to being one half of one of the greatest defensive partnerships the Premier League has seen, with John Terry for six years. The remarkable thing about Ricky was that his expression never changed no matter how hard José went with the criticism. On the pitch Ricky was a warrior. Off it, he was a gentle, friendly, softly spoken soul. José's most famous tirade against Ricky was in essence a long list of all the players and auxiliary staff José said he would rather pick ahead of Ricky. It went something like this:

Ricky you've been so effing shit that if John Terry or William Gallas aren't fit next week you're still not playing. I'll play Robert Huth. If Robert Huth isn't fit, I'm going to play Michael Essien at centre-half. If Michael Essien isn't fit, I am going to play Stevie Watt [a promising young lad at the time who never made it through at Chelsea]. And if Stevie isn't fit, I am going to play the kitman at centre-half.

Ricky's face was impassive throughout. The rest of us were trying desperately not to laugh, and wondering if José might go on past the kitman, to the catering staff and perhaps a selection of the groundsmen. Did José really resent Ricky that much? Or had he just decided that was the way to get the best out of him? José won the Champions League with Ricky at Porto. He signed him at Chelsea. He signed him at Real Madrid. Ricky was one of the best centre-halves of his generation. José just wouldn't let him rest.

Was it around this time I went to see Roman to tell him I wanted to leave? I can recall the meeting, if not the date. My agent David Geiss had advised against it. So did others. But I ploughed on nonetheless. Roman was in his office at Cobham with Eugene Tenenbaum, one of the directors at the club and his close aide. Wherever Roman was, Eugene, a Russian-Canadian, was never far away. They let me talk, and so I said José and I were not getting along and that it would be better for both of us if I just moved on. I wasn't trying to play a game or assert what little power I might have had. To me it was just simple: José and I didn't get on and so I had to leave. The truth was that I just really wanted José's approval.

'Hmmm,' said Roman, 'but Joe – we want you to stay.'

There was a long pause, as all three of us looked out of the window across this beautiful new training ground. I wasn't sure whether to break the silence. Roman and Eugene seemed quite happy to sit there saying nothing. My mind started to wander. Was this how billionaire Russians got their business done? Was I on the clock? Was there a magic word, or sentence, that would unlock all this? Roman spoke again.

'José,' Roman said, 'he is sometimes too quick from here.' He pointed to his heart. 'To here.' He pointed to his mouth. Again, a long silence. This was the moment when, if I had the necessary resolve, I would have stood my ground. I needed to say something assertive. I just had no idea what that was. I wouldn't have been much use in those long negotiations over

Soviet aluminium plants. I think they knew my heart wasn't in leaving.

'Okay,' I caved finally. 'I'll stay.'

My new contract was agreed in March of that year. To say I was a hardened negotiator might be overdoing it, but from a financial point of view I was very lucky to have been a footballer in this era. The one card we did have was that I was the favourite player of Roman's then second wife, Irina. We knew because Irina had told my mum at a game when they had a chat. My dad, ever the schemer, had treated that as potentially useful information in any negotiations that might follow. Unfortunately, it did not prove to be the clincher I might have hoped it to be. By the time I was hoping to embark on the third contract negotiation of my time at Chelsea, in the summer of 2008, Roman had divorced Irina and had a new partner called Dasha Zhukova. Who her favourite Chelsea player might have been, I never did find out.

A lot is written about footballers' salaries. How much is accurate is hard to say. Even though that newspaper report on my first pro deal contract was way off the mark in terms of the numbers, my parents, my agent David and I took the view that it was easier to ignore than to explain. Now, all these years on, none of this really matters. In the interests of transparency, these are the first four contracts of my professional career, covering my first twelve years as a professional from November 1998 to my departure from Chelsea in June 2010.

- £1,000 per week, signed at West Ham on my seventeenth birthday.
- £16,000 per week, rising to £19,000 per week, signed at West Ham in the summer of 2000 after my first full season was ended by injury.

- £55,000 per week upon signing for Chelsea in August 2003.
- £87,000 per week, rising to £92,000 per week – a new four-year deal agreed in recognition of my new status in March 2006.
- Just less than £100,000 per week at Liverpool, as a free agent signing.

We will get to the rest later. Great money. I take none of it for granted. Although as a point of order, I never earnt as much as Frank, John, Petr Čech and Didier Drogba as far as I was aware. Never did I believe I should. There is always a hierarchy. These are big numbers whichever way you cut it. I was content with what I got.

That 2005–06 season was the high point of the first Mourinho Chelsea years. It was also Didier's big breakout season when he established himself as one of the best strikers in the world. He had not quite convinced everyone in that first season in which he had arrived as José's main pick as striker. Although inside the club we knew we had a brilliant goalscorer. Our form in that season was so good I first started to understand what it was like to see a team beaten in the tunnel before the game. I would enjoy watching some of the opposition casting little sideways glances at us. The champions have an aura and it takes some discipline not to have a gawp at the country's best players. They were not looking at me, I hasten to add. Although the form I was in meant that on the pitch players were standing off me more and more because, if they lunged in then I could quite easily make them look foolish. In the tunnel they would look at John Terry, our leader, and then they would be looking for Frank, but in the end it was Didier who got them most anxious. Off the field he was an easy-going, happy soul who would chat and crack jokes and then, on matchday, you could see this gradual change in him as kick-off got closer. The jokes stopped, the smile faded. He would become a different person. He was ready to take on responsibility and to demand that others do the same. He would enter the tunnel with his shirt off, an oiled up and glistening Adonis who towered over the opposition. They couldn't stop looking at him. When Didier headed a ball, he did so with such ferocity it made a noise I would recognise with my eyes closed. It was like a whipcrack. He won the ball from attacking corners and defending corners and on his day he could throw good centre-halves around. It was a privilege to play with him. There were times that season when, with Didier, we felt invincible.

There was more competition for me on the right side of the attack. Chelsea had signed Shaun Wright-Phillips, a friend of mine who I had known since our childhood when his south London side had come over the river to test themselves against my Chapel Boys team on Coram's Fields. As the son of Ian Wright, Shaun came with huge cachet and he was an exceptional talent in his own right. One of his teammates in those early years was the formidable Adebayo Akinfenwa – we knew him as a kid as Bayo – who would have his own distinguished professional career. Shaun had been the main man at Manchester City in the days when they were just another Premier League mid-table club. At Chelsea it was much harder for him to establish himself in the side. He had some big moments for the team but there were four wide midfielders, or more orthodox wingers – me, Arjen Robben, Damien Duff and Shaun – competing for two starting places. That was the nature of the Chelsea team in those years. We were relentless and if you had a bad forty-five minutes under José you could be out of the side. It might take a few weeks to get back in again. The standards were fierce. Shaun is a good friend. Ultimately, though, we were all competitive and we all wanted that starting place.

We didn't lose a game that season until 6 November, in the Premier League at Old Trafford, and we didn't lose again until 22 February against Barcelona in the Champions League. They had got better since the previous season and it was the first time I came up against Leo Messi, a fresh-faced sensation on his way to winning his first Champions League with Barcelona. He had a glow about him. You see it immediately in the way a player moves and the way he shifts his weight around when he's on the ball. Messi can do it so fast. You think you've got him in the crosshairs and then suddenly he's on a different course, and your original calculation is all wrong. He has either gone past the defender – or the defender has just got a piece of him and it's a foul. When people ask me to describe Messi, I often think how Sir David Attenborough might narrate some footage of Messi in full flight, looking at him and identifying a strain of super species. He would have to draw the conclusion that Messi has attributes other humans just don't have – and chief among them is to see the game around him in a way the rest of us can't. I am convinced Messi knew what was going to happen before anyone else. In its simplest terms, the example I would use is like trying to swat a fly. You think you've got it but the fly observes – and the fly reacts. All of it much quicker than the swish of your rolled-up copy of the sports pages. Messi is the same. Tackle imminent? Bodycheck incoming? He's already seen it. He's seen it so early it can make you feel like he can see into the future. But maybe Messi sees more frames a second than the rest of his species. The other aspect to Messi – as well as the fly-vision, the skill, the pace, the shooting ability and the astonishing ability to find pockets of space – is the strength. It may not be immediately obvious but if ever you are sharp enough to get within striking range of him, he puts down a foot, leans into you and is as strong as anyone on the pitch.

Of course, this second Champions League epic between Chelsea and Barcelona ultimately became a story about the referee Terje Hauge. I thought there was another side to it. As a team, and with Messi, Barcelona had improved since we had blown them away at Stamford Bridge the previous season, and tactically we had not moved with them. At left-back, José picked Asier del Horno, a new signing the previous summer from Athletic Club of Bilbao, and Messi had him on toast. Asier's red card was the killer blow for us in that game and from the moment he committed that second foul on Messi I knew that in the reshuffle that would come I would be substituted. Del Horno had a lovely left foot but he wasn't a one-against-one defender. However good you might be as a full-back, against Messi it was inevitable that he was going to make you look daft at least once. He liked to cut inside on his left foot. You knew what was going to happen, the question was whether you could keep the damage to a minimum. A much better option would have been to switch me to the left wing and pick Gallas at left-back. We would have doubled up on Messi and tried to restrict him as best we could. Again, I wonder if my reputation worked against me. I knew how to do that job and after almost two seasons of José, I was impeccably drilled in the positions to take up. I knew I didn't have the pace to get out of trouble. I needed to be in the right spot to track runners, and I could do that.

Barcelona also took more risks. They pinned us back. Once again, Giovanni van Bronckhorst was taking up positions high up the pitch, and I would go with him. It would be the same on the other side. It made us defensively solid but it also meant that Barcelona knew we only ever had one out pass, which was a ball clipped up to Didier. We could have risked more. We could have risked Paulo Ferreira against Ronaldinho on his own and Essien dropping in to help out, but that wasn't our style. José had made us defensively sound and we were very well organised. But there was less of that when it came to the attacking side of it. Today the leading teams all have patterns of play. They rotate into midfield and get the ball, and then back out again. The wingers are encouraged to take up high, wide positions. They are told to stay there and wait for the ball to be moved to them. There was none of that. It was still quite basic. We broke with pace and that was it. The training methods José brought with him were revolutionary and they changed the sport. Every great manager makes some major change. Ten years earlier it had been Arsène Wenger and his emphasis on a new lifestyle for his players. Now it was Barcelona and their risky attacking play. We lost that first leg at Stamford Bridge, drew away at the Nou Camp and went out. Another year went by without the Champions League that Roman wanted us to win.

We had beaten Liverpool 4–1 at Anfield in October and 2–0 at Stamford Bridge in February in the Premier League but still lost to them in the FA Cup semi-final on 22 April, one week before we won the league for the second time in that game at home to Manchester United. Again, we changed our usual system when I felt we would have been better off going at them with the best we had. José switched to a diamond formation in midfield. I didn't exactly help myself by blasting one over when I came on in the second half. The lads didn't want to play that diamond midfield but you go with it because the manager is all-powerful, or at least José was then. There was a feeling that even for all the wins José racked up against Rafael Benítez, that Benítez had his number in certain games. That might have contributed to how José set up the team that day.

By the end of the season, Duffa and I were the two first-choice wingers. By now Robben was coming in and out of the reckoning with injuries and José was starting to lose faith in him. It was me who scored that goal against United at the end of April to seal the second Premier League title at home, against the team we had deposed as the best in the country. By then we were used to playing in big games, and the team was used to the pressure. I was well accustomed to the pre-match habits of my teammates. Frank barely communicated with the rest of us or the staff. He was calm. He was also very content just being left with his own thoughts. He would do all his own strapping, the kind of thing most players leave to the physios out of a general sense of laziness. I'm convinced the strapping makes no real difference apart from some kind of mental reassurance. Luis Suárez played with strapping on his wrist for months. I'm sure he kept it on long after there was any problem.

There were very few other superstitions as far as I could see, although I have to give John Terry an honourable exception. John had lots of them. One of which was that he only ever wanted to eat five potatoes – no more, no less – for his pre-match meal. Every pre-match dinner I would observe John in deep conversation with the server on the team buffet potato station, being quite specific about which potatoes he wanted. Some were scooped up and then subsequently rejected. Others were moved aside in search of better potatoes. I guess if you're going to limit yourself to only five potatoes, you want to make them good potatoes. Why did he limit himself to just five? I'm afraid to say I never asked.

Our rivalry with United was deep-seated. We didn't like

them and the feeling was mutual. Frank and I had played with Rio Ferdinand at West Ham and later that summer of 2006, my old friend Michael Carrick would join them too. We all played for England together, but none of that really mattered for most of the time. It was, in truth, pure animosity. We would barely look at each other before the game and if Rio was tempted to glance at Didier, then he kept it well hidden. It was more difficult for the bare-chested pre-match Didier to intimidate the likes of him and Nemanja Vidić.

In the current day there is much greater friendliness in the tunnel before matches between players on opposing sides. I know that all players of my era, and many of those from before, find that perplexing. It just was not like that in our day, which is not a phrase I ever expected to find myself using. All the cheery greetings and cosy chats these days, where does it come from? I think social media has a lot to answer for. My reading is that players from different clubs who may not have seen one another for ages, or only briefly played together at other clubs or in national teams, feel like they know one another better. But that is not what you are there for on the day of a game. Michael was my room-mate at West Ham. We had won the FA Youth Cup together. We had broken into the first team at West Ham within a year of one another. Yet when we were on opposing sides for Chelsea and United, we were not asking after one another's families in the minutes before the game started. If we wanted to have a chat there were six other days in the week and I had his phone number. The tunnel before the game with the cameras in your face and a big game on the line was a time to be focused on your job.

I had come a long way in my three years at Chelsea. Many players had come and gone – some big names, and among them those who might easily have reduced me to a footnote if I hadn't hung in there. I had done more than that. I had thrived. I had a new four-year contract. At the end of the season I had scored that goal, the best of my career, to defeat Manchester United. I had dribbled past Vidić, Ferdinand and Mikaël Silvestre and smashed one past the best goalkeeper United had had since Peter Schmeichel. All that was missing that season was a sense that José appreciated me. When he came to me at the final whistle after the win over United I had long since stopped wondering what the reaction might be. He said to me that day if Ronaldinho had scored that kind of goal then the world would have stopped. What he seemed to be saying was that people didn't appreciate me, or that they underestimated me.

Someone at the club, who was in the know, had told me that I had been voted player of the season. Even though I had never chased individual awards, it felt like vindication for the way I was playing. I did feel quite proud. I was told with such certainty that I let others know too, Carly and my parents. The day before the award ceremony at the Grosvenor House Hotel on Park Lane, I was told it was not me but John Terry who had won it. A worthy winner who had a great season. But no-one ever told me why the change of heart. Maybe they just miscounted the votes the first time around. But really these moments just flit across your horizon and are gone. I knew I was playing well in a golden era for the club. José would be there after the summer's World Cup finals, welcoming me back like the prodigal son. Chelsea would have two of the most famous players in the world join that summer. We had won back-to-back Premier League titles and the rest of the world was waiting for this team and this manager to finally blow up. We didn't disappoint them.

9

Old School:
West Ham in the 2000s

If you wanted a snapshot of West Ham in 1999, my first full season as a professional footballer, then let me take you back to half-time at St Andrew's in late November of that year, shortly after my eighteenth birthday. We had twice fallen behind to Birmingham City in the League Cup fourth round, and by the time we were back in the changing room, we were losing 2–1 to this side in the division below. Things were about to come to a head. At the end of the twentieth century, English football was slowly starting to change, but in the West Ham dressing room at half-time, the range of nationalities aside, things were as they had always been. Paolo Di Canio, our fiery Italian creative talent, blamed Shaka Hislop, our giant London-born Trinidadian goalkeeper, for the first Birmingham goal. An argument ensued. Paolo tried to throw a table over. Shaka, rarely anything but calm, fired back. Paolo launched a kick at the wall, right next to my head as it turned out. Shaka lost it and grabbed Paolo. Suddenly wayward punches were being thrown, and virtually the whole team was in a tussle in the middle of the away dressing room trying to drag goalkeeper and striker apart.

Enter our manager Harry Redknapp, who took stock and

started shouting at us. 'Effing fighting? Effing fighting? You should've shown some effing fight out there on the pitch. Losing to this effing lot.' Harry had our attention. He was furious. 'You effing go out there and sort it out,' he said. 'You put it right.' We went back onto the pitch with his fury ringing in our ears. We won this midweek cup tie in the last minute, 3–2, with a cross from Paolo to create the winner. Our travelling fans were jubilant. Paolo and Shaka embraced one another in the dressing room afterwards. The game had been broadcast live on Sky Sports and for that night we felt like the centre of attention. Sky wanted to interview the match-winner – which was me, the last-minute goalscorer with the first goal of my professional career.

It was an evening of such vivid memories. The fight between Shaka and Paolo at half-time. The feeling of possibility as we came back into the game, and then as I read Paolo's intentions with that cross from the right. A run stolen across the defender and the finish from close in, the droplets of rain falling off the net as the ball struck it. A demented celebration, so close to the fans and then with my teammates piling on top of me. I had scored many goals before for youth teams and for England schoolboys but none like this. None when such a great surge of emotion had engulfed me. I came back to earth moments later as if awakening from a dream, the music that played in my head now loud in my ears, in time to concentrate on the final few minutes of the game. I felt such joy. Joy in the long walk round the pitch to find the Sky reporter, accompanied by the kitman, who was the media officer before such a role existed at West Ham. Joy at the group of Birmingham fans who, rather than hurrying home on a cold night, had stayed behind to call me a see-you-next-Tuesday through the wire fence that separated us. It was all wonderful.

We finished ninth in the Premier League that season, fifteenth the next, seventh in 2001–02 and then relegated the year after. That was the West Ham way. That February 2000 we would embark on one of the greatest Premier League comebacks of all time, from 4–2 down to 5–4 winners over Bradford City. On that occasion Paolo, enraged at the referee's decisions, would try to leave the pitch in protest and had to be manhandled back on by Harry and Frank Lampard senior. There would be a few games when Harry raged at us at half-time. He knew his players well, though. There was conflict and recriminations, but it often seemed to work. The West Ham of the late 1990s feels like a distant land now. There was precious little done in the way of tactics, and we were as likely to sit down to analyse what we had done in previous games as we were to sit around painting watercolour landscapes. If you wanted to see any video analysis of how you had played, you watched *Match of the Day*. Given how few West Ham games featured on the show, which I would record every Saturday night, I took to going to the club shop where, a few weeks after the event, you could buy a VHS of the home games. It was the first time I was able to watch my games in full, and all my involvements that did not make the highlights packages.

The first team training ground was like a hectic bazaar with hawkers coming to sell whatever they could to the well-paid first team pros. Players still in their boots, just off the training ground, would be checking out the merchandise. Jewellery, suits, food hampers, as well as tickets for any game, big fight, concert or West End show. There was a well-known tout who had been selling West Ham players tickets since the days of Bobby Moore and had a reputation – deserved or not, I don't know – for his seats often turning out to be of restricted view. John Moncur once claimed he got an injury from a couple of hours craning his neck around a pillar during a night at a show. On the way home from away games we would still eat fish and chips on the bus. In fact, in my days as a youth team player, I would be part of the operation to collect the takeaway in time for departure. Travelling with the team to Anfield, I was tapped on the shoulder about ten minutes before full-time by the kitman Stan Burke and told to follow him. We walked out of the stadium with the early departures, through the gates and found the nearest fish and chip shop where Stan ordered thirty-odd portions of cod or sausage or whatever – all of it with chips. The first Liverpool fans out of the stadium will have encountered the pair of us, in our West Ham tracksuits, leaving with this huge order in plastic carrier bags. My final act was to place the right order on the right seat on the coach, like a ceremonial offering to the returning first team player. Needless to say, the West Ham of that era didn't have a nutritionist. Actually, they didn't even have a coach driver – Stan did that job too.

We won the Intertoto Cup that season, a competition of so little consequence it didn't even have a proper trophy. We all stood around waiting on the pitch after the second leg of the final against Metz and in the end we just assumed that UEFA had forgotten to bring it.

I had ended the previous season after my debut against Swansea in the FA Cup as part of the first team, albeit back with the Under-18s for our FA Youth Cup games. Eight days after Swansea I was on the bench at Old Trafford with another of my youth team peers, Izzy Iriekpen. I came on at half-time with us 2–0 down. This was the United team that would be European champions and treble winners by the end of May and they were just on a different level. You could feel the change in quality. But I hung in there. I smashed into a tackle with Jaap Stam who seemed to regard me as most people would an irritating mosquito. But I had a role in the goal that Frank Lampard junior scored in the final moments of a 4–1 defeat. I felt I had held my own. Then I came back into the dressing room and caught Izzy's eye. He didn't look right. Izzy was six months younger than me, and still just sixteen. I asked him what had happened. Izzy said that he had been told by Harry that he was coming on but then he couldn't get his coat off. The zip had stuck. As he had struggled with it, Harry had lost patience and eventually the referee had blown for full-time. Izzy looked distraught. He would have been the youngest ever to play for West Ham. As it turned out, his chance would never come again. He never even played one game in the Premier League. He had a bad knee injury and it was testament to his ability that, after that, even on one knee, he had a good career. He became captain of Swansea City. But I often think of Izzy's unfortunate twist of fate and how lucky I had been.

Izzy was my teammate in the West Ham youth team that would go on to win the FA Youth Cup in 1999, pulverising Coventry City 9–0 on aggregate over the two legs of the final. If I was being targeted by the opposition for some physical treatment, Izzy would respond in kind. He was my minder in the team. That semi-final second leg 6–0 win in front of 18,438 fans at Upton Park is the stuff of legend at the club. All I can say is we were playing like Barcelona ten years before Pep Guardiola took over. We were a dominant team in our age group, which was remarkable for a club like West Ham that would inevitably be behind the likes of Arsenal and Tottenham when it came to attracting the best players. Seven of that side would go on to play for the first team. I was already in by that stage. Michael Carrick would be a Champions League and

Premier League winner with Manchester United. Yet I look back at it differently. It makes me wonder – why didn't more of my mates have better professional careers?

There were others in that team with the ability to do so. All the side were given a pro contract of some description, which was unheard of for a whole youth team. We would not have had the success that we did without a very high calibre of player. Adam Newton, a skilful, lightning-fast attacker would have been a certainty in my teenage reckoning to have a Premier League career. But he never did. Izzy had his injury. Bertie Brayley – Basildon Bertie – was a striker with a brilliant left foot who these days would have gone on to a Premier League contract at seventeen. His Football League career totalled seven appearances as a substitute for Swindon Town. Youth team football is hard and these boys had, through their teenage years, climbed all the way to base camp. But then you face the mountain. At eighteen, all that work only entitles you to a place in first team training. A chance to take on the experienced professionals for their place in the team – a place they will do everything to keep hold of. At West Ham, we had Stuart Pearce, Igor Štimac, Neil Ruddock, Moncur. For us in the youth team, those players were closer to our fathers' generation than ours. Our youth was our advantage, but they had years and years in the game.

As a young pro you have to be prepared for it all to go wrong, and to go wrong for a while, and keep going nonetheless. You have to be prepared to be told you're not ready, to do all the right things – and for none of it to work out. Most of all you have to keep going. Easy for me to say, I guess, because my ride was relatively smooth. But the further you get in football the more it is obvious that there are lots of very gifted players. There are fewer with the kind of mindset required. Frank Lampard junior is the clearest example. He had a willingness to keep going, whatever the criticism and there was so much of it for him at West Ham. Every training session, every game. A bloody-mindedness to continue in spite of it all. It takes a lot for a young person to do that, without the certainty that things will get better, and in your early days in football you need that steel. I am not talking about any of my West Ham youth teammates in particular here. I just know that in two decades as a footballer I saw a lot of players who looked for excuses. Who found the pain of a poor performance, or their own shortcomings, too difficult to take and blamed it on someone or something else. It is a defence mechanism. I understand why it exists in people. It is the same as the guy on the bar stool who tells you how he could have had a football career had he not discovered women and booze. At its heart that is not a joke. It is someone reassuring themselves that it wasn't their fault. It's a deflection. It's the same with those players who would diminish the game or its importance when things went wrong. I met players who would say that none of it really mattered anyway. I can tell you that I encountered that kind of character right through my career and into the England team itself.

I was lucky. I could never pretend football didn't mean anything to me. When we lost, and when I played badly, it really hurt me, and my sense of myself. I worried at times, at West Ham, Chelsea, England, Liverpool, whether I was good enough. But looking back, that was fortunate. It meant that I could not tell myself that none of this mattered. Or that it was someone else's fault. I loved football more than anything and I trusted football to tell me the truth. Either I would be successful or I wouldn't, but when it came that verdict would be fair and I couldn't blame anyone else. There was also good fortune with the people I met. John Moncur was such a technically gifted footballer from the East End of London who would have made it at Tottenham, where he was an apprentice, but for the fact his path to the first team was blocked by a certain Paul Gascoigne. Moncs is also a very good person. It was effectively my emergence, along with that of Frank and Michael Carrick, that meant Moncs lost his place in the West Ham team. He could have been really difficult about that but he was never anything but encouraging to us all. That was an example I took into the latter stages of my own career.

Another was Neil Ruddock – Razor to friends and colleagues. Another talented footballer who never got the recognition he deserved. Razor and Harry Redknapp rarely saw eye to eye. Razor was a drinker and by the time I got in the first team it felt to me that Harry believed Razor had served his purpose. In one of our training exercises we would play defenders against attackers with the numbers weighted in favour of the latter. Harry would put Razor up against me and Jermain Defoe and let the phase run and run. It was for fitness, but every player knows when a manager is prolonging the torture. I could see Razor's legs going. He would back off us. Razor might have felt like booting me, or Jermain, for our cheekiness and our irrepressible youthful energy. Yet he never did. There were plenty of senior players who made it their business to kick the youngsters in training.

In the meantime, I was learning what it meant to succeed at the game at the very highest level. First of all, how to use my attributes against others. My strength was my touch, and my ability to take the ball on the half-turn and glide past an opponent. If it came to a grapple in close quarters with a giant like Patrick Vieira then he was going to win. But if I could be away before he had the time to pin me then I had a chance.

In those early days I had a very good game against Vieira who was the best midfielder in the world at the time. He asked for my shirt afterwards and I was delighted. I felt I must have been doing something right if Vieira was asking for my shirt. Then Ashley Cole told me Vieira was only asking for it on behalf of the chef at the Arsenal training ground, who was a West Ham fan.

Secondly, I learnt you have to know how to buy a foul. This was how it was in late 1990s English football. If you dived around and held your ankle screaming for medical attention then you were looked upon with a high degree of scepticism – chiefly as one who had absorbed what some considered too many of those dubious foreign ways. But if you were a centre-forward skilled in backing into a defender and artfully tricking them into contact that looked as if you had been tripped or fouled – that was fine. And if you were Alan Shearer, you almost certainly would get the free-kick. Shearer was capable of that split-second judgement. If he felt the contact he would use that. The man was an absolute master at it. I played in games against Newcastle when it was hard to tell who was refereeing the match – the actual referee or Alan Shearer. He was not alone in that. Tony Adams would address the referee with the considered formality of a nobleman arriving in the court of a distant kingdom to deliver a vital communication. Then other times you would see the lad from Dagenham erupt in him, incandescent at a decision. John Terry became very good at influencing referees by the time he was Chelsea captain. No referee is immune from a bit of manipulation. All of them are human.

Third. Before you can be creative, you first have to fight to keep the ball. This was the key problem with football in that era. Before you could play you had to come through a small war to get the ball. In a Pep Guardiola team, the midfielders tend to get a ball into their feet and then they play from there. What a luxury. When I was delivered the ball I might have first to wriggle out of a tight gap or bounce off a couple of hard tackles – only then could I think about finding a pass. In the meantime, I knew it would have to be a hell of a foul on me for the ref to give a free-kick. That environment benefited the kind of midfielder without much of a touch to speak of who spent the whole match crashing into people. They wouldn't survive in the game as we know it now.

At West Ham under Harry we were not geared up to have a structure that got us the ball in certain positions. Out of possession, like most teams, we knew our positions. In possession, you passed only if it was safe to do so. If we were under threat then defenders would err on the side of caution and clip it long. There was no imperative to play to feet regardless of the pressure. There was no notion that the manager would tolerate mistakes in pursuit of the bigger picture to play through the lines. If a defender risked a ball into a midfielder under pressure, and he lost it, then the blame was placed on the defender. So he tended to avoid it.

My point was that I wanted the ball all the time. I trusted my touch was good enough. I knew how to use my body and the strength I did possess, after years in the cages of Camden. I knew how to hold off opponents, to get low and use my arms and my core to protect it. But that did not always mean I got that ball into my feet from the full-back. West Ham had two greats of the game in the full-back positions. Both Stuart Pearce and Nigel Winterburn would often look at me, and then look at the players around me and calculate that they would be better served clipping it up the line. Or slinging it into the striker's chest. Rather that, than risk me being robbed. In the early days, Nigel would talk me through a game defensively. I recognised, out of possession, that if I just did what he said then I would be fine. He could see the game unfold from his position and anticipate the runs of opponents or the overloads that might develop. If he told me to come off the touchline and close down a central midfielder because he had read the ball from the opposing full-back, it got to the stage where I was confident enough to know I didn't need to check over my shoulder. I just needed to get going as quickly as possible. Those players who can guide a younger teammate through a game are that much rarer now. Jamie Carragher was one of the last I played with who was confident enough to do it.

It was a strange existence. I knew I was at heart a creative player, but there was a tax on that. First you had to win a physical contest. At the early stage of my career I would often be the smallest player on the pitch, or at least it would be rare for there to be two players smaller than me across the two sides. By the end of my career I was about average in size for the kind of footballer playing the game. The pitches were much better. The managers wanted you to play out from the back. The referees were stricter. As a result the spoilers and the crashers, the midfield colliders with the dubious touch were being driven out of the game. Certainly those players of that lower technical level just couldn't play the position they once did. You only have to look at one of the greatest midfielders in the game: Luka Modrić. When he arrived at Tottenham I could see he was a wonderful player. But most weeks the mood seemed to be that he should play as a number 10 with two others to crash around him further back in midfield. Now it is recognised that Modric is a playmaker. And while he is still doing it at the highest level, the attitude in coaching has changed. It's not just that those small technical players are much more prized. They're much better understood.

Harry's teams were much less structured than some of those teams who were more dedicated to a direct English style of playing. Harry's way was more suited to the way in which I preferred to play, and that in itself was a benefit. But even so, no one could argue it was easy. In response I developed a style of play in a midfield four. We always had two strikers, or three forwards if Trevor Sinclair played right wing-back. My job was to roam around, get on the ball and then get it through what was the no man's land of the midfield and drive it up the pitch. I was effectively doing the job of a modern-day midfielder but in the war zone of an English midfield. If I played well, Trevor, Paolo and Freddie Kanouté would have more of the ball. I also had to try to score some goals as well.

The second goal of my career came in that famous game against Bradford in February 2000. We were 1–0 down, 2–1 up, 4–2 down and then eventually 5–4 winners. It also encapsulated in ninety minutes why that West Ham team at the turn of the millennium was so fondly remembered by the fans. It could be chaos but it was always entertaining. At 4–2 down, Paolo wanted to come off the pitch in protest against the referee's decisions. When he stayed on he had an argument with Frank over the penalty that made it 4–3. I remember thinking at the time how like a dysfunctional Sunday league team we could be. My goal made it 4–4 and then Frank scored the winner. My friend from the youth team, Stephen Bywater, was in goal and it had been a difficult day for him. He was at fault for the two goals Jamie Lawrence scored. At one point, after a period in which we had piled on the pressure, Stephen had got distracted. He was watching the game on the big screen which was a few seconds behind the action on the pitch and he hadn't noticed that Bradford had the ball again. We used to call Stephen the Boy Wonder, partly because his mind wandered so much. He had a good Premier League career and without injuries would have played for England.

It was while out with the team one night that I stayed over at Trevor Sinclair's house in Epping in Essex, on the other side of London from the flat at Donnington Court in Camden where I still lived with my parents and Nicky and Charly. I woke up that morning and had a bit of an epiphany. Why couldn't I live somewhere like Trevor? I was earning money. I had a new contract coming that would make me and my family wealthier than we could ever have expected. I was a Premier League and England footballer still living in a council flat and it was becoming a bit of a problem. On the estate you would get a lot of visitors over the course of a day but now there were a lot of people asking for money. The assumption was that I just had so much of it. I was well paid, sure, but I also had no intention of becoming a cash machine.

Increasingly I wondered if I wasn't a little bit more at risk. I had lived my life in Camden but now I was different. Having been beaten up in the stairwell when I was home on a break from Lilleshall, I was more attuned to the dangers of life on the estate. There was another incident when I had been playing pool with Ossie and his dad Metin and a few others in St Mary's working men's club in Camden and someone had a call from Paul Ellis. He had got in a fight in a nearby pub and was holed up in the gents' toilets while hostile parties massed outside. We all ran down there. Being the fittest I got there first and found myself in the middle of a confrontation. There were snooker cues and bottles all with a lot of drink in them, flying around. Looking at the carnage, I had a moment of clarity. What was I doing there?

That was it. We moved out of Camden to a faraway land and a new culture. I'm joking. We moved to Romford. A lovely detached house in a cul-de-sac. I said to my parents that whatever happened, this house would be theirs. My brother and sister went to new schools. I was a short drive from the West Ham training ground. Michael Carrick lived a few doors down, so there would often be a few parties after hours but I could always walk back up the road to my own bed and wake up to a breakfast made by my mum. It was perfect. Hard for my dad, though, who left behind all that he knew in north London. I say that he left it behind, it wasn't like he was departing Plymouth on the *Mayflower*. It was half an hour's drive. But it was significant, nonetheless. By then I had my first car, a Volkswagen Golf. In fact, I had two. In my first negotiations on a boot deal with Adidas, my dad's sixth sense told him that the other side were more desperate to sign me than we had realised. He tried his luck. 'Joe has just passed his driving test,' he said. 'He wants a BMW too.' So Adidas gave me a brand new BMW.

Towards the end of the 1999–2000 season, a new head of education at the academy turned up and, having checked the regulations for the development of players, discovered that the club were obliged to provide me with some form of post-sixteen education. Harry was incredulous. 'But Joe's learning to be a footballer,' he said. The head of education was insistent. On a Thursday afternoon I had to be involved in some activity that would contribute towards a qualification. 'Well, what do you like doing?' Harry asked me.

What I liked doing was playing football, meeting girls and driving around in my VW Golf listening to Oasis. I just blurted out one word: 'golf'. I had barely ever played it. At the time it must have seemed sophisticated to me. 'There you go,' said Harry, 'golf lessons.' So that is what I did in Lea Valley every Thursday afternoon. The rest of my fellow young pros couldn't believe my good fortune. Those golf lessons were, sadly, the sum total of my further education. Also, I'm still hopeless at golf.

My first full season as a professional footballer ended abruptly when Rory Delap broke my leg at Pride Park on 15 April. Had it not happened I am sure Kevin Keegan would have selected me in the England squad for Euro 2000, as I was playing well enough. There are the times when you know you have hurt someone with a tackle, and the times when the opposite is the case. I kicked Luke Young by mistake on one occasion and I could see he was in pain. I got his phone number and called him after the event and apologised. This time, I was facing away from my goal, with Delap behind me, and feinted to turn left. I turned right with the outside of my right foot and knew immediately I'd beaten him. When he kicked me across the shin there was a flash of white light behind my eyes. I've done them all in my career – ripped ligaments, broken bones – and you know immediately when it is serious. The pain is of a very different flavour. The foul would have been a straight red card under today's interpretation of the law.

They took me off on a stretcher and although my instinct was that it was a bad injury, at the front of my mind was – what if it isn't? I was most conscious of looking weak at having gone off too easily because that was the culture in English football at the time. The next day I went in to the training ground and all I could think of was – what must the physios think? By Monday morning I could move my toes. The West Ham physios had a foolproof way of checking how serious an injury was – they took you for a run. After thirty yards there was intense pain shooting up my leg and it was then they conceded it might be time for a scan. They found a crack in the bone, and that was my season finished.

I got kicked and elbowed a lot. Sometimes worse. The next season David Batty would be sent off at Upton Park for smashing me in the face with his elbow. It looked like a move he had picked up from cage fighting. My head whipped back and I went down. It was worth about three red cards. When I got back on my feet, as per the requirement of the era not to show any weakness, I gave Batty a gentle shove in the chest. What amazed me the most about all this, was the reaction. Later I watched it on *Match of the Day*. There was little or no condemnation of Batty. Just a bit of wincing when the slow-motion replay showed how violent he had been. Instead the BBC commentator reacted with disbelief to my shove. 'Oh, young Cole reacts rather foolishly,' he said. 'You've got to get used to challenges like that.' At the time, even I ended up apologising for my reaction when I was asked about it afterwards. There is not a chance a young player would be treated the same way now.

David O'Leary, the Leeds manager, piled in as well. He said I had helped to get Batty sent off. Just to be clear, the only person that got Batty sent off was Batty. But that was the game then. It was very physical. There were even some players – who I won't name – whose job it was basically to run around smashing into people. I don't include Batty among those. Whatever our differences he was a good footballer who won a league title and represented England.

If you were a creative footballer who wanted the ball to your feet, you could forget about that. First, you had to fight for it. The game has changed in those twenty-five years. I'm glad. It never felt right to me at the time. I knew we were doing it wrong.

10

We Can't Play like Barcelona

During his first two seasons at Chelsea, José Mourinho would build me up with praise and then demolish me with his criticism, but for his final fifteen months he picked me in his team every time he could. He would stop me in the training ground when I was injured and ask when I would be fit again. He wanted more and more from me at a point in my career when, for the first time, my body was starting to protest. I came back from the 2006 World Cup finals, the best of the three I played at from my point of view, to a hug from José when I first saw him at Cobham. I should have known then that things were going to change. He wanted to know all about the fallout from Wayne Rooney's red card. He told me not to worry about all the criticism aimed at England. He told me to forget my disappointment because we were going to win things again at Chelsea. We had signed Andriy Shevchenko, the great Ukrainian striker from AC Milan who had won the Ballon d'Or. Michael Ballack had come from Bayern Munich as a free agent. Ashley Cole had finally arrived from Arsenal. Chelsea were twice Premier League champions and – we thought – either the best team in Europe or the second best.

Yet what we did not know was that the days of José were coming to an end – a dramatic global news event kind of end, but an end nonetheless. I believed I had been the club's best player in the previous season. I had scored one of the best goals at the World Cup finals against Sweden in the group stages. I was ready to push on – and then I got injured. It was the first big injury of my year. I had broken my toes on that moped in Marmaris. Rory Delap had cracked my leg. But this one was different – a lingering, stubborn, evolving problem that would change the season.

It is always the games you least expect. My injury was sustained in Illinois playing on Chelsea's pre-season tour in the United States against the MLS All-Star team. Injuries change your life. You find yourself managing their effect. You try to work around them. Nothing is the same any more. I was at the top of my game and then everything changed. One problem led to another and for a long time, no one knew exactly what was wrong with me. In the US I was taken onto the plane home in a wheelchair and dosed up on painkillers. The scan found medial ligament damage in my right knee and suddenly I was out of the game for three months. The process of rehabilitation is very boring. You don't just miss the matches and the training. You miss being around your teammates. The constant competition, the gossip, the arguments, the friendship.

It was then that the injections started too. At first a little cortisone to bring the swelling down and then more and more. Later in my career the injections of anti-inflammatories would become such a common ritual that the pain in my stomach was agonising at times. I was diagnosed with damage to the stomach lining because of the quantity I was taking. Yet even after that I would carry on with the tablets and injections. Why did I do it? I wanted to be fit to play. A gift that through my childhood and early professional career I had taken for granted but now seemed like such a privilege. The other problem is that I hate needles. Later in my career at Aston Villa, my old midfield rival Roy Keane, by then my coach, would look at me in disbelief when I had to sit down and try not to faint after the sports scientist used a finger pinprick to take my glucose levels. It is not the sight of the needle that turns me funny – although it doesn't help. It is mainly the thought of the needle. When I was a child, Mum says it took four doctors and nurses to chase me around and hold me down at St Mary's Hospital in Paddington to get a jab in. I don't suppose the memory of that helped either. But injections would become a regular part of my life.

Chelsea had problems. They weren't terrible problems, but we felt them. We had been a winning team and now, with our new signings, we were not the same. Damien Duff had been allowed to leave, which I felt was a mistake, so Didier Drogba would sometimes play off the right wing to accommodate Shevchenko. With Ballack in midfield, trying to play the same game as Frank Lampard, we were not the same there either. Yet even so, there is a difference between defending champions who slump and those who lose out by fine margins. We were the latter in 2006–07. It was so close to being an incredible season. We finished second by six points in the Premier League to a resurgent Manchester United. We lost only three Premier League games all season. We played Barcelona, the Champions League winners the previous season, in the group stages and took four points off them. We lost in the semi-finals again to another mediocre Liverpool team. We won the FA Cup and the League Cup. Yet, for all that, the relationship between José and Roman Abramovich was falling apart.

In the meantime, José and I were getting on better and better. My ligament injury in the US meant that I did not play much at first. When I was available José wanted me in, or he wanted me to play off the bench. I came back as a substitute in mid-September and did not play again for a month. When I played for England against the Netherlands in late October it was only my ninth game of the season. The pain was now in my right foot and it was excruciating, so I was taking injections to manage it. The scans were not telling the doctors anything new. The assumption was it might be related to my knee ligament damage, but no one knew for sure.

When finally we played at Old Trafford at the end of November, I was in agony. We stayed in Manchester ahead of a game against Bolton Wanderers that week. In the morning, I couldn't get out of the hotel bed. The doctors sent me for another scan and finally they found what they were looking for. I had a stress fracture in my foot. I had cracked the navicular bone and no one had noticed. My running style had been changed by the knee injury and in the rush to bring me back as swiftly as possible that had caused the stress fracture. I don't blame the doctors and physios. That was their job. As players we were pushed hard, injured and then pushed just as hard to get back playing. I was complicit in it all because I was so eager to play. If I had my time again, I would have asked more questions. I would have taken my time, like my old teammate Arjen Robben always did over injuries. As I got older and the injuries got worse, I got better at managing my body and knowing my limits. I also became more assertive with managers about what I could do and what I couldn't.

At the end of 2006 a delicate little cracked bone on the top of my foot seemed to have a hold over my life. I was told bluntly that if it snapped then that would be the end of my career. When it comes to surgery, the club can advise you on treatment and offer options, but in the end it has to be your decision – and your choice of surgeon. One surgeon told me to rest and recuperate. Another told me to get the procedure done. That procedure was a bolt drilled into both pieces of the bone to fix them together. I went back and forth in my mind between the two options. I felt I was making a decision that would either sustain my career, or possibly end it. The question was on my mind constantly. Looking back, it was a coming-of-age moment. I was twenty-five and life had been relatively kind. I had succeeded in what I had always wanted to do. I had my parents to fall back on and the love and support of Carly. Now I was on my own in this decision. It weighed heavily on me. I woke up one night struggling to breathe and Carly was pretty sure that I was having a panic attack.

I chose to have the operation. I chose the surgeon, Professor James Calder, because his confidence was reassuring. I was to have surgery on 1 January 2007. It was the first available day. I called the professor a couple of nights before and tried to bring the subject round to a small detail that was playing on my mind. It was a bit awkward, but I needed to know. Was he planning a boozy New Year's Eve? He reassured me that he was not. James's expert work on my foot did the trick. He told me to be patient. José, on the other hand, just couldn't wait. He asked me constantly when I would be back. United were resurgent. We were fighting them for a third Premier League title. Chelsea won the League Cup in February with me watching from the stands. We went all the way to the Champions League semi-finals. As bad seasons go, this was a very good one. Looking back, if this wasn't good enough for Chelsea in 2007 there cannot have been many managers working under such exacting demands. But three straight draws in the Premier League over New Year put a gap between us and the leaders United.

I had not played since the end of November and come

150

April, José could wait no longer. He put me on the bench for the first leg of our Champions League quarter-final against Valencia. I played fifteen minutes as a sub and then three days later another seven minutes as a sub against Tottenham. It's a strange thing being a half-fit footballer. I was in a lot of pain. James was telling me that the bone was strong. I had all sorts of worries about what might happen. But once you are on the pitch, the assumption from everyone – fans, pundits, media – is that you're fit. You don't get to put an asterisk by your name in the player ratings in the newspapers, there's no:

Joe Cole 6/10*
*in agony after surgery and suffering anxiety that the bone might break again.

Instead, you get judged by the standards that everyone else lives by. In Valencia for the return leg, José brought me on at half-time and I played well in what was another Champions League epic against a great opponent. We won 2–1, with a last-minute goal from Michael Essien to take us through to the semi-final. But the result seemed secondary. All I could think about was my navicular bone. Was the bolt still in place? Was my career still viable? At the final whistle I was called into drug-testing when I just wanted to get some ice on my foot. The painkilling injection was wearing off and I was in agony. I started pouring bottles of water into a bucket to soothe my foot which for reasons that weren't quite clear really angered the Valencia team doctor. We had a big row. The key thing about drug-testing is that you cannot go anywhere until you have peed. So after the argument we had to sit there together in this little room in an awkward sulky silence trying to ignore one another.

José was doing what most managers do. He needed what he considered his best players in the team if they were fit enough to play. That is how football works and we all sign up to it, one way or another.

As the title slipped away, it never occurred to me that change was coming soon. I thought José would be there for ever. I looked at what he had done and couldn't imagine that Roman would sack him. At last, José seemed to approve of me and although I was in pain, I was eager to play whenever asked. There were some big moments. I started the FA Cup semi-final against Blackburn Rovers. I scored the winner in the first leg of the Champions League semi-final at Anfield, a tie we would eventually lose on penalties. I played in the worst FA Cup final in living memory.

That was our 1–0 win over United to deny them the double, with a goal from Didier Drogba in extra-time. FA Cup finals should be glorious days of great football in May sunshine. The FA Cup finals I had attended as a kid – and a Chelsea fan – in 1994 and 2000 were reference points in my childhood. Compared to those, I'm afraid 2007 is much less memorable to me – and I actually played in this one. It was a horrendous game. I was still in pain but keen to repay José's now un-wavering faith in me. He came to me before the game and asked if I could play and of course I said I could. Winning the FA Cup is a great moment in any player's career and I did so more than once. But I was focused on getting through the game and managing the pain more than anything, and then on us squeezing out a win by any means necessary.

As we came into the tunnel at the newly opened and rebuilt Wembley, with the United players growling at us and Didier no doubt somewhere at the back with his shirt off looking magnificent, I spotted Mick Jagger. The actual Mick Jagger.

Right A North London boy from the Camden estates. Here I am near our flat in Donnington Court on the Clarence Way estate. I played football every day of my childhood.

Right My mum, Susan, and dad, George. They gave me and my siblings everything. Life was not always simple, but we laughed a lot together. They gave me love and security.

Below With my dad, George. I presume the beer on the bar was for him. He and my mum watched me play all over the world once my professional career began.

Left While training with Manchester United, me, my mum and my brother and sister, Charly and Nicky, got to meet Eric Cantona. He was serving his ban at the time for kicking the Crystal Palace fan. On this day he told me he was off to do his community service.

Left As a West Ham junior, running out the famous old tunnel at Anfield. You could have fit me twice over into that Pony shirt.

Below On tour with the England schoolboys team with some of my friends from the FA centre at Lilleshall. Football meant that I saw a whole new world outside of Camden.

Above Size XL Pony shirt tucked in. Game face on. I made my West Ham debut at seventeen and my football apprenticeship there was ideal. It was one of the last of its kind.

Above right With Michael Carrick and Frank Lampard. We all made it through the West Ham youth system and played for England, but sadly never repeated the World Cup win of West Ham's boys of '66.

Right Paolo Di Canio was a fabulous footballer. One of many West Ham teammates who taught me so much, and he always let me know if I didn't pass to him.

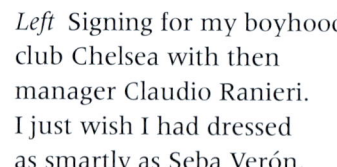

Left Signing for my boyhood club Chelsea with then manager Claudio Ranieri. I just wish I had dressed as smartly as Seba Verón.

Middle From the moment he arrived, José brought the future to Chelsea. I could see it from his very first training session. He got the best out of me – even if at the time I could not understand why he gave me such a hard time.

Below left After we beat Barcelona on that great night in 2005, José sought me out for praise. I craved it from him.

Below This was taken by one of the fans watching me and Didier Drogba celebrate the 2005 Premier League title outside Bolton's stadium. I almost slipped on the champagne that had been sprayed on the roof of the coach.

Right Luiz Felipe Scolari used to say I was more Brazilian than English. We just could not turn results around and he paid with his job.

Right With Carlo Ancelotti, a brilliant manager who always knew how to keep his players calm. He always took time to speak to me when I was injured.

Below left Just one season under José and at last I had some more trophies to add to the legendary 1999 Intertoto Cup triumph with West Ham.

Below right Slipping past Paul Scholes in the 2008 Champions League final. I was so sure we would win the shootout I took my contact lenses out ready to celebrate.

Above It took me a long time to win Sven-Göran Eriksson's confidence. I did like him – he never took life too seriously.

Above Drifting away from a tackle against Sweden at the 2006 World Cup. I was at the top of my game and I scored one of the goals of my life that day.

Left Jamie Carragher, a great Liverpool defender and one of the few then left in the game with the personality to organise his teammates in a game.

Right Celebrating with my Lille teammates – a wonderful season in my career. It meant I got to play alongside Eden Hazard, the most talented teammate I ever lined up with.

Right At Aston Villa my body felt like it was falling apart. I had to lift my leg out of my car on one matchday.

Below My swansong in English football at Coventry City. I just wanted to play football and Tony Mowbray gave me the chance.

Left With my Tampa Bay Rowdies teammates – a great time in my life in Florida. We flew economy and finished training by 10.30 a.m. I loved it.

Left My brother-in-law, Mitchell Cole, with his daughter, Rhys, and son, Georgie. Leni was born weeks after his death in 2012.

Below My precious family, from left: Harry, Carly, Max and Ruby.

One of my heroes. Not many people could have disturbed my cup final focus in that moment. But Mick was one. Amid the tension and the brooding machismo of the pre-match tunnel I called out: 'Awright, Mick!' And the great Jagger looked over and said, in that great Jagger voice, 'Hi, Joe!' I just wish he had done one of his little claps as well. In person, he is much smaller than I imagined. In my mind he was a giant. Yet he was built like a nippy little number 10. Either way, a moment of FA Cup magic.

Despite winning the FA Cup, the League Cup and finishing second in the Premier League, the discussion in the newspapers about José's future did not subside. On tour in the United States that summer we encountered a new figure on the scene. This was Avram Grant, an Israeli coach who was in the inner circle with Roman and his people. In our hotel in Beverly Hills it was obvious that José was unhappy with it all and that Avram, now our director of football, was Roman's guy. I had no personal issue with Avram but there was a paranoia in the group that you did not want to be seen hanging about with him too much. José's people distrusted him. They were unsure why he was there – although they could guess. This is the politics of a football club. You have to realise that, sometimes, who you talk to matters. If Avram was reporting back to Roman then no one wanted to be seen as the informer. After all, José was still picking the team.

On that tour, José and his staff played a friendly game against a team from the English media who were in Los Angeles en masse to report on us as well as David Beckham's arrival at LA Galaxy. The game took place before one of our training sessions on the campus of UCLA and so we sat and watched. José played in goal, as his late father Felix, a one-cap Portugal international, had done. As ever, José was smart. When the game went to penalties he substituted himself for his assistant Silvino Louro who had played more than twenty years as a top goalkeeper in Portugal. He was Benfica's captain in the 1990 European Cup final. He had won twenty-three caps for his country. Silvino duly won the shootout for the staff team. José was a good footballer, despite him never having had a career as a professional player – which was constantly cited by people trying to undermine him. He never wore shorts, so I can't tell you if he had the classic footballer's legs or not, but he did well when he trained with us, often in the four against four games. That said, none of us would dare tackle him.

He picked me as a false nine, before false nines were a thing, in the Community Shield, another dreadful Wembley game between us and United. For the first league game of the 2007–08 season against Birmingham City he left me on the bench, and then never brought me on. By then, I felt more confident. I followed him into his office at Stamford Bridge afterwards. I confronted him: 'Why the effing hell was I not coming on in a game like that?'

Looking back, José had been right. He had brought on Steve Sidwell ahead of me to see out a 3–2 win. Siddy, a good friend of mine, was new and José wanted to ease him in. But I had got used now to being one of José's main men. José interrupted me mid-rant. 'Eff off, Joe,' he said.

I said, 'You can eff off. I want to leave.'

He replied, 'You want to leave? Fine. Call your agent. We will sell you for twenty-five million pounds.'

This absurd conversation, which was mostly my fault, continued for a while, but I couldn't conceal my smile. 'You really think I'm worth twenty-five million?' I said. That was a lot of money in 2007. 'If I'm worth twenty-five million, why the eff am I on the bench?'

'Eff off, Joe,' José said again.

I was almost twenty-six, in my prime, but worried about injuries. José had been the top dog in English football but could now see the writing was on the wall for him with Roman. Ours had been a complex relationship to say the least. We had won so much and come close to winning even more in Europe. We had gone from that original meeting at Harlington when he came closest to defining me as a player as any coach had managed, to tearing into me on television – and then praising me. Then finally he had come to rely on me. Now we were in our last days together, and I would hate for him to think I did anything to get him the sack that September.

He was dismissed the day after a 1–1 draw with Rosenborg at home in our first Champions League group game of the season. By that point, we had won three, drawn two and lost one of our first six Premier League games, which is hardly a disaster but it felt like José's relationship with Roman was beyond repair. I go back to the point – Roman wanted us to play like Barcelona. That wasn't possible. Barcelona played that way because of years of a certain style of coaching and academy development and buying a certain style of player. For Chelsea to do it, on a small pitch at Stamford Bridge entirely unsuited to that approach, would have taken years of transition and a lot of new players. José was there to win trophies by any means necessary. As for the final step in Europe, he had reached two Champions League semi-finals. He would have got there eventually. Although he wouldn't have done it playing like Barcelona. In the aftermath of José's sacking, in the newspapers it was all about how the players had forced him out. Maybe some of them had. I never spoke to Roman about José other than that one meeting earlier when I had asked to leave. I was not in the inner circle. I was never asked my opinion. To knife a manager like that would have gone against everything I had learnt as a kid. What I had to say about José, I said to José. Even at the end of my career, when a club owner asked me for a discreet opinion on the manager of the time, I refused.

José came to Cobham to say farewell. It was like the introduction of the dignitaries before an FA Cup final. He came down the line shaking hands and embracing his players. He blanked Shevchenko. As it got close to my turn I began to worry. Is he going to blank me too? If someone had told him I was in some way responsible, I was going to have to put him straight. The worst thing he could have accused me of – among all the things he had accused me of in the past – was being a manipulator. I readied myself for one last confrontation. José got to me, grabbed me in an embrace and wished me all the best, and within a minute he was out of the door and gone. I have seen managers come and go, but I have never seen so much emotion as when José left. Frank Lampard, a man whose feelings were locked away deep below the surface, was crying. In the world outside the media was poring over every last detail of the drama. Then quickly, after all the tears, it was over. The king is dead, long live the king. We had United at Old Trafford on Saturday. And into the chaos walked the new man: Avram.

I was stunned that it wasn't Steve Clarke as a temporary replacement for José. But then I guess I had not read the politics. Avram was tight with Roman. Avram was smart when it came to the team. He didn't really change anything – and he didn't need to change anything, because there was nothing much wrong. It was obvious that Shevchenko was not working so he gradually took him out of the side. He played one up top, which was usually Didier. Nicolas Anelka might start up there as an alternative or off the left. I would be on the right, although Avram did rotate me with Florent Malouda, Shaun

Wright-Phillips and Salomon Kalou. In midfield we always looked more settled with Frank, Michael Essien and Claude Makélélé. Michael Ballack had some big games and scored some big goals, but Essien and Maka allowed Frank to get forward and not worry about the defensive work. One way or another, things settled down.

We lost to United in Avram's first game, but after that we lost just one more league game the whole season. Ask Avram and he will tell you that he has the best win ratio of any Chelsea manager in history. Later, another new manager, Luiz Felipe Scolari, would make the mistake of trying to change the José system. Avram just went with it, all the way to the Champions League final. Avram's approach was to pick the team and do the team-talk, but Clarkey continued doing the coaching. We knew our roles at set-pieces to the last detail thanks to José's drilling. Clarkey barely had to write the details on the board. The players were accountable. Then another twist was added to the plot. Chelsea appointed the Dutch coach Henk ten Cate, who had been part of the staff at Barcelona under Frank Rijkaard when they had won the Champions League in 2006, as assistant first team coach.

Ten Cate was clearly a very good coach. He was an expert in the Dutch way, which had been refined at Barcelona by their manager Johan Cruyff during the 1990s, and he was there to help fulfil Roman's dream of us playing like Barcelona. The problem was we didn't have the players and Clarkey, schooled in the José way, saw the game very differently. Ten Cate and Clarkey were at loggerheads over how we should play and Avram sat benignly in the middle. There were times when I would look at Frank or John Terry as if to ask: 'What exactly is the plan?' We would sort it out ourselves. The José way versus the Barcelona way. It was usually José's way that won out.

WE CAN'T PLAY LIKE BARCELONA

I would like to have played like Barcelona. That had always been my dream. I am just not sure all my teammates would have been on board, or indeed capable of doing so. Frank, for example, was a dynamic, forward-thinking midfielder. He wasn't interested in slow build-up from the back. Neither was Essien. We didn't have Xavi or Andrés Iniesta. Besides, for four years, our patterns of play had become so ingrained that when Frank or Essien got the ball I knew where I had to be, and they expected me to be there. Just as when the opposition were in possession, I had specific responsibilities. To ignore that felt reckless, especially when Clarkey's coaching was all about the systems that we had developed under José. Ten Cate would tell us one thing. Clarkey would tell us another. Ten Cate's approach, as far as the wingers were concerned, was much like what Pep Guardiola's would become at Manchester City. You stay high and wide and wait for the ball to come to you. It stretches the opposition and creates the spaces for passes through them. You do not, for the most part, drop back looking for possession. It is the structure of the midfield and defence that works the ball up to you, and from a high position on the pitch you can attack the opposition's defence. I was a substitute for the second Champions League group game against Valencia in December, having scored in our win at the Mestalla in October. When Ten Cate told me I was coming on, I thought – I'm going to give this guy's ideas a try.

It felt strange standing on my own on the touchline, resisting my instincts to track back or try to win the ball. At times I felt like a spectator. But this is what Ten Cate had told me to do. I waited and I waited. 'Patience,' Ten Cate shouted at me, in what I thought was an encouraging sort of way. Just when I was thinking about taking a seat in the East Stand the ball came to me at last. I felt fresh. I hadn't had to run fifty yards to win it and then turn around and join the attack. I dropped a shoulder, beat a player and had a shot which the keeper turned onto the post. It felt good. On the touchline I could see Ten Cate was delighted. He gave me a thumbs-up.

It never really caught on at Chelsea, although it was a nice idea. The spine of our team was not really suited to this brave new world. Deco, who would not arrive from Barcelona until the following summer, could have done it. Deco was an excellent player – Paul Scholes but with a couple of yards of pace. I liked the ideas that Ten Cate had. I liked the idea of getting the ball in more advanced positions, unencumbered by defensive duties. But it was too soon for the team. If you put that Chelsea team in a veterans' league now with John, Frank, Čech, Didier, me and Essien we would still play the same way José had drilled us. Avram should have told Ten Cate and Clarkey how he wanted the team to play but it never felt like he knew. As players we made our own minds up and it worked well to a point. We only lost the league to United by two points. We got to the League Cup final and the Champions League final. The conflict between the two key coaches was not a big drama because as a team we knew how to play. My job was essentially what it had always been. Get the ball in tight situations, keep it and get us up the pitch. And do the defensive work. But I was also playing with freedom. The 2007–08 season was quite a joyous time in spite of the occasional confusion about how the hell we were supposed to be playing. There was also a part of me that, for all the freedom I craved, and that Ten Cate's way of playing promised, was still proud of the defensive work I did. I had learnt that before I had met José, but under him I had become so much better at it. In my mind's eye, if I slacked off, I could still imagine him on the touchline flapping his arms and shouting at me.

WE CAN'T PLAY LIKE BARCELONA

Avram phased out Shevchenko, and by the time we played the Champions League final in May the once-great striker was not even in the matchday squad. I was sad to see him struggle. He was a lovely man and popular with the players. Football is a brutal game. I feel like we treated him with respect as teammates. There is no hiding place in the game. You are good enough for the team until you are not and then you're out. There was one occasion when John Obi Mikel tore into Shevchenko in frustration during one of our hyper-competitive training ground games. I had great fondness for Mikel and so I spoke to him. I said that I understood his competitiveness but whatever he felt, we had to treat Shevchenko with respect for what he had done in the game and for the way he behaved around us as a teammate. John went on to be a great player for Chelsea and Nigeria. It is important that, whatever a team-mate's limitations as they decline as a footballer, you treat them as you would wish to be treated yourself in the same position. Because the only certainty is we are all going the same way. I would find out later in my career how hurtful it can be when younger teammates dismiss you.

Avram dropped me to the bench for the League Cup final against Tottenham, which we lost. He went for Anelka instead and Aaron Lennon got to run at Wayne Bridge too often. Avram apologised and said he wouldn't do that again. I appreciated his honesty. I had come on in extra-time although the final was also notable for another Cole on the pitch. That was my cousin Justin Cole, son of my dad's brother Billy, a Spurs fan who had been in the Chelsea end with a ticket I had got for him. That branch of the family are devout Spurs fans, and they have history for running on the pitch. At White Hart Lane, Billy Cole once tried to get to an opponent who had kicked his hero, Jimmy Neighbour. As I went over to clap the

Chelsea support, I saw a Spurs fan run onto the pitch and thought, with a sinking feeling, that looks like Justin. By the time I turned my phone on in the dressing room there were a lot of messages about it. Justin had been on TV as well and it was not long before the newspapers got hold of it. That is life in the Cole clan. You can get angry about it or you can just accept the occasional moments of madness.

No Chelsea player managed more than my fifty-five games that season. I was finally – officially – named Chelsea's player of the season. I had come back from an injury that might have ruined my career. I had thrived under José, and at times I had just about survived José. I felt like I was back at the peak of my powers and not just for Chelsea but for an England team that had stumbled and fallen in Euro 2008 qualifying. We had not won the league but we had finally got past Liverpool in the semis to reach the Champions League final. I had seen off so many new players and challengers for my position in the team. What I really wanted was another Chelsea contract. I believed the club would offer one soon. We were one game away from winning the Champions League. The trophy that, if the stories were to be believed, had inspired Roman to buy a football club, and the one that he coveted above all. The final was to be played in Moscow, the city in which he had made his fortune. We were playing United, our great rivals of the era who we had beaten in the league in April, in the first ever all-English final in the European Cup. Surely, nothing could go wrong.

11

The Academy of Football's
Missed Opportunity

I came to realise for good that West Ham were not going to compete for trophies when they sold Rio Ferdinand in November 2000. My world view had been pretty simple at first. I thought I was going to win things at West Ham and I would do so alongside youth team graduates like Frank Lampard and many of my mates from the 1999 FA Youth Cup-winning team. By the time I turned nineteen years old, the same month that Rio left, it was becoming very clear it would not be like that.

West Ham sold all of us in the end: Frank, Rio, me, Jermain Defoe, Glen Johnson and Michael Carrick. All within the space of four years and one relegation. People talk about the Class of '92 at Manchester United; what they achieved together, from three different age cohorts, was incredible. Our West Ham generation was from four different age cohorts and as a group of individual players, overall, I think we scored more highly. Yes, they had great players like Paul Scholes, Ryan Giggs, David Beckham, but put us against them in both our respective primes – seven-a-side, pick your best goalkeeper – and we win. There was one major difference. They had been young pros at Manchester United under a manager who had them at the centre of his planning. We were at West Ham who were not financially stable enough to keep that group together.

Rio was the first to go and that was the sign that this generation of West Ham players was available for sale. I realised with clarity that if I wanted to achieve all that I could as a footballer I might not be at West Ham for much longer. I stayed until we were relegated in 2003. We were almost relegated in 2001, losing eight of the last eleven league games. Harry Redknapp was sacked just before the end of that 2000–01 season, along with his friend and assistant Frank Lampard senior. And so Frank junior left that summer for Chelsea, at £11 million one of the biggest bargains in the history of football. By contrast, when Rio left for Leeds United the widely held view was that £18 million was a fortune for a defender. But what looked like a good deal gradually turned out to be a terrible deal for West Ham. Rigobert Song, the immediate replacement, was a signing that never worked out. We spent a bit more on Christian Dailly, and then Tomáš Řepka, and then Gary Breen, but none of them solved the problem. There is one Rio Ferdinand in every generation. A defender who can do everything, who can play at any level. When you sell him, you have lots of money but then you have to replace him. There is no guarantee that you'll get another Rio in the next twenty years. The same goes for the rest of the West Ham generation. When a club is lucky enough to develop a group of great young players with an emotional connection to the club, they have to understand that this is an exceptional moment in the club's history.

If I had been in the place of Terry Brown, the chairman at the time, I would have spent as much as I could to keep us all at the club – even if it was only long enough to win one major trophy. That would have made it a historic era. We would have achieved something. But each of our sales felt like they were made out of desperation. When Glen and I left for Chelsea three years later, the fees paid by Roman Abramovich effectively saved West Ham from financial catastrophe. West Ham always seemed to be a distressed seller.

By the age of nineteen in November 2000, I was still not at the two-year anniversary of my first team debut and yet I was already a senior player. That probably said more about the eclectic mix of the dressing room than anything else. We did have Davor Šuker, a man with a mighty CV, including the likes of Real Madrid and Arsenal as well as a 1998 World Cup semi-final appearance and a golden boot from that tournament. I was fascinated by what Davor had to say about playing alongside Raúl or Roberto Carlos or against Zinedine Zidane. Davor was the first player I had ever seen wear flip-flops when he went for a shower, and given the state of the showers at West Ham's training ground he may have adopted that custom just for this stage of his career. We all followed suit.

We had some moments. In January 2001 we won an FA Cup third round tie against Manchester United at Old Trafford. That was me, Frank and Michael in a three-man midfield against the quartet of Beckham, Giggs, Butt and Keane. The three of us were nineteen, twenty-two and nineteen years old respectively. We set up with five at the back and were outnumbered in midfield but not outplayed. It was that cup tie in which Paolo Di Canio scored the famous winner. Fabien Barthez pretended that the game had stopped and pointed to the referee. I have to say he would have kidded me but Paolo called his bluff and stuck it in the goal. By the end of the match, United had Andy Cole, Dwight Yorke, Teddy Sheringham and Ole Gunnar Solskjær all on the pitch together trying to get the equaliser.

In defeat, United were generous. When I got on board for the long bus journey home, I was told that the crates of beer being distributed had been gifted to us from the United players' bar. A lot of clubs just wouldn't have extended that courtesy, but they knew how much it meant to us and I guess they had won enough over the years. Even Harry, who did not like us drinking, allowed us to celebrate on the way home. The coach took us straight back to Essex and to the only place anyone would have suggested to celebrate a win that momentous on a Sunday when most of the pubs closed early. That was Charlie Chan's nightclub under Walthamstow Stadium, famous for its dog track. Possibly the most quintessential east London venue ever. Chan's is gone now, and so is the dog track, but the memories remain.

That same season we beat one of the best teams in Europe at Old Trafford, we lost at home to Ipswich Town. That was the measure of West Ham in that era. We would even rebound the following season, 2001–02, under Glenn Roeder and finish seventh but the downward momentum was even stronger after that. The 2000–01 season, in which we narrowly survived, was a dry run of the relegation that would eventually envelop us two years later. I thought we did enough to save Harry's job that year. A team under threat of relegation can go two ways. By the end I understood what people meant when they say certain players give up. You only see it if you look closely. A player who might be able to get back from an injury in three weeks takes four weeks – to avoid a tough away game. If contracts are coming to an end, some players won't put their bodies on the line. Rather than showing for the ball their movement says they don't want it. Strikers don't want the chance because they don't want to be the guy who misses the chance. In the privacy of the dressing room, lots of players try to diminish what relegation means. These are the deflectors. There are others who seek scapegoats to try to avoid being blamed themselves or they try too hard to show they care to avert any blame from themselves. In reality, when you break it down, any goal conceded usually involves two or three mistakes. I have seen players point fingers at others when, really, they should look at themselves.

It would also be fair to say that West Ham was somewhat behind the curve when it came to its facilities. Our medical room was one physiotherapist, John Green, who had access to one heat lamp, and any number of injured players to treat. Each of us would have to wait for the lamp and each player that would come in would immediately demand it was taken from whoever was being treated. The lamp took on a significance beyond any medical benefit it might have offered. But it was all we had. One doctor that worked for us would always steady the nerves with a couple of glasses of wine before the game. When Darren Moore pinged me with an elbow my mouth filled with blood and I could feel the rough edge of torn skin with my tongue. As the doc came over to stitch it up at half-time I could smell the booze on his breath. During the second half I could feel the flap of skin working its way loose from the stitches and at the end of the game he had to do it again. I can still feel the scar. When I got to Chelsea, I learnt that if you wanted something prescribed – sleeping tablets, strong painkillers – there was a process to go through. At West Ham, they might just drop it off at the house on request. There was a certain informality in everything we did.

Terry Brown called me when they sacked Harry. I imagine there were a few who got the call ahead of me but even by that point I was playing every week. It was a big change. Harry had been there since 1992, and he had been manager since 1994. The West Ham fans had never taken to Frank junior in the same way that they had to other academy kids, including me. That had been less than ideal for him, but it never changed Frank's unerring determination to succeed. I think every West Ham fan can agree that the club lost a great player that summer. There was no love lost between Frank and the fans from that moment on. I have been luckier. I went back to West Ham much later in my career when the injuries were taking their toll on me, and I was grateful for the appreciation. Sometimes you get it at a club, and sometimes you don't.

Glenn Roeder took over for the final game of the season and ended up in charge for almost two years until he was diagnosed with a brain tumour in April 2003. He had been promoted by Terry Brown from the academy and may have thought he was only going to be there to guide us through that final game of the 2000–01 season. Rio and Frank were gone. Glenn inherited a West Ham squad with a lot of cult heroes – although probably not enough actual heroes. There were players like Paolo Di Canio, Řepka and also Sébastien Schemmel, our French right-back, who won the Hammer of the Year award that season and now owns a burger bar in a shopping centre in Luxembourg, inevitably called Upton Park.

For Michael and me, it was an opportunity to play lots of games. That is not something that every young footballer gets these days and yet at West Ham it felt normal. I just expected more of my FA Youth Cup-winning teammates to join us. Adam Newton, our brilliant winger, would leave at the end of the season having never made the breakthrough. Shaun Byrne, the talented Irish left-back from our youth team, was in the first team squad but also could not hold down a place. As kids I had rated Shaun as highly as his youth team coun-terpart at Arsenal, Ashley Cole.

Don Hutchison was signed as Frank's replacement and generally he played in midfield with Michael and me. By now

I was playing progressively deeper and the 2002–03 season, my last at West Ham, I would often be used as a defensive midfielder which is not how anyone thinks of me in those early teen prodigy days. But that was the reality. I had to learn to do every job in midfield and my growing seniority meant that I could demand the ball from full-backs much more successfully than I could in my first two seasons. We almost didn't go for Don. Instead we almost ended up with Pep Guardiola. He was leaving Barcelona that summer after eleven years and an agent had offered him to Glenn. The manager rang me and asked me what I thought of signing Pep. I told him to go for it. I liked the idea of playing with one of the Barcelona greats of the 1990s who had won a European Cup. Glenn was worried that Pep might stall Michael Carrick's progress in midfield and, as much as that sounds daft now, I guess he did have a point. Sadly, we didn't sign Pep. He hasn't done badly since. But just think how the course of history might have changed. Schooled in the great Johan Cruyff tradition of Dutch total football, he could have come to Upton Park and learnt about playing in midfield for a West Ham team battling relegation when the pass was often aimed at your neck and you had two opponents trying to kick you. I like to think we would have added something to the greatest manager of his generation.

As a club we had some strange results in 2001–02. In October, we lost 7–1 to Blackburn Rovers – a game I am glad to say I missed through injury. In the three wins that followed we beat Chelsea at Upton Park, when Frank came back for the first time as an opposition player. We then won again at Old Trafford in October against a United team that had been Premier League champions three seasons in a row. In January we then lost 5–1 to Chelsea at Stamford Bridge. We played them four times that year, including an FA Cup fourth round tie and the replay that followed when John Terry scored a winner in the last minute. That February we played Blackburn in the return fixture after our seven-goal stuffing and won 2–0. We were an unpredictable team. Watching the side from the stands during my period injured, I came to recognise our many vulnerabilities.

Playing against Frank for the first time was an odd experience. I had known him from childhood, ever since I had started playing at West Ham. A couple of years older than me, he preceded me into the first team. Our development with England had been around the same time and although my international career started later it picked up steam quicker. I got to ten caps before him and then at Euro 2004 his England career took off. He became one of the team's biggest stars. Playing against him was tough. I knew his qualities well from the years we had played together, and yet that still did not help me. I knew what Frank was likely to do. Whether I could stop him from doing it was another question. You face Frank with a feeling of anxiety that at any moment he will disappear from your field of vision and reappear with the ball in a scoring position. I called him the ghost.

Frank waited for that moment you looked away. That glance to check over your other shoulder and in that second he would make his move. In that first FA Cup tie in January 2002, I lost him for a split-second just after half-time. The ghost was gone. I had been on it all game and it had taken just a moment. He just clipped the post with a shot. Frank never called for the ball. He liked to leave few clues as to his whereabouts for those who were trying to mark him. I came to prefer that, playing with West Ham. In fact, there's much less calling for the ball at the top level than you might think. My view on any teammate who called for the ball was simple. Mate, I can see you. I have been doing this all my life. If I decide to pass you the ball, I will pass it. If I don't, I won't. Besides, my suspicion was that when players are screaming for the ball the reality is that secretly they might not actually want it.

Paolo Di Canio was a fabulous footballer. If you missed the chance to pass to him, he, and the crowd, would let you know. Many times I found myself working the ball out of midfield and breaking the lines. Perhaps a dip of the shoulder, perhaps a one-two, then get the ball to Paolo. I'd make a run forward beyond him to try to get him some support. Sometimes he would give it back. Other times he might lose it and have a moan at someone while I went sprinting back in the other direction to cover. But, all the same, I embraced my defensive responsibilities and, as for Paolo, he won us so many games.

My midfield transformation in the last two seasons meant I played against Roy Keane a lot. Like Patrick Vieira, he was the midfielder I measured myself against. He was much more than just the uncompromising competitor that some now see him as – perhaps because of his punditry style. He was a very accomplished passer of the ball and had a great awareness of the way space opened up and closed on a pitch. I was always looking to break the lines and more often than not Roy would be in my way, occupying the pocket of space that I wanted to reach. He read an opponent's intentions well. I once said something to him I shouldn't have done (sorry, Roy). I could hear him coming after me for the rest of the game. The pace of his breathing changed. God, he was angry. He was waiting for a chance to put one on me. I don't blame him. Roy wasn't a dirty player and we kicked each other a bit. In fact, United used to kick me a lot in the days when you still could. A few years later I left one on Cristiano Ronaldo at Stamford Bridge and saw Sir Alex Ferguson jumping around on the touchline waving his arms at the referee trying to get me sent off. I thought that was a bit of a liberty given how many scars I had on my legs from his players, mostly Scholes and Butt. Either way, there is much less of that in the game now. I bet even Ronaldo can't recall the last time he was properly kicked by an opponent.

As the absence of Rio became that much more telling at West Ham, I tried to persuade Glenn to sign a Dagenham boy I knew from my youth team days. That was John Terry, an east Londoner wanted by every club when he was a kid and who had subsequently ended up at Chelsea. John was the only defender I knew who would put it all on the line every minute of every game. He was so good on the ball. He read the game like he had been playing at the top for twenty years. And I knew he was frustrated at Chelsea. In that 2000–01 season it was still Frank Leboeuf and Marcel Desailly starting most games. We would occasionally bump into one another in Essex on a night out. He even came to watch us train the morning after a few beers. I asked him if he fancied it but he desperately wanted to make it at Chelsea. Besides, Ken Bates, the Chelsea chairman, wasn't daft. He would never have sold a kid they had beaten Manchester United to sign. We certainly tried a lot of alternatives to Rio. Ahead of 2002–03, we signed Gary Breen who was supposed to be joining Inter Milan that summer but instead joined us which, much as I love West Ham, always struck me as an odd choice even then. He would later say he had failed a medical at Inter.

The seventh place in 2001–02 had been the club's best finish since West Ham came third in 1985–86, an achievement that is celebrated so enthusiastically that you could be forgiven for thinking West Ham had won the league that season. I remember looking at the squad that summer and thinking that if we had injuries we might be in trouble. Sure enough, Paolo and Frédéric Kanouté were injured a lot. Defoe had just turned twenty and he played more games than anyone. We won only three of our first twenty-four games. We played a part of the season with the centre-half Ian Pearce up front.

That development with Pearce gives you another insight into the way football was played, coached and organised even at the start of the 2000s. There was not that much difference between a centre-forward and a centre-half. It was still very much considered a role where you had to be good with your head. I salute Ian for his application to the role but I don't think a centre-half of his style would be considered to do that job now. In those days you still didn't have to be a great receiver of the ball. I think of the likes of Paul Warhurst, Dion Dublin, Gary Doherty. All centre-halves who became centre-forwards. In the meantime, the smaller players got overlooked. Leon Britton was in the West Ham youth system in the years that followed my own. He always struck me as a really talented player capable of doing many things that others could not and there was no question that his small stature held his career back. Leon eventually made it to the Premier League with Swansea City but it should have been much sooner.

Glenn started to introduce a few of the younger players as the team started to slide in the second half of the 2002–03 season. That was when Glen Johnson came through. Richard Garcia, one of the youth team boys of 1999, and Michael's best friend, played. I got on well with Glenn Roeder and I appreciated the way he consulted me on decisions around the team. The problem was that he and Paolo just did not get on. Glenn loved football and his coaching background, especially with young footballers, meant that his passion was for improving players. He was very straight in giving his opinion. Some footballers can take that level of feedback and others can't. While some managers might have been a bit more circumspect with their opinions and tried diplomatically to get the best out of a player until he could be moved on, Glenn was more likely to tell them exactly what was on his mind. Apparently he had told some senior players that he didn't believe they were up to it. I think he lost a few hearts and minds with that.

A strange time. I felt I was playing as well as ever. There was lots of praise for my performances, but the drudgery of defeat was hard to take and the downward momentum was hard to ignore. As a youth team player and an England schoolboy international I was used to winning. Now, as a senior West Ham player, I was having to get used to losing. On the pitch I was trying to do it all myself. I didn't have the maturity to try to galvanise the rest of the team with anything other than my performances. I couldn't really find the words or the tone.

In the background, my agent David Geiss was speaking to the clubs interested in signing me. Arsenal and United, the leading Premier League clubs in 2003, were both interested in me. From Spain there was an expression of interest from Valencia and also Barcelona. I had a contract at West Ham until 2004 and the chairman Terry Brown was not offering me another one. I don't think he could have gone to the level of wages that I would have expected and certainly not if the club was relegated. I asked David to leave me out of the discussion because I could not look any further than keeping West Ham in the Premier League. Sometimes people ask why you have an agent. This is one of the reasons why. There are times in football when you have to do two things at once that aren't necessarily compatible. I couldn't afford to think about life beyond the end of the season and beyond West Ham. I had to be completely committed to the club. But at the same time I had to plan my career.

I was very lucky to meet David. He was an accountant and

a man with a healthy scepticism about people who told me they could invest my money better than him. He never took risks. He treated his clients like his sons. Dad realised early on that I would need people around me with greater expertise than he could offer, so his idea was that I should get an agent and an accountant for the simple reason that, in his view, they could keep an eye on one another. Not that I ever needed to worry about that. The pair of them, David and my accountant Malcolm Webber, have become family friends. I recognise that I could have encountered much less scrupulous people over the course of my career, but David and Malcolm have put me and my family in a position where we are secure and confident in our finances. The promises they made to me at the start of my career have all been kept. I don't think you can ask any more than that.

It started to get precarious at West Ham at the start of 2003. United got their FA Cup revenge on us with a 6–0 pumping when we drew them at Old Trafford in the fourth round. I came back into the dressing room and found Breen apologising. He had been given the runaround by Ruud van Nistelrooy. He hadn't been the only one, but I could sense a desperation in him that was a bit troubling. I wanted to offer him some reassurance. Later in my career I would see what the effect of great success had on certain characters. Early in my career I was learning what defeat did to a player. 'Breeny,' I said, searching for the right thing to say, 'we were all s— today.'

It had been a bit of a catastrophe after late October. We won once in seventeen games. At the start of February at home to Liverpool we were 2–0 down within ten minutes. The next weekend Kanouté got sent off at Leeds United. This was something of a miracle for a man who was a very talented footballer but rarely ever made a tackle. Then it all changed.

We won six of our last eleven games and lost only once – to Bolton Wanderers who were, unfortunately for us, our direct rivals for relegation. That defeat was pivotal. We finished on forty-two points which is the highest all-time total for a relegated Premier League team in the thirty-eight-game era. In seventeenth place Bolton had forty-four.

The Bolton defeat in Lancashire in April was notable for a scuffle that would get me a ban that I would end up serving as a Chelsea player. It was a lesson in how obsessed certain people can become with footballers – in this case a senior off-duty police officer who was at the game that day. It was he who pursued the case with a truly fanatical zeal. Short story, there was a bit of an argument at the end of the game which I tried to sort out and during which Ian Pearce was given a red card. The Bolton full-back Bernard Mendy tried to land a headbutt on me so I punched him with a jab that was unlikely to do any lasting damage. Bear in mind, Mendy never mentioned the punch to me later, and it did not appear in the referee's report. There wasn't even any footage of it – or a picture for that matter. Yet the police officer in question, who had been watching from the stands, told the Football Association that if they did not pursue the case against me, he would tell his officers to open a criminal investigation into me. I had not helped myself by having a tantrum on my way off and kicking the side of the tunnel which ripped a section of plastic. I assume that was relayed back to him by one of the police officers in the tunnel. Either way, I don't think it met the usual benchmark for a police investigation.

When it came to the hearing in November, my solicitor told me the only evidence of my conduct, wrong though it was, came from the senior police officer and they took his word. The hearing had become a bit of a circus. The referee on the day, the late Uriah Rennie, turned up even though he had not been called as a witness. The FA gave me a two-game ban and a £17,000 fine. Summoning all my legal expertise – which is to say none, apart from my dad's occasional brushes with the court system – I asked them to consider fining me a larger amount and annulling the ban. I was playing well for Chelsea and I knew that once I lost my place in the team I might struggle to get back in it. As I made my case, I could sense that the vibe from my solicitor was: shut up, Joe. There was to be no leniency from the FA.

Back at West Ham in April 2003, we won our next game against Middlesbrough, and it was in the period after that game the club secretary Paul Aldridge called me to say that Glenn had collapsed with what turned out to be a brain tumour. Glenn survived although in the immediate aftermath no one knew how serious it would be. Glenn was a good man. He loved football and that put the pair of us on the same page temperamentally. As a centre-back in his playing days he was known for his fondness for a stepover. He would have been appreciated more in the modern era when central defenders are expected to be comfortable on the ball rather than just asked to head and tackle. Glenn went on to manage Newcastle United and Norwich City after West Ham. He died in 2021.

In his place came Sir Trevor Brooking, a legend of the club, a famous pundit and also at different times a key figure at the Football Association and within British sport. Management had never been among Trevor's ambitions, and he took on the job on a caretaker basis out of a sense of duty to West Ham. He called me into an office and asked me what had happened between Glenn and Paolo. Glenn had been trying to bring Jermain Defoe into the team and Paolo was the kind of man who wanted to play every game. The fallout had meant that

Paolo hadn't been in the side. Trevor put him back on the bench.

Trevor won two and drew one, and we were in contention to stay up until the last day but couldn't catch Bolton in seventeenth place. We were relegated. To say there was a rush for my signature might be overdoing it, but there were definitely interested parties. Arsène Wenger had the first refusal on both me and Michael, but turned us both down. Manchester United were hoping to wait all summer and drive the price down while they sold Juan Sebastián Verón, or so we heard. But, with Glenn Roeder back in charge, I was still at West Ham come July and although I fully expected to leave that summer I played a full part in pre-season, preparing for life in the second tier – then known as the First Division. We embarked on a tour of Sweden where I was obliged, as club captain, to make a speech – a very bad one it turned out – at a post-match banquet in our honour. I scored two goals against the mighty Atvidaberg. We played the Swedish champions Djurgårdens in a small town outside of Stockholm because their own stadium was being used to stage a Robbie Williams concert. Robbie was evidently regarded as a hotter ticket than West Ham.

Back in England we lost to Wycombe Wanderers at Adams Park. My last game for West Ham, the club of my teenage years, was a defeat at Upton Park on 1 August 2003, to a PSV Eindhoven team that included Mateja Kežman and Arjen Robben. Five days later I signed for Chelsea. I would be playing Champions League football at the club I supported. I never asked David, or my dad, what the contract offer was – I just felt I was ready to go. Money was not important to me compared to my key preoccupation – which was getting into the team. Even these days, I don't have much that I desire to buy. I put very little thought into what I wear. I get my spectacles from

Boots because the expensive pairs I've bought just seem to break as regularly as the cheap ones. I do like a nice holiday. My brother Nicky laughs at me. He says I should do something decadent – like buy a monkey as an exotic pet.

12

Turning Point: Moscow 2008

Didier Drogba had a green bike that he liked to ride to the training ground some days and, occasionally, when the mood took him, he would pedal around the Cobham site to warm-up. Didier wasn't going to win any stages of the Tour de France on his green bike – it wasn't an expensive one, just a standard hybrid – but it had another significance for him. It was his lucky bike and, as we know, superstition sits heavy with some players.

As we went head-to-head with Manchester United in the 2007–08 season, and as our paths would converge in the Champions League final in Moscow that May, we had some bad news. Didier's green bike had disappeared from Cobham. Who took it, whether by mistake or design, we never found out. I used to joke that Sir Alex Ferguson had sent some secret agents to grab it. And as we counted down to the biggest game of our lives, anything and everything would crowd into our minds.

Didier was sent off in the final. John missed what would have been the winning penalty when he slipped as he struck the ball. We lost the Champions League final, and I would never get to another with Chelsea. I would never win the Champions League. Four years later I would be watching on television as the club I loved and many of my old teammates won the Champions League without me. Jealous? You bet I was. But I loved 2012 too, as a Chelsea fan who had been there in the days when they were just happy to be in the First Division.

In Moscow in 2008, the night before the final against Manchester United, you could feel the tension. It was just different. This was a game that would define many of our lives. We had our rituals. The team meal made by our own chef. Our famous masseur Billy McCulloch – known as Bill Blood and beloved of the players – would get up to tell a couple of jokes. Often terrible jokes which he would laugh at himself and in turn make us laugh. It was childish but footballers need that sometimes. Anything to break the tension. The chef would get his guitar out. Didier would get up and sing 'La Bamba'. When he did so that night in Moscow we did what we always did: we joined in. We twirled our serviettes above our heads, we threw bread rolls at Bill Blood, but this time the serviettes were twirled a little faster, the singing a little louder. I'm not saying it was good behaviour in a five-star hotel. Just that we needed something to bring us together and people like Bill and Didier sensed that. Bill is a great friend of mine. He is still at Chelsea, kneading and soothing the muscles of another generation of players. You may see him pitchside before or after games and you will recognise him in part by his giant hands, made super-human by all those years of massaging. He has been a constant at Chelsea through changes of players, managers and even owners. He's one of the people who I admire greatly.

The Luzhniki Stadium is a forbidding ground, built in the era of the Soviet Union and that night in 2008 it felt like we were still in that era. The changing room was small, ramshackle and panelled with dark wood. I had played hundreds of matches in my career but this was the big one. The bell rang in the corridor outside, signalling the teams should come into the tunnel. There was a pounding on the door. It was the UEFA official responsible for getting us out on time and keeping the global TV broadcast on schedule. Someone slammed the door shut in his face.

No Chelsea team in history had ever made it that far in Europe's greatest club competition. We had lost once that season since 16 December. Our team was full of big hitters: Petr Čech, Ashley Cole, John Terry, Frank Lampard, Michael Ballack, Didier Drogba. We were straining at the leash. We were told to wait. Our manager, Avram Grant, insisted on bringing a television into the room. When it arrived, it looked like it might have been manufactured in the Soviet Union. Avram was fiddling around with the remote control. I could feel the energy in the room. It was restless. The mood was: let's get out there. We were ready. Finally, Avram got the TV working. He put on a DVD and on the screen the movie *Gladiator* flickered into life. Avram seemed to say that we were going to watch a certain scene. There was bemusement in the room. What was going on? Some very famous players were ready for the game of their lives and desperate to get going. No one wanted to watch the telly. I think it was Didier who just said: 'Lads, let's go.' And we walked past the television, out into the corridor where the bell was ringing and United were waiting. Usually, we would joke about something like that, but the game was so big, and our focus so intense, it felt wrong.

I was· so into the game it wasn't until I watched it back years later that I realised how heavy the rain came down by the end. I was up against Patrice Evra – early on he was getting enough of the ball that I was often deep in my own half and not involved in the game in an attacking sense. I did not play badly. I was still very much José's player, for good or for bad. Which meant one thing above all: I was not going to be the one who made a mistake. As a game it was not much better than the FA Cup final against United one year earlier. The big selection call for Avram was Florent Malouda – the choice had been between Nicolas Anelka, Salomon Kalou and Malouda. Malouda didn't get tight on Wes Brown when he crossed it for Ronaldo to score. Avram made a mistake not starting Paulo Ferreira at right-back. Instead he tried to get his best players into the team so with a midfield of Frank, Ballack and Claude Makélélé, he went for Michael Essien at right-back. Paulo had marked Ronaldo out of the game when we had played United before.

It was part chess match, part war of attrition. I was absorbed in the game. That era was so cagey and the top Premier League teams would play one another cautiously. This game was no different. Frank gambled on following in Didier's shot and scored for 1–1. I got into the game more in the second half and was able to start driving at Patrice Evra. I dropped a shoulder and went past him and whipped in a cross that Didier was just an inch from putting into the net. Then Didier hit the bar. I felt then we would win it. I went through on goal and nicked the ball ahead of Rio Ferdinand. He caught me in the face with his knee. Today with VAR it would have been a penalty. I should have gone down and milked it. Naively I bounced up and tried to get a shot away which gave the referee a way out of making the decision. I got an elbow from Evra that could have been a red card. I was confident we would win the game right up to Didier's late red card. Physically, a game like that is very demanding and you do your best not to show your opponent how much it takes from you. The cramps that you feel are your body's way of telling you that you are pushing it hard. I had been on the original list of penalty-takers, but by the time penalties came I had been substituted.

It is a strange feeling when the game is in the balance and you know it is going to penalties. No matter who you are – you cannot stop your mind wandering. In Petr we had one of the best goalkeepers in the world. Even so, we had lost our last two shootouts, to Liverpool in the Champions League semi-final the previous year and then to United in the Community Shield at the start of that same season. We missed all three that day. But by the time John stepped up, with Ronaldo having missed and just one penalty needed to win it, I felt it was written in the stars. How confident was I that John would score? So confident I took my contact lenses out. I thought that in a few seconds I would be running to John to celebrate. Experience had taught me that those big bundles of players are a nightmare for contact lenses. Fingers in eyes, shoulders in faces, you can end up losing one around the back of your eyeball very easily. Then of course there would be the champagne later and that also plays havoc with contact lenses. So I thought, let's get ready. Big Tel – Terry Ellis, the kitman – helped me get them out. So it was with a squint I watched our captain prepare to take the penalty that would win the Champions League.

Just put this one away John, and we can start the party.

I had never seen John slip over in all the hundreds of penalties he had taken in training. From that moment there was a feeling of dread. A foreboding that we were going to lose. When Anelka stepped up, the man who had come on for me, I thought: that could be me. You don't blame the man who misses the penalty that loses the final. That happens. No one wants to miss. But all of a sudden I wasn't running with my teammates celebrating the greatest night of my football career.

I was standing in the rain in Moscow – cold, wet, despondent and, in my case, with a very fuzzy view of things.

In the dressing room no one said anything. John was distraught. I felt a strong sense of sympathy for John. That could easily have been any of us. I remember looking around at my teammates and feeling a great deal of affection for them – and also pride. I was surprised by the strength of that emotion. Some do say that defeat bonds you. I remember that feeling well. It was very rare in my career. Where were these feelings coming from? What did they mean? I responded in the time-honoured way familiar to many blokes ambushed by their feelings. I didn't tell anyone and pushed them away to the edges. I'll save that conversation for my therapist a few years down the line.

When later in the hotel I met with Carly, my family and all the friends that had come, I didn't stay long. My dad just leant in and told me to go to bed if that was what I wanted to do. The next morning, I bumped into the lads who hadn't been named in the matchday squad. They had gone straight out after the game and stayed up all night. Most of them were still drunk. They cheered me up with their stories of a surreal night out in Moscow. Among them were my two good friends Wayne Bridge and Shaun Wright-Phillips. Shaun had reason to feel hard done by. It had been his best season at Chelsea. The strangest thing about losing a final is that the after-party tends to be that much boozier for it. The fans may think that you have to pay lip-service to the mood of disappointment. I see it differently. Many of us will have wondered if we would ever reach a Champions League final again. Some had got all the way there and not even got changed into their kit. But the world keeps turning, the sun comes up and you go again.

Shaun's and Bridgey's stories of their night brought me out of my funk.

I would have stayed at Chelsea for ever. I had been the club's player of the season. I had played in most of the games. We were a cigarette paper away from winning everything. I had two years left on my contract and I expected a phone call to say they had a new contract for me. But it never came. In the end my agent David called the club and the response was that they were going to wait until my deal had eighteen months to run. I was a bit peeved. I felt I had given them the best of myself. A five-year deal would have taken me to thirty-two years old. I would have bitten their hand off. One theory is that Roman was so furious at us losing the final that all those contract talks were put on hold. By the time eighteen months came around it would be too late for me. My biggest injury was less than one year away although even after that I could have played twenty-five games a season. Maybe I would not have got injured had we won that final? I often think how different life would have been if John had scored that penalty. It was all about to change again.

Just after Portugal played their last game of the Euro 2008 group stages – the tournament England had failed to qualify for – Chelsea announced that the new manager would be Luiz Felipe Scolari. Big Phil was how he introduced himself. He had taken over Portugal after winning the 2002 World Cup with Brazil. He was a short pugnacious man with a moustache and a twinkle in the eye. I liked him immediately. From the moment we met, Big Phil was always very encouraging to me. He used to joke that I should, given my style of play, have been Brazilian which is what every player likes to hear. I felt I was part of his plans. His English was a lot better than the English spoken by Fabio Capello. But for Big Phil at Chelsea it never turned out how we hoped it would.

First of all there was talk about the Brazil international Robinho coming to Chelsea. He ended up at Manchester City, who were keen to sign some big names just after the Sheikh Mansour takeover that summer. But once again I was confronted with the possibility of a player coming in to replace me. There is part of you that has to accept it comes with the territory at Chelsea, but I did tire of this notion that there was always someone better than me out there. Of course, eventually that happens to us all but at the time I was playing as well as anyone in the team. We had fallen short the previous season by fine margins. Robinho was just the latest one. I had seen off plenty of others. I knew that when it came to playing for Chelsea in the Premier League, he wouldn't be able to give what I could. And yet the club still hadn't offered me a new contract.

Scolari and I would often chat about the great Brazilians. He would tell me about managing Ronaldo and Ronaldinho. He told me we were going to win the Champions League and have a lot of fun doing it. But it was never like that. Instead we did a lot of running. It was like the old pre-seasons at West Ham. I had moved on from all that after the José years when everything had been with the ball, and now I was back on the cross-country runs like those days chasing Frank Lampard senior in his spikes. This was not my strength. Frank Lampard, Bridgey and Ashley Cole were at the front. John Terry and I would plod along in the middle of the pack. It was not conducive to creating football fitness. Scolari had not been in club football for seven years and things had changed. Once Scolari was sacked we would go back to the José way. That was the short, sharp, intense sessions that focused the decision-making, the tactical and the physical all in one. But under Big Phil there was all this running, and my body was really struggling.

The first pre-season tour post-José was a disaster. We had games in China and Malaysia. The heat was uncomfortable and the pitches were bad. With José out of the picture it felt like the commercial side of the club had taken control. We understood that we had a growing number of supporters out in this part of the world but as preparation for starting an intense Premier League and Champions League season it was the wrong idea. Big Phil didn't know how hard the Premier League was and he went along with the schedule.

I was not in the right condition. I had an ankle problem on the same leg in which I had the operation on the navicular bone at the start of the previous year. I tried to treat the pain with the same anti-inflammatories I had always used, which in turn did my stomach no favours. Having tried to manage it with tablets, when the pain got too much I needed a local anti-inflammatory injection. That would involve a guided scan while a needle would go around the back of my ankle and spray it with an anti-inflammatory around the bone. After twenty-four hours it was blissful but the damage was still there. I never gave myself enough time for it to heal. It meant that I missed a few games, but Big Phil was fully invested in me and when I was fit I was straight back in the team. When I played I felt I was as good as anyone on the pitch but it was a struggle to get out there. I scored the first goal of the season against Portsmouth. Big Phil would ask me what I wanted to do when it came to playing minutes. It was perfect in that regard, but the question was whether my body would hold out.

Big Phil was sacked on 9 February 2009. People say we failed that season. But there are many teams who would have loved to have failed the way we did. Big Phil's run to the sack was this: four wins in a row with two in the Premier League and two in the FA Cup. Then we lost at Anfield and drew 0–0 with Hull City and he was out. There was a bit more to it than that, of course, but it's not like we were in freefall. We had been top after thirteen games and then fell away and we could never get it back. From a home defeat to Liverpool in the Premier League on 26 October our form was so up and down. When we drew with West Ham and then Everton before Christmas the whole place was despondent. Standards were so high. We knew the manager could well go.

At the same time Carly and I had made a couple of big decisions. First, that we would try for a baby. Then, that Carly would give it a go on the reality television show *I'm a Celebrity . . . Get Me Out Of Here!* We can come to that later but it was a weird time for her, and also for me. Watching from home I could see she wasn't comfortable in the jungle. Big Phil was fascinated by the show. For all the pressure he was under he would often whistle the theme tune to me before training. I did like the guy.

Those were two huge factors in our lives. The third was what would happen on a miserable cold and wet Wednesday night in Southend in an FA Cup replay on 14 January 2009. I would finally suffer the big injury of my career and in that moment, life became that much harder. You could draw a line through my playing career at that moment. All that came before 14 January 2009 was different to what came after it. I would seek solutions from all sorts of weird and wonderful people – faith healers and reiki masters – as I sought to stay fit and manage my body in the years that followed. I would play on for another nine years – and I would have some good games – but I would never again be the player of the first ten years of my senior career. All of a sudden it became much, much harder.

By that day in January 2009 I had been playing a lot. Big Phil wanted me in the team whenever I was fit. Yet I knew my body was not right. I was twelve days past the ten-year anniversary of my debut as a professional aged seventeen. I'd had ten solid years of being kicked by a variety of opponents and it was taking its toll. There had been those two big injuries and one major surgery. The change in the demands of Big Phil's training methodology had an effect. I probably needed a rest. But the pressure to be fit and available was too hard to resist. By the time we went to Roots Hall for that replay we had won just one of our last five Premier League games and there had also been an embarrassing draw at home to Southend in the FA Cup third round. Peter Clarke, an old Lilleshall teammate of mine, had scored a late equaliser and so we were obliged to make the journey to Essex for the replay.

The game was almost called off. The fog was dense. When we went for a nap in the hotel on the afternoon of the game, our assistant manager, the late great Ray Wilkins, told us to prepare regardless. He talked to the referee that afternoon and, as Ray could, persuaded him the game should go ahead. We fell behind in the first sixteen minutes and so the pressure went up again. I went to turn on the ball in the first half and it felt like my right knee snapped out of its socket and snapped back in. It made a noise I won't ever forget. For a brief moment I wondered what it might have been but by that point I was in full denial mode. There was no pain so I carried on. I didn't even come off at half-time. After the break I hit a nice, volleyed pass into Salomon Kalou and he finished it for 2–1. We were on our way to a win, but I didn't know that I was hurtling towards the great crossroads of my career.

I made a run behind Anthony Grant, a Southend player I had known from West Ham, and just as my foot hit the floor, unfortunately he tried to pull my shirt. In that moment my knee twisted and I felt a shooting, agonising pain – like a knife stabbed into my knee. The strange thing was, in the moments after I hit the floor the pain went away. I was confused. The physio came on, checked my knee and said he didn't like the look of it. This is the crazy part: I had just blown out all the major ligaments and yet – I played on. The ball came to me immediately, I went to do a stepover and my knee gave way as if the leg wasn't even attached. There wasn't huge pain, but I knew something was wrong. Despite hanging on to the last crumbs of hope, this time I knew I had to come off. My last act of defiance was to refuse the stretcher and embark on a slow trudge around the pitch at Roots Hall, while the good people of Southend told me what they thought of me and of Chelsea. That's one of football's enduring rules. Injured at an away stadium? You need a really gruesome injury to get a sympathetic round of applause from the home fans. My limp just didn't meet the threshold. In the dressing room, I focused my attention on the doctor's face as he examined me. I could see he was worried.

I knew when he accompanied me to the scan the next day that it was likely to be serious. I had been to scans before and gone in on my own. The club doctor would call me at the end of the day when he got round to looking at the results. This one was different. We were going to do the results there and then – and the results were not good. Medial collateral ligament, posterior collateral ligament, anterior collateral ligament. All gone. Medial ligament? Hanging by a thread. As a bonus the doctors suggested that I have both cartilages repaired. I was going to be out nine months to a year anyway. They might as well mend the lot.

Managers only want to know one thing: are you fit to play? Once you say you are then generally you get treated – and judged – like you are in prime physical condition. There would be times over the years that followed when I would like to have stopped the game and announced to the crowd: Look, I'm struggling here and doing my best. But I know that no one cares. You're either fit to play or you're not. No in-betweens. Ultimately, after 14 January 2009, I never played another game in my career without pain. For all that, it wasn't like I was going in for a cancer scan. It was my football career, not my life, that was in the balance. There was no panic attack as there had been in the build-up to the surgery two years previous. I was also very lucky to have the great knee surgeon Andy Williams operating on me. Andy was straight with me. He said in isolation all these repairs to my knee were very simple. But the four or five together were a different proposition. He said he couldn't say for sure how it would end up.

Even so there was still an irrational part of me thinking: we are still in the Champions League and maybe if we reach the final in four and a half months, I could do it. The doctors told me that they wanted to take me down to the operating theatre on a bed. As with my departure at Roots Hall, I protested. I wanted to walk down there on my crutches. They told me, legally I wasn't covered. I insisted. Why? A last bit of control, I guess. By that moment I don't suppose I was thinking straight.

There was a lot of cutting and stitching in my knee during the surgery, so the painkillers had to be strong. I drifted in and out of consciousness for a day. Carly and my parents were obliged to sit by my bed while I was under the influence of industrial grade opiates where I talked, I am reliably informed, utter nonsense for quite some time.

I won't bore you with all the details of rehab. All you need to know is that it is boring and repetitive and very long indeed. The old approach was that they put a cast on your leg and months later took it off. With time, doctors and physios realised that the leg muscles would waste away during that period and getting the leg moving again as it should do was much harder. The new approach is to put weight on the knee immediately, that tells the brain it is still a functioning part of your body, but the pain is intense as the tramadol wears off. Once the swelling went down the first challenge was how quickly I could straighten my knee. The pain took my breath away. Doing it six times in a row felt like the hardest thing I had ever done. For the first two months I had to make these tiny incremental steps all of which were accompanied by astonishing pain. It really was not much fun.

In the meantime, Big Phil had been sacked. I had missed all the drama. He was a good guy and I felt sorry for him. I never once played in a team managed by his temporary successor Guus Hiddink. Guus came in to see me working in the gym in his first few days and asked me how I was. I said: 'Guus, I'm a bit effed.' We had a laugh about it, we both knew he wouldn't last beyond the end of the season and I wouldn't be back before then. He invited me to watch training and I wish I had, if only to observe how he worked. At the time I just couldn't face it. I did notice on matchdays, however, that we were getting better. Guus did the sensible thing. He went back to the José way that Avram had continued and that Big Phil had tossed aside. Training was small-sided games, intense, and the players responded. They quickly looked fitter and stronger.

I went back to watching games from different parts of the stadium as I had done as a kid. Sometimes I watched having had a few beers beforehand. Sometimes I went cold sober. None of it really worked for me. I hated not playing.

I suppose I was jealous of my teammates too. I had played football every day of my life since I was a very young child, into adulthood, and now that was taken away from me. Meanwhile my teammates were able to carry on every day. I watched them come off the training pitches laughing and enthusiastic, and I wanted that life back. I felt like a kid placed in an endless detention, looking out at the schoolyard. But that was in private. In public, every injured player has a responsibility to his teammates not to sulk.

I was at Stamford Bridge sitting behind the benches the night that we played Barcelona in the Champions League semi-final second leg. It seemed obvious to me that we were going to the final. The tie felt like it was won. I sat with my crutches, making my peace with it in my head. Happiness, frustration, jealousy. Chelsea were going to another Champions League final but this time it would be without me. I knew I had to pull myself together and celebrate with the lads when the moment came. Whatever sadness I felt at missing out was just not important. It was just a bundle of my own insecurities. I also knew that the jumping around and general pandemonium at the final whistle would not be good for my knee, so I went down the tunnel and sat in the dressing room on my own waiting for the boys to come back in. On my own I pulled a beer from the fridge and popped off the lid. I looked up at the TV just in time to see Andrés Iniesta score an injury time winner. By then we should have been 3–0 up. The referee had been, by any objective measure, absolutely dreadful. In that moment the world changed again. I poured the beer down the sink and chucked the bottle away. It wouldn't have been right in the circumstances. I felt the pain that the boys went through.

Day after day, week after week, I worked the knee back to health. My pact with the physio was that I would never do anything less than they asked of me. In turn the physios told me that I had to schedule breaks into the programme, and they would adapt. I went to Las Vegas with Carly to watch Ricky Hatton fight. I had a few nights out. Then it was back to the grind. I ran on the treadmill that sits in one of the hydro-pools at Cobham. I wore out the pedals on the watt bikes. All of it intensely boring. Yet I could feel my body getting stronger.

By the time the FA Cup final came around at the end of May I was just desperate to play some football and struggling with being on the outside on another big day for the team. I went out the night before and a few drinks became ten, became twenty, became all the Camden lads back at mine and still drinking at 7 a.m. Luckily, Carly was in New York getting her wedding dress fitted. So, I began FA Cup final day absolutely spangled and was woken by my dad banging on the front door of our house in Chelsea. He had tried to call me but my phone was ringing out, so he had dutifully got in the car and driven over from Essex.

'Dad,' I said, 'I'm still drunk. I can't go to Wembley.'

'Get your suit on, son,' he said. 'You're going.'

'I can't, Dad.'

'If you don't go, you'll look like you don't care. You're feeling sorry for yourself.'

'Dad, I feel dreadful.'

It went on like this for some time. Bear in mind I was twenty-seven years old at this point, but I still didn't like to argue with George Cole. By the end of the argument, he had started to deploy some of his deep supply of c-bombs to get his point across. 'Don't be a [redacted], son. Get in a cab and go to Wembley.' Dad had to drive back to Essex and fetch others who were also on the way to Wembley. Faced with the hangover, and an angry father, I decided to fight the former rather than the latter. I went to Wembley in my Chelsea suit a disgrace. I was sick out of the cab window a couple of times but somehow I got there and into the stadium. Sweating, dehydrated, no doubt stinking of booze and desperate to lie down, I finally arrived in the changing room. I wished the lads well while trying not to breathe on any of them.

Fortunately, the next person I encountered was Mick Roberts, kitman, confidant and discreetly efficient in dealing with wayward footballers. 'You look terrible,' he said. By this time we were almost alone in the dressing room with the team warming up on the Wembley pitch.

'Mick,' I said, 'if I have to sit behind the benches I might end up throwing up live on TV on cup final day.'

'Follow me,' he replied. He moved a couple of kit skips into a far corner of the open plan rooms and from one of them he lifted piles and piles of towels. From there he arranged the towels into a bed behind the kit skips. He gave me a training kit to change into, in case I was sick again. I kid you not, I fell asleep to 'Abide With Me' playing outside. Through Louis Saha's early goal and Didier's equaliser, through the half-time team-talk, and Frank's winner, I slumbered peacefully. I woke with Mick gently shaking me by the elbow. 'A couple of minutes left,' he said. 'Get ready. We're going to win.' Then he cracked open a bottle of beer and handed it to me. 'Straight back on it, Joe,' he said.

That's an elite level kitman.

13

The Unflappable Don Carlo

Only in my final few months at Chelsea, the double-winning season of 2009–10, did I finally see Roman Abramovich get angry. It was a meeting none of the players would forget although I suspect that Roman himself had moved on five minutes after he left the room. We had been eliminated from the Champions League on 16 March by Inter Milan who, critically, were managed by José Mourinho. Our new manager, Carlo Ancelotti, was delivering in the title race and the FA Cup, it would turn out, but not the Champions League. José's Inter team would win it that year against all the odds. Inter eliminated us, then José did that famous number on Barcelona in the semi-final and beat Bayern Munich in the final. But that week in March, Roman was furious. It was only the second time under his ownership we hadn't made it out of the round of 16. In those days, Chelsea not being in the latter stages of the Champions League was unthinkable.

I didn't play in the tie at San Siro and had come off the bench late in Stamford Bridge. We lost both games. The day after the second defeat the word went around Cobham: Roman wants to speak to all the players. We took our seats in the press auditorium and waited for him to join us. We had a pretty good idea it wasn't going to be great news. It certainly was not going to be like that night at Highbury seven years ago when we had tried to bounce Roman, then ecstatic at our win, into a new bonus schedule. There was an interpreter on hand that day although Roman spoke to us in English. He didn't waste his words. Roman asked us a simple question: 'Are you top players or are you just players with top salaries?' He was uncharacteristically angry and quite emotional. I understood that. Football can affect us all that way. He was the man who had paid for all of us to be at that club, on those big contracts. His investment had helped pay for the training ground and the perfect pitches outside and everything else down to the nice seats we were sitting in. But I had to say that I disagreed with him. By that stage I was in and out of the team and so I had less skin in the game than I might have done in seasons past. I wasn't pleased about that either. Nevertheless, I thought Roman wasn't fair on the team that day.

Winning the Champions League can come down to moments that either go your way or do not. The margins can be fine. With the benefit of hindsight, we knew that José would also find a way to beat the great Barcelona team of Pep Guardiola that season. Without Inter's win Barcelona could easily have swept three Champions League titles in a row. Of the eleven games left that season in the Premier League and the FA Cup we lost just once, at White Hart Lane. We did not fall away as Chelsea teams would do in the years that followed.

It was interesting to watch Carlo handle it. He stood to the side of the room, knowing there was no point in intervening. His job would begin the moment that Roman had left. Then Carlo would manage the discontent and soothe bruised egos. A lot of managers would have felt the pressure of an owner pushing them aside and taking matters into their own hands, but it didn't seem to bother Carlo. An emotionally unstable manager could have let that affect them. He had the confidence that he could roll with these kinds of owner interventions. Sooner or later, he knew it would all be over. Sure enough, once Roman got back in his helicopter it was business as usual.

There was a lot of complaining afterwards. Of course, no one was ever going to say it to Roman's face. Still, a lot of the lads thought it was a liberty. They said, look, we've won a lot of trophies. Although at that point there was still no Champions League among them. Roman could well argue that his intervention worked. We won the Premier League and the FA Cup. I have also learnt that in football, especially with ambitious owners, there is always a period of grieving after losing a big game. Even when that period is over, people in football tend to hold grudges a lot longer. The big decision-makers – people like Roman – find it very hard to admit they are wrong. José had come back and made his point in the most emphatic fashion. I say that no one had the balls to tell Roman he was wrong, although that was not quite accurate. At the end of the season, when the champagne was flowing, Ray Wilkins did remind Roman of that meeting. Legend has it that Ray said to Roman: You told them they were not top players. Now they have won the double. Ray's contract was not renewed the following November.

At the start of that season, I had fought my way back to fitness. I doubled down over the summer of 2009 and after eight months out I was back into full training as the season approached. In the first session back with my teammates, Michael Ballack cleaned me out with a tackle. That is football. That was certainly Bally's character. In some ways I had to admire the brutal logic of the game. You're back training? Then you must be fit. And if you're fit then you're going to be kicked like everyone else. Not that I saw it that way at the time. I lost it in that moment and in the seconds that followed I took my chance to go through Bally with both feet. I straight-legged him, as the football parlance has it. I did it so recklessly I could have injured myself. We went at each other in the aftermath and just as the punches were about to be thrown, Ray popped himself in between us. Immediately we were mollified by his soothing words and irrefutable logic.

'Chaps. Do we really need to go down this route? We're all friends here. Let's just take a moment and think this through.'

I was furious. Bally was a six-foot-three lump of East German muscle and I thought he was taking a liberty. Most of the time I got on with Bally. He was a direct character. He just said what was on his mind. I used to ask him about growing up on the other side of the Iron Curtain and he would tell me funny stories about his childhood. He told me the GDR used to send every child a present on their birthday. Or maybe that was just Bally who got special treatment.

I was insecure about my knee and what my career would be like. Although in my heart I knew that I would have to be durable enough to survive this kind of challenge if I was to have any hope of continuing. After working intensively over the summer, I was two months ahead of schedule. The surgeon and the medical team had made the decision to suture my cartilage in the hope that it would help me in the long term but there was always a risk that it would not hold. Shortly after that scrap with Bally I caught a cross on the end of my toe and the impact on my extended leg meant the cartilage went. It meant keyhole surgery and another four weeks out but given I had been prepared for that eventuality, I took a deep breath and got on with it.

As I prepared to go into surgery – and another argument with the doctors about whether I should walk into theatre or not – I got a call from Ray. He asked me how I was, as Ray always did, and then he did something new. He passed the phone to Carlo. 'Joe,' said Carlo, 'you're a big part of what we are going to do at Chelsea. We are going to get you fit. Good luck.'

That meant a great deal to me. There had been no call when I went into surgery in January that year or for the first time back in 2007. It was that care for his players that made Carlo such an effective manager. I don't think he did it because of that – he did it because that was his personality. In football's macho world, where you were expected to take your medicine and get on with it, I found him a completely different proposition. It had started when Carlo first got the job and by way of introduction, and for a team bonding session, he invited us all to a meal at an Italian restaurant in Chelsea. I was last there. Even though I lived in Chelsea, I had cut it fine and then my taxi didn't arrive, and before I knew it, I was jogging down the street worried about being late. The only seat left unoccupied was next to Carlo. The rest of the lads watched me slip into it, enjoying my discomfort. I didn't really know what to expect from Carlo. He shook my hand, poured me a large glass of red wine and started chatting like we had known each other for years. My head was spinning. Didn't we have training the next day? Then we moved on to shots of grappa. After a few drinks I was thoroughly enjoying myself. We were chatting about Serie A in the 1990s and I couldn't help but notice the wine was really quite excellent. Now the lads were looking at me differently. I could feel their pangs of jealousy. In the past, I had never been the manager's pet. I had never been in the inner circle under José, so I was determined to enjoy this for as long as it lasted. Later John Terry would call me son of Carlo. To be honest, I would have been quite happy with that.

I loved Carlo and Ray. But the problem with the club was still the same. I had deserved that contract in 2008 after the Champions League final but the summer had passed by and then the injury had come and now here we were in 2009 and I was less than a year away from being a free agent. I never asked to be on the same money as John, Didier Drogba, Frank Lampard or Petr Čech. I knew I wasn't regarded as one of them, but I felt I deserved to be on the second tier of earners and I was never sure that I was. I couldn't get it out of my head that if we had started negotiations in the summer of 2008, we would have reached a reasonable middle ground. Now my ego was nagging away. I felt my ability was being doubted and as I did so the stakes got higher and higher.

I missed the first six weeks of the season but when I came back on 23 September I played well. At last, the club started talking about a new contract. We were winning games and it looked like we were improving. Still at the back of my mind was the thought that the club held all the cards. They had just waited to see in what state I came back from the injury. If I had been wrecked by the damage to my knee, I know they would have binned me. I understand that is how football works, but it didn't stop me from resenting it. I was earning around £87,000 per week. I should add the usual caveat here that we are lucky to earn these huge wages, and I don't take that for granted. Nevertheless, this should have been my peak earning point in my career and I wanted to maximise this contract. My argument was that I could play and contribute enough to justify between £92,000 and £98,000 per week. Before the injury I would have got that. Now Chelsea were offering me the same terms as I was already on. It would be structured as a two-year contract with an option for the club to renew on the same terms for another two years after that. We worked out that the tax implications would effectively reduce my net pay. All this was important. By this stage of my life, I was involved in the financial management of my career. Above all I wanted to feel that as a senior player at Chelsea, who had achieved a lot with the club, I was appreciated. I was capable of playing my part. I knew what it took to get Chelsea over the line to win trophies. I wanted to be wanted. So, I told the club I wanted a four-year deal. By the time we got to January they had gone cold on any kind of deal. I even wondered whether, if I had accepted their original proposal, that would ever have materialised.

The Africa Cup of Nations that was taking place in January 2010 meant that we would be without a lot of our players: Didier Drogba, Salomon Kalou, Michael Essien, John Obi Mikel. I viewed it as a good chance to show the club how important I was to them. For that period, I felt I was one of Chelsea's best players. We won 5–0 against Watford in the FA Cup and 7–2 against Sunderland. I was creating chances. I knew in my bones that I deserved to be in the team and that meant that when those players were available again, I would see what the club thought of me. As it transpired, as soon as they returned I was left out. That was when I knew. It felt like the club were telling Carlo that I was the past. I was still playing but I was coming off the bench rather than starting. I played, and scored, at Old Trafford when we won the title, but I was in the team because of injuries. It was a huge game in that period of the season and my selection showed that I was still important to Chelsea. I felt vindicated. I came off the bench against Inter Milan when José knocked us out of the Champions League. Winning that Premier League and FA Cup double was another great Chelsea experience, my last at the club as it turned out. I deserved to be in the side for the cup final but I was only a substitute. By then I knew I was leaving. I didn't want to go. There was part of me that was fearful of the prospect. And I guess I was grieving for the end of my time at Chelsea and all the success and satisfaction being at the club had brought me. I also believed that Carlo wanted to keep me and that he was under pressure from the club to bring through a group of young players who – and this is not easy to say – simply were not good enough.

The club was being run then by Frank Arnesen, the Danish sporting director Roman had hired, who had taken special interest in the academy. Chelsea were not the first club to invest heavily in young footballers from other clubs in England and across Europe but they were the first to do it on such a large scale. I felt that Arnesen and, to a lesser extent Michael Emenalo, who had come in with Avram Grant and went on to be the technical director, wanted me and a few others out to make room for the next generation. They wanted to move on and they thought they had the players who could replace us. I left that summer of 2010 along with Ballack, Deco and Juliano Belletti. We were experienced and we had a few more years left. The next generation of Chelsea players were supposed to be Josh McEachran, Jeffrey Bruma, Sam Hutchinson, Gaël Kakuta, Nathaniel Chalobah, Fabio Borini, Jacopo Sala. I could have told you in 2010 they would not be good enough for Chelsea. That is no slight on them. They had decent careers in football but not Chelsea careers. Sure enough, next season Chelsea finished seventh. Carlo got sacked. Yet Carlo has not done too badly since he left Chelsea. It is just the three Champions League titles he has won since then in two spells at Real Madrid, and there could yet be more. It is not inconceivable to me that, if things had been different, he could still be at Chelsea now, winning Premier Leagues and Champions Leagues. After 2010, Chelsea did not win the league again for five years. I felt Arnesen's motives were all about self-preservation. He wanted to justify the investment in young players. Yet it was the accountability that rested with the manager. I liked Michael Emenalo. I thought he was a fair man. But by the end Chelsea didn't even offer me a new contract. It seemed that they had just decided it was over and the direction had been agreed with the boss Marina Granovskaia, who was the closest connection to Roman.

I was dawdling along. Out of contract at the end of June, for the first time since I had signed schoolboy forms with West Ham, before I went off to Lilleshall, I was not affiliated to a professional club. With David Geiss, my agent, I tried to line up my next club. Mark Hughes was manager of Manchester City and he had wanted to sign me in the January transfer window of 2010. That really appealed to me, given that City were doing the same as Chelsea had in 2003. They had been supercharged by the Abu Dhabi takeover of Sheikh Mansour. I met Mark at my parents' new home in Hertfordshire. Not long after, I got a call from a number I didn't recognise and answered it. The guy on the phone introduced himself as an agent. His name was one I had read in the newspapers. It would be fair to say he was well known. This agent told me that if I wanted to go to Manchester City, I would have to go through him. I told him to speak to David. I never did get an offer from City. It did not help that Mark Hughes was sacked in December 2009 before the window opened. Perhaps they just went cold on me. I did do one deal with Mark eventually. He bought my house in Chelsea.

For the second time in my career, Arsène Wenger turned me down on a free. I also met some nice people from Juventus at a restaurant on the King's Road, but I never pursued it. I could not shake the feeling that I had it in me to win more titles in the Premier League and really it was Chelsea that I still wanted. I guess it was like being dumped by a girlfriend I was still in love with. I didn't want it to be over. There was a part of me thinking that once we had won the Premier League they would offer me something. As the season ticked down, I hung on to the belief that I would play the last few games and we would come to an agreement. But I wasn't reading the room. Manchester City must have been getting some encouragement from Chelsea to have believed they had a chance of signing me in January. I could not see what was obvious to others. It was over at Chelsea.

That left interest from Tottenham and Liverpool as the last two on the table. I wasn't sold on either of them. The appeal of Spurs was that Harry Redknapp was in charge there. The downside of Spurs was: it was Spurs. They are the club Chelsea fans hate the most and I just couldn't bring myself to go there. It would have been nice to stay in London, and that was Carly's preference. Our daughter, Ruby, had been born in March 2010 and it would have made life easier for us to be near both our wider families. But going to Spurs? I just felt it would ruin much of my legacy at Chelsea and the Spurs fans would probably dislike me regardless of what I did there. They still sing a rather unflattering song about me and Frank. My Spurs-supporting friends and family delight in singing it to me every now and then. Spurs really wanted to sign me and so David did explore what might be offered. As a result, Daniel Levy called me directly. The Spurs chairman said that we were close to a provisional agreement on my salary package but that we had a problem. He urged me to cut my agent David out of the deal. I told him there was absolutely no chance of that. Neither David nor I heard from him again.

Comparatively, Liverpool were really struggling at the time. The club was owned by George Gillett and Tom Hicks, the Americans who eventually lost control as the finances spiralled downwards. So Liverpool were in the kind of place where a free agent signing made financial sense, which perhaps allowed them to look past my reluctance. By the same measure I was just trying to convince myself that it was a good fit when in my heart I knew otherwise. I would try all sorts of things to convince myself. Playing in front of the Kop as a home player was one. I even wondered if the fact that the city was the home of The Beatles, their music always on in Donnington Court when I was growing up, should count as a sign.

Liverpool never wavered in their determination to sign me and the club itself was always honourable in its dealings with me, even later when it became clear that I was surplus to requirements. My England teammates Steven Gerrard and Jamie Carragher were enthusiastic about me coming. So, in the end, I agreed to meet Roy Hodgson, who I liked a great deal as a person, but felt we had different views when it came to football. He was keen on the two banks of four and working to stop the opposition playing. I was more interested in what we could do as a team. I met with Roy and the then chief executive of Liverpool, Christian Purslow, at Christian's house in London. I liked them both, but whenever I steered the conversation onto football it just got very vague. I believed that for them the most important thing was that I came without a fee attached. I never got the impression from Roy that he was excited about me joining and I understand why. I am not really his sort of player.

Liverpool had finished seventh that season, twenty-three points behind Chelsea in first. That worried me. I tried to push that aside as the irrational fear of someone who had spent seven years at Chelsea and was just a bit afraid of change. My dad was a lot more pragmatic. George Cole was not a football fan and not sentimental about the game. He understood that I loved football, and that I wanted to feel like I was appreciated, but he kept coming back to the key point: someone's offering you the chance to earn millions. Sign the deal and you will never have to worry about money again. He was right, of course, but just as when I signed for Chelsea the first time, the salary was not uppermost in my mind. I wanted to be paid what I was worth. I was just not sure that my heart was in it. I left my house in Chelsea to go to Liverpool for the medical, trying to convince myself all the way there that it was the right move. I feared that Liverpool were not going to be able to challenge for trophies in the next few years. I wasn't wrong about that. I asked my agent David if we could include a get-out clause in the contract so that if I hit the ground running I could perhaps get back up to a team challenging for the Premier League or Champions League. I wasn't really thinking straight.

I know for Liverpool fans this might be infuriating to read. I am just trying to be honest about the factors that contributed to a decision that did not work out for both parties. I know that part of it was that I struggled to stay fit. I tried my best to do so but my body was starting to break down and I had not learnt to manage the training and the games in the way that I would do in the years to come. However, I was interested in learning about the club and the city. I lived on Merseyside, which few of the current squad do now. It just did not work out. I bought a house in Formby with its beautiful beaches. Over the years that followed once I had left, I rented it out. Every one of my tenants seemed to be players who had the same struggles as me nailing down a place in the Liverpool XI over the long term. At different times it was lived in by Stewart

Downing, Alberto Moreno, Rickie Lambert and the super-sub Divock Origi. Perhaps its most successful occupant, in terms of games played, was Richarlison, although he played for the other club in the city. Perhaps the house was cursed?

I signed for Liverpool in July and went straight to meet Roy and the squad in Austria for our pre-season camp. As I was checking into the team hotel, I bumped into George Gillett, then Liverpool chairman, in the lobby. He and his fellow US owner Tom Hicks were at loggerheads by then and they would no longer be in control of the club come the end of October that year. They had sacked Rafael Benítez that summer, and the club was under pressure financially. George was very friendly and seemed delighted that I had decided to join.

George said to me: 'You've got a great room, Joe.'

'Thanks,' I said.

George said: 'I'll show you to your room.'

I said that was very kind but it really wasn't necessary. He politely insisted. So the pair of us crammed ourselves into the lift with my bags and George proceeded to show me to my room. Not only that, he showed me how the curtains closed automatically and how the air conditioning functioned. I cannot recall if he took me through the TV channels or recommended anything from the room-service menu, but it was certainly a bespoke check-in from the man in charge of the club. In charge, at least, for the time being. I thought to myself: blimey, this is a bit different to Roman. George was effusive about me, in a kind way. He said the club were very pleased to have signed me and he expected great things from me at Liverpool.

I never saw him again.

14

England: How Can I Get in Your Team, Sven?

At the party for the England squad and our families after Brazil knocked us out of the World Cup in Shizuoka, Japan, on 21 June 2002, I was unique among the players in that I didn't have any family there. I was twenty years old, no girlfriend, and my mum and dad had headed to the airport already. The World Cup had not gone very well for me. I had played just sixteen minutes in all. I decided that, all things considered, I would like to get drunk.

By about 4 a.m. Japan time, I had accomplished my mission. I was waiting for the lift back to my room and caught sight of myself in the mirror. On my head a jester's hat, acquired from I don't know where. My shirt unbuttoned. A bottle of champagne in my hand. I might also add that I was sharing the lift with a woman a few years older than me who I had been chatting to at the party. The lift pinged, the doors opened and there stood none other than the manager of the England team, Sven-Göran Eriksson – with his partner at the time, Nancy Dell'Olio. I could see how this must have looked. What to do next? As football problem-solving exercises go, they certainly don't teach you this at Lilleshall. For a moment Sven and I stared at each other and then I chose what I considered my best option. I raised my fists in celebration and shouted, 'WAHEYYY'. And Sven laughed and shouted 'WAHEYYY' back at me. In my memories of the late England manager that moment looms large. Sven was a fun-loving guy. He was never going to criticise a player for leaving a party in the early hours with an attractive woman he had just met, because that was exactly what Sven planned to do himself most of the time.

I played fifty-six times for England. I went to three World Cups. I was there when Kevin Keegan quit in the toilets of the old Wembley Stadium. I saw Beckham-mania close-up. I saw Rooney-mania close-up. I was there when the WAGs invaded Baden-Baden in 2006. I was on the pitch when Steve McClaren unfurled his brolly. I saw close-up the consequences of Fabio Capello banning fun. I loved playing for England and when it all ended abruptly in 2010, I always dreamt of a comeback. In fact, I was promised one when I was thriving on loan at Lille in 2012 but unfortunately the man who made that promise, Harry Redknapp, never got the England manager's job. Like many England players, I look back with regret. Not just the tournaments we didn't win – or didn't qualify for – but because of the football we often played. We were so slow as a nation to develop and I knew it from the start. Right from those days at Lilleshall as a kid, and then as an England schoolboy international standing around the piano practising singing the national anthem. From my days with the Under-21s, up to Capello in South Africa, we never innovated. I watched other nations learn to keep the ball and adapt to hot summer tournament conditions. They made us look so ordinary. I watched other England players get caps I don't think they deserved, or crumble under the pressure. The culture of English football is set, to a great extent, by the England team and it is much better now for players who, like me, want to take the occasional risk and play creative football.

I lived through one of the most entertaining decades in the history of the England team – the 2000s. Scandal, celebrity, glamour, and we won a few games too. I was, by some estimates, the last member of the Golden Generation, as it was described by the former Football Association chief executive Adam Crozier. Depending on your view, that generation encompasses sixteen players from the oldest, Paul Scholes, born in November 1974, to me, the youngest, in November 1981. I arrived in the England squad at the age of seventeen in 1999. Not officially. Keegan had continued the tradition started by Terry Venables of calling young lads into the squad in addition to the selected players for a bit of experience. I had only started playing for West Ham's first team in January but I was already stirring some interest. I had played a lot for England's junior teams. My love for football had been kindled watching the 1990 World Cup at home at Donnington Court. Like all my friends, I loved Paul Gascoigne and Gazza put the idea in my head of what England meant and how the team could fire up the whole country.

I bounced into the England camp as a very naive seventeen-year-old, full of enthusiasm and desperate to make friends. I put on the kit laid out in my hotel room and set out to explore. The first thing that happened was that Keegan took me aside and told me I was wearing the wrong shorts. I suppose it was the old story of assuming the flash Londoner thought he could wear what he wanted. The flash Londoner accusation was one that had already surfaced at Lilleshall and would follow me around whenever I was outside of London. I was certainly a Londoner. As for being flash, anyone who knows my dress sense will immediately recognise that is not the case. But I *was* wearing the wrong shorts. I just didn't have a clue what the right shorts were. And my eagerness to find out what was going on downstairs meant I didn't stop to think.

What was going on downstairs was an unofficial England squad horseracing betting night. It was my first taste of the culture of the England football team and its love of betting: horses, cards, you name it. I was a teenager and keen to get stuck in. The evening's entertainment was organised by Teddy Sheringham and Alan Shearer. We were betting on pre-recorded horse races that were played on a VHS. Looking back, I can see the issue with that – although the emphasis was on having a laugh. There wasn't big money being wagered. A tenner on a race to Sheringham and Shearer who would set the odds. Keegan joined in. There wasn't much else on offer. In those days there was no social media or PlayStation to absorb the lads. I might not have been legally old enough to stake money on horse races that had long since been run with a collection of famous footballers I had been watching on television a few months earlier – but I didn't see anything wrong with it. I was still living on a Camden council estate. Plus, all these famous players, and Keegan, were very kind to me. They made me feel welcome.

I had quite fancied my chances of getting in the Euro 2000 squad until Rory Delap broke my leg. The tournament went badly for Keegan and his players and the qualifying campaign for the 2002 World Cup began in October 2000, a month before my nineteenth birthday. I was called into the squad proper for the first time for the games against Germany and Finland. One last chance to play at the old Wembley, staging its last game before it was demolished. I had played there for England schoolboys against our German counterparts and won 2–1. I loved the place. What could possibly go wrong?

The first time you get on the coach to go to training with a new team there is one big issue to negotiate: where do I sit? Every team bus has its seating hierarchy and when you're eighteen you don't want to sit in the wrong seat. As I surveyed my options with some degree of trepidation, Tony Adams popped his head up from over the top of the broadsheet newspaper he was reading.

'Young Joe!' he said. 'Come and sit down next to me.'

I felt like I was going in to see Father Christmas in his grotto. Tony was huge and I was tiny by comparison. As he chatted away to me about football and asked me about my career, I struggled to reconcile the friendly man sitting next to me with the great warrior I had watched playing for Arsenal on TV. He was so easy-going.

Training was skill exercises and then a game, which was right up my street. I loved it. Keegan was full of energy. I got to see some of these players close-up. The teammate that always sticks in my mind from that era was Andy Cole. I had him down as a goalscorer. A tap-in merchant. But in our small-sided games he was brilliant with the ball at his feet. Athletic. Lovely technique. I think Andy is one of the most underrated players in the Premier League era. None of his goals were penalties either. Although I never understood why a striker would not want to take penalties.

I didn't make the matchday squad for the Germany game. When Keegan flipped over the page with the team on it, Gareth Southgate was in midfield. That was surprising but not a shock as the newspapers had already reported that was the way that Keegan was going. I presume Gareth knew the plan because we hadn't done any tactical work as far as I was aware. I was expecting a classic along the lines of England against Germany at Euro '96. The reality was a really drab game. I was in the stand and although I was disappointed not to be out there on the pitch or among the subs, I knew my time would come eventually. Then I was still purely an England fan like everyone else around me at Wembley. We lost. Didi Hamann's shot skidded past David Seaman. At the end, they played 'Always Look on the Bright Side of Life' on the stadium sound system. I guess someone at Wembley had a sense of humour. We were told to get back down to the changing room because Keegan wanted to speak to the players and I trudged around the old pitch in the rain. The fan in me was still thinking then: what if we don't qualify for the World Cup? The fans in Wembley were angry and they let us know in a passive-aggressive sort of way. Effing tell them to sort it out. That sort of thing. By the time I got to the tunnel my football brain had kicked in. I thought: if he changes the team maybe I get a chance to play against Finland. It turned out there was something bigger in store.

In the tunnel I saw Keegan talking to the Football Association official David Davies. I could hear Keegan saying something like, 'I can't do it, I can't do it'. And I could see how worried Davies looked. I saw the FA people around Keegan panicking a bit and it was clear to me that something big was going on. Someone got us all to shuffle into the dressing room, but the old Wembley rooms were so small I was stuck outside the door in the corridor trying to get on my tiptoes to peer over shoulders and catch the conversation. Keegan was talking and there were faces looking on in disbelief. Tony Adams said something like, 'Just stay calm, Kevin.' The one thing I remember was the confusion. By the time we got back to our hotel, Bisham Abbey, in Buckinghamshire, someone had explained to me that Keegan had resigned. Legend has it he had told the FA in the privacy of the home dressing room loos. There was so much going on I was kind of forgotten about. Having been chaperoned through most of it I was left to my own devices. A few players went to the bar for a drink. I'm pretty sure we were told we could go home for a night. My first England call-up had ended with the manager quitting after one game. That might be a record.

The FA brought in its technical director Howard Wilkinson to take the next game. I liked him in the same way I liked Keith Blunt, my coach at Lilleshall. They might both have been chiselled out of the same Yorkshire rock. That is not to say I agreed with their vision of football but I appreciated their honesty. Howard had won the First Division with Leeds United in 1992. He had previously been the coach of the England Under-21s, so I knew him before we headed off to Helsinki for the second of our two World Cup qualifiers amid the fallout from Keegan's departure. Dogmatic is the best way to describe Howard's beliefs about football. He looks through you when he addresses you which can be a little unnerving the first time. Keegan had been bubbly in meetings. Effervescent is the word I would use – and, yes, I learnt that one myself. Howard was a completely different prospect. In our first meeting he was rambling on about what we were going to do about Finland and then, with his pen literally on the whiteboard, he suddenly stopped. He said: 'Everyone stop what you are doing. I can sense you are getting agitated. You're not listening. Go outside. Have a fart. Have a drink. Have a bit of food. We will do the meeting in ten minutes.'

Have a fart. I remember that phrase clearly. So we all walked out of the room and there was a buffet waiting outside. Back in after a break and – would you believe it – Howard said we were going back to 4-4-2. The game itself was dreadful. Ray

Parlour hit the bar. I watched from the bench with Steven Gerrard wondering whether one of us might come on. Stevie had already made his England debut. By now I had trained under two England managers, witnessed one of them resign, played a full role in the betting evening, worked hard in the training sessions. The only thing I didn't have was a cap.

After Howard came the third manager of my England career – and like his two predecessors, Peter Taylor also saw no compelling reason to cap me. He appeared to pick every young player in the country apart from me, including Seth Johnson. There was a huge clear-out. Shearer had already retired after Euro 2000 and a fair few followed him out of the door: Tim Sherwood, Dennis Wise, Paul Ince and Tony Adams. In their place were Kieron Dyer, Frank Lampard, Gareth Barry and Stevie. What irked me about Peter Taylor was that I was obviously playing well at the time. Taylor seemed to be saying to me that this was the new England and that I wasn't a part of it. He gave Seth Johnson a cap against Italy, rather than me. I have no ill-feeling towards Peter but I would say that if he thought Seth was a better player than me, especially then in late 2000, then our views diverge significantly on what makes a footballer.

It was Sven, my fourth England manager, who eventually gave me my debut in 2001. I was in his first squad, which was encouraging. I might have played against Spain but in my enthusiasm during training I chased a ball from Ugo Ehiogu that was running out of play and rolled my ankle. Despite the swelling I thought I might just be able to hide it from our physio Gary Lewin but he was too observant. Gary spotted it and they pulled me out of the game. I was furious. I finally made my England debut as a substitute against Mexico at Pride Park, Derby, in May 2001. I was nineteen years and six months old. Michael Carrick made his debut that night as well as Alan Smith, then still at Leeds United, and his teammate Danny Mills. This felt like a huge moment for me. I had only really understood the concept of England at Italia '90 watching on the sofa at home as an eight-year-old. It was Gazza and the impact he had on me that changed my life. I had wanted to play for England then, and now, eleven years later, I was coming on for David Beckham.

England changed a lot under Sven. The first time Michael and I were in the squad together we were approached at the team hotel by an old chap who was friendly and easy to chat to. Lovely bloke, I thought – perhaps he worked at the hotel? He looked like he might be there for a bit of gardening, although nothing too strenuous. He seemed so old. It turned out it was Sven's assistant coach Tord Grip. No one had told us who he was and he never wore any of the England branded tracksuits. In the first meeting Sven had with the squad, he kept pronouncing Emile Heskey's first name as 'Emily'. I had to pinch at my skin to try to stop myself laughing out loud. It was made all the funnier because Emile tried politely to correct Sven on the pronunciation but because Emile is so softly spoken, Sven didn't hear him. The tension in the room was unbearable as everyone tried desperately to contain the laughter that welled up every time Sven said 'Emily'.

I should have scored on my debut from a Robbie Fowler cross. I took it on the wrong foot. I'll admit it – it still bothers me. I also won a free-kick that Teddy Sheringham stroked in. Bursting with confidence after the ref had given it, I told Teddy that I wanted to take it. Teddy explained to me very calmly and very firmly that I could eff off. I then didn't play for England again until the following February and come the next month I felt that I needed a performance against Italy at Elland Road if

I was going to have a chance of making the World Cup squad that summer. I came on at half-time, lost the ball and, from the move that came out of that, Vincenzo Montella scored their equaliser. Italy ended up winning it 2–1. For that I felt Sven gave me a bit of criticism in his post-match press conference that set up the general mood that I was unreliable. I thought the opposite. I had helped to set up the goal for Robbie Fowler. I felt I had been one of our better players. I was creative. But the focus on mistakes would become a regular theme in the years to come. I hadn't given the ball away in front of goal. There had been plenty for Italy to do after that.

At the same time, I was playing central midfield for West Ham every week in the Premier League – and a West Ham team that would finish seventh that season. AC Milan had even enquired about signing me. I knew I was playing well. The notion that I was unreliable was largely advanced by people who just did not watch me every week. AC Milan would have been a great move – another case of the path not taken. I had watched the Italy players turn up at Elland Road. Gianluigi Buffon, Fabio Cannavaro, Alessandro Nesta, Francesco Totti. They all looked so cool in their Italian suits. The contrast with us lot in our Umbro tracksuits was painful. We looked like a bag of spanners by comparison.

For all Sven's scepticism, I did well for him again in April against Paraguay at Anfield, coming off the bench. That and my form for West Ham meant that at the age of twenty I made the World Cup squad in May 2002. By then the team under Sven was pretty settled. There was nothing radically different about the way we played. It was 4-4-2, and the Manchester United players were running the show. In place of the old guard of Shearer, Adams, Ince and Sheringham was Beckham, the captain, and the United core of Nicky Butt, Paul Scholes and the Neville brothers, Gary and Phil. As a young player from a club that only had a handful of England players I couldn't see a problem with it at the time. I figured that these guys knew how to win games. I hadn't won anything. If they liked the manager and the tactics then maybe we would be fine. But the 4-4-2 did not really excite me. I looked around at the quality of players we had and felt that we could do more. Whereas at West Ham it could be a battle against more talented teams, I thought that with the quality of England players it should be easier.

There were many experiences from that World Cup that I will not forget, starting with our friendly against the co-hosts South Korea in the Jeju Stadium. I was blown away by the energy of the Koreans. It is one of the few times I have come off a pitch and felt that the standard of the opposition's fitness was, to put it bluntly, inhuman. They blitzed us. We just about held on to draw 1–1. When you compare the two sets of play-ers, and even allowing for the climate and their home advantage, we should have won that game. What usually happens in games such as these, against opposition you would expect to beat, is that you get a great early burst of energy unleashed at you. The question is how you deal with it until gradually the intensity drops and you can make your greater quality count. But in this game the intensity never dropped. I came off totally exhausted and I had only been a half-time substitute. It was relentless. There was just no space anywhere on the pitch for ninety minutes. They never seemed to run out of steam. The whole game felt like the first five minutes over and over again. South Korea had suspended its domestic league to get the players in camp with Guus Hiddink to prepare for the tourna-ment and they eventually reached the semi-finals. So whatever they were doing worked. There were a few of that team that went on to play in England or in Europe although you would be hard pushed to say that any of them became major stars. Maybe tactically they were so well drilled physically – and so buoyed by patriotism – that it made the difference.

I loved the World Cup and you learn so much at the tournament – about how it should be done and, at times, how best not to. On the bus to the second warm-up game against Cameroon in Kobe in Japan we had no air conditioning. Even in shorts and T-shirts we were sweltering and desperate to get off. This was to be my first start for England and when we saw the Cameroon players, playing music and singing and dancing, you saw just how much more comfortable they were with the pressure. They had a good team: Samuel Eto'o, Lauren, Geremi, Marc-Vivien Foé. They knew how to play in the conditions and once again we were just hanging on. I was one of four in the starting XI who played the whole game and we only nicked a late equaliser, scored by Robbie Fowler.

Sven did give me a chance in our first group game against Sweden as a sub with about fifteen minutes left. My enthusiasm got the better of me. I flew into a tackle in front of the benches – the red zone as they call it, because chances are that much greater you might get a red card if you make a mistake with a challenge. Luckily, I timed it well but still it was full-on. The reaction from my own bench was telling. I could see Sven, Sammy Lee and Steve McClaren wincing. The score was 1–1 and their instinct was to keep it safe in the first game of the tournament. In the heat of the moment, my instincts were very different. I had visions of Gazza in my head and that a good tackle and quick attack might just lift us. As soon as I saw Sven's face, I knew I had got it wrong. I didn't play another minute after that.

It meant I spent a lot of time observing the squad and the staff. As one of the staff, Sven took a Dutch fitness coach,

Richard Smith, who seemed to be there just to treat Beckham. The captain was struggling to be ready in time with his infamous broken metatarsal injury. Richard would be ready to treat Beckham twenty-four hours a day. Richard was a long-haired surfer-style Dutch guy who when he wasn't treating Beckham was treating Michael Owen who also wasn't fit, or Kieron Dyer, who was ahead of me in the pecking order. When he was not treating those two, Richard was persuading us to do yoga exercises. He was probably ahead of his time. Beckham bought into it because he was – against all the odds – playing. I walked into the treatment room and asked why Richard was massaging Beckham's calf if the problem was in his foot. Richard told me to relax and watch him work his magic. The game is full of these guru types. No doubt much of it is in the training and the experience, but when you get a character like Richard it is also about the confidence they transmit. He would just tell people he was going to make them better and perhaps that is half the trick. I started off very cynical but then after a while I quite liked his energy. He was a funny guy and he just oozed confidence. He was like Beckham's shadow. Every time Beckham sat down, Richard was massaging his right leg.

I was fascinated by the power of Beckham's huge fame. By that stage he was already one of the most famous footballers on the planet and in Japan, where we were based, they were obsessed with him. The FA organised a night out to a TGI Fridays restaurant for a change of scene from the hotel and by the time we had finished our dinner, word must have got out that Beckham was there. The crowds had grown so big, and so frantic to see him, that the police had to close the road just to get our bus out. At the time I just thought that was normal working with England. But it wasn't – it was normal for Beckham. Every day people would follow the bus to training in cars, on bikes or just running along. It was a wonder no one got hurt. The older players like David James and Teddy explained to me that this was different. Tony Adams or David Platt didn't get this kind of treatment. It didn't really bother me but I imagine some players felt differently. To put it in perspective, over the years I saw people shoving the likes of Steven Gerrard or Frank Lampard out of the way – and I mean literally shoving – to get to Beckham. These fans would barely even notice that the blokes they had just pushed past were some of the greatest Premier League footballers. But Beckham had a mystique that no one else could match. I went out on my hotel balcony in Japan one afternoon and a huge cheer went up which did my confidence no end of good until I realised Beckham was on his balcony sunbathing in his briefs. People would wait outside for Beckham to come out on his balcony just to shout to him. As a player, there were certain parts of Beckham's game that were, simply, excellent. The guy had a lovely strike off that right foot, and it was not just all those free-kicks and passes. Before the Argentina group game in Sapporo, we were directed to a huge indoor warm-up area inside the stadium. Someone who had clearly never worked with foot-ballers before had hung a clock on the wall. Immediately the lads started peppering it with shots. Beckham came in and had a go. His first one hit the clock. His second attempt hit it again. His third clipped it at a slightly different angle so it spun off its screw and shattered on the ground. Job done, we all filed out to play Argentina at the World Cup.

During the tournament, Teddy must have got the sense that everyone was nervous. Before the first game against Sweden he had laughed at us for all earnestly shaking hands and wishing each other good luck. For the Argentina game I got the sense of the intensity going up a level. They had players like Pablo Aimar, Seba Verón and Walter Samuel that I had watched as a kid. If Beckham felt any pressure – given his red card four years earlier when he reacted to a Diego Simeone tackle – you could never tell. Beckham had that poker-face before matches. A guy whose emotions were hard to read.

As ever, people expected us to win it. A lot of that was down to the Beckham phenomenon. He was more famous than the best players in football – Zinedine Zidane, Alessandro Del Piero, the Brazilians Ronaldo and Ronaldinho. Lots of people who didn't know much about football had heard of Beckham. But we weren't a better team than Brazil and France. Beckham was not truly fit. Owen was nowhere near full fitness. Even by the first knockout round against Denmark I got the sense that we were patching players up to play. We had nothing like the strength in depth of other nations. A quarter-final felt about right for England, although many of the fans and much of the media felt otherwise.

As for my own chances, I came to realise that Sven wasn't going to use me. I didn't come on against Argentina or Nigeria when the games were in the balance. Sven was just very conservative and he clearly considered me too erratic. My fondest memento of the 2002 World Cup is a sketch that David James did of me in the coach when I fell asleep and my head ended up resting on Robbie Fowler's shoulder. Jamo was such a talented artist. I loved playing with Robbie. He was past his peak by 2002 and injuries had cost him, but he was a wonderful player. After the Brazil defeat I went to get drunk. I stayed out so late that even the barman went to bed and left us to it. As I remember it, Robbie and Nicky Butt were the last men standing. Ashley Cole overslept and missed the coach. He had to get a bullet train to the airport. That moment at the lifts with Sven will always stay with me. Sven had his strengths and one of them was allowing players to let off a little steam. It wasn't like I had hit the ice bath, drunk a protein shake and gone to bed early to get ready for Euro 2004. Maybe had my manager been Capello or Roy Hodgson I would have tried to bat differently. I will always love Sven for the way he just laughed in that moment. We didn't always see eye to eye on football and the teams he selected, but Sven had a great attitude towards life.

For all its rewards, professional football is much about how you handle the pressure. If you always took it as seriously as we did when we played as little kids – well, your legs wouldn't stop shaking. You have to give it your all. You have to prepare, which I always did. And once it is done, life moves on. It just becomes part of your life's story. Some you win and some you lose. I was always good at moving on. Every big defeat hurt me. But you have to go out and have a drink afterwards. I probably did more of that after defeat than victories. I also love hearing the stories of my family and friends who followed me around the world. My mates would be out getting up to mischief. My old Camden pal Jason Richardson was in Japan with my mum and dad and ended up playing pool against Beckham. Jason is a good player but he lost that one – his cup final.

World Cups are different to cup finals. As footballers we know that if you miss a penalty or get sent off it will be there for ever. In twenty-five years' time when you are getting the groceries, someone will make a remark about it. That's the pressure. What you are doing in that moment affects so many people, although it is irrelevant in the grand scheme of things. You are not performing lifesaving surgery or curing cancer. You are playing football. But that is where the pressure comes from – being able to perform in that single moment. I look back again to some of the players I grew up with and who didn't make it. The ability to handle that and focus is the difference more than anything. Not every England player was the best in his age group at Under-13s. You have to be able to cope with that pressure, and the possibility of failure and all that comes with it. With England it is ever present.

15

England: Risk Averse

The England team had what some might call a gambling culture. Whether it was a gambling problem depends on your point of view – or how much money you lost. As one generation of players passed into retirement the card school continued with the next generation and the sums that were staked rose as wages went higher, fuelled by the Premier League's ever rising television rights. In the Under-21s we were prepared for life in the senior team – and not just on the pitch. I started in the Under-21s card school, staking a few thousand pounds although the limits of what was won and lost were never more than about five thousand. When I got into the senior squad I was still a West Ham player and I was smart enough to realise that I could not live with the kind of cash that was being staked. Some of the lads might lose sixty thousand pounds in a day. Then win it back. Then lose it. The turnover of money was vast. People gasp when I tell them but in that strange little bubble in the early 2000s, as we chased the hit of victory in our card school, it was about the money and then also it wasn't – it was mainly about the risk and the rush of winning. As any gambler will tell you.

It was at the 2002 World Cup I realised that, on a West Ham contract, I was out of my depth. I lost a few grand and thought – eff this. Instead, I joined the masseurs who were not on silly football wages and passed the time playing Cluedo. They didn't wager money on that. I played board games, as well as table tennis and pool and, of course, watched the tournament on the television. But the card school kept going. There was always cash on the table but mostly losses were recorded in a notebook, and the payment of debts was negotiated. Immediate cash payments were offered in return for a discount on the total losses. That sort of thing. Indeed, one of my teammates from that era – he shall remain nameless – still tells me to this day that he is owed gambling debts from the 2002 World Cup from another of our teammates in that squad. The cards were always there. On the bus to training. On the bus back from training. After dinner. It was usually three-card brag that was being played. With it would come the chatter. I might sit down at breakfast with Frank Lampard and John Terry and they would be chatting about the card game the night before and how much one person had lost. It was all-pervasive.

Michael Owen was the squad's bookmaker at the 2002 World Cup. You asked him for the odds on a game and he gave you a price – taken from the real bookies, I presume. I liked putting a tenner on a game and backing my judgement. We would debate the fairness of the odds, lay our bets and then watch the game. For me that is what gambling should be about – a few quid to back your judgement and give the outcome of any one game a bit more of an edge. But at times in my life I have had to check my habits. I like to think I can gamble responsibly. But I have lost big money when I have been betting. I find myself even now at home watching a game and unable to resist backing my instincts. I lost about £70,000 in one run once. When that happened, I deleted the betting apps and banned myself for a year, but I was surprised how strong the pull would be when I was sitting in front of the television watching a game. Even when I have imposed a betting ban on myself, I can feel that itch to wager a couple of hundred quid on a game. I look back and wonder how I would have handled a card school had I been the manager. I would certainly have talked to the players and asked them to be honest about whether they thought the numbers being lost were out of control. I would have given the players the responsibility of policing it and making sure that it was sensible. But back then, we just did whatever we wanted to do.

After the 2002 World Cup I won another senior cap against Portugal and then found myself back in the Under-21s as West Ham succumbed to relegation that season. I was still just twenty but I found it demoralising. I could not understand why Kieron Dyer was ahead of me. Kieron was a good player, and he had blistering pace, but he did not have what I had. He got thirty-three caps for England and while some of them were at full-back the vast majority were on the left side of midfield which I felt was my position. I would like to have had more caps, and every team I missed out on was an opportunity I could never get back. I ran the show against Slovakia in October 2002 but I did not play for the England senior team until the end of the season when Sven-Göran Eriksson called me into the squad late. Carly and I had gone on holiday together for the first time and I was in Dubai when I had a message to call the FA. Someone had got injured and I had been called into the squad for two matches. For Carly, who was only eighteen, it was an early introduction to the weird world of football where all it takes to end your holiday is one phone call. In those days I was so single-minded that I just wanted to get back in the squad and win another cap. I am sorry to say I probably did not take Carly's feelings into account as I should have. We went back to our room and packed our bags.

The England team were off to South Africa to play a friendly in Durban. David Beckham had his hair braided into corn-rows for the occasion. Beckham's ever-changing hairstyle was all part of the show and he certainly went for it in South Africa. Why did he do it? For the attention. He loved it. We were given the opportunity to meet Nelson Mandela the day before the game with a Football Association delegation that would fly to Johannesburg and back. I felt it was not going to help my chances of playing well but as a young player I was worried about the politics of it. When I saw Gareth Southgate was not going I felt I would be fine with my decision. It was optional. Gareth seemed like a sensible bloke. Obviously, Beckham went with a few others. The FA found itself having to explain why some of the players were not going to see Mandela. Another situation where it felt we lost either way. A couple of hours on a plane a day before a match would usually have been judged total madness. On the other hand, it looked like we were passing up the chance to meet one of the greatest figures of twentieth-century history. Only the England football team and the FA could get itself into that situation. I had learnt about Nelson Mandela at school. As for my dear old dad, he might not have had much of a grasp on the polit-ical realities of South Africa but, in the 1980s, George Cole knew that the students and tourists coming past his stall on Inverness Street market in Camden didn't half buy a lot of Free Nelson Mandela T-shirts. At least as many as the Ralph Lauren shirts that kept coming his way.

In the second game, against Serbia and Montenegro in Leicester, I was on the bench with the seventeen-year-old

Wayne Rooney who had made his England debut in February. I was blown away by his talent and also the way in which in that first year, the twelve months leading up to Euro 2004, he just seemed to get stronger every time I saw him. Sven brought me on after 62 minutes. He had to give me a cap this time because he had brought me back from holiday in Dubai. We had a late free-kick and luckily for me Beckham wasn't playing that day. Rooney wanted to take it. As the senior man – I was twenty-one – I pulled rank. I caught it just right. It was my first England goal. A moment of pure joy for me. I was channelling Italia '90 and David Platt, my old Under-21 manager, scoring against Belgium. When I came back into the dressing room fifteen minutes later I was still euphoric. I saw Beckham, and for reasons I cannot explain shouted, *'That's you off free-kicks now, Becks!'* No one really spoke to Beckham like that. Sven certainly didn't. I noticed it all went quiet and a bit awkward although I was too pleased with myself to care. I had just been through a bad few months with Glenn Roeder's collapse and then the relegation. Now I felt better about my own abilities.

Having signed for Chelsea, the next season I found myself in a fight to get in the team for my club as well as for my country. With England it always seemed that much harder. Sven just did not seem to believe that a right-footed player could operate on the left side of midfield. Over the course of 2003 he even gave Alan Thompson of Celtic a cap, solely on the basis he was left-footed. But the problem seemed to me to be bigger than that. As I got into the Chelsea team that went all the way to the semi-finals of the Champions League, the discussion was always about what I couldn't do rather than what I could. That old English sense returned of not trusting a player who wants the ball. At West Ham I had been the boy wonder who could do no wrong but now, with all the expectations people had of me, I felt the perspective on me went the other way. For reasons I never understood, Sven seemed to go with it. By the time I got to the end of the season the newspapers said that Phil Neville and I were in competition for one last place in the Euro 2004 squad. In the end injuries meant that we both went but even so – how could it be the case that two such different players were considered rivals for the same kind of role? I never felt that I deserved to start ahead of that Golden Generation midfield that was first choice at that Euros – Beckham, Scholes, Gerrard and Lampard. But I did think that I would get some good time off the bench.

Before the tournament our new club manager José Mourinho came to speak to those of us from Chelsea – me, John Terry, Frank and Wayne Bridge – who were in the England squad based in Manchester. I suspect he felt we may have still been feeling sorry for Claudio Ranieri. José wanted to get us onside. He said to us: 'I am a champion. We are going to win the Premier League and this is how we are going to do it.' I was taken aback with his confidence. He just seemed to be so sure of himself. Not a bit of doubt. We said goodbye to him and then headed back to the dining room. None of us quite knew what to say. In fact, the natural reaction was just to laugh and shake our heads. We had never seen anything like it. The vibe was: wow, he really rates himself, doesn't he? Footballers tend to make a joke of new and uncomfortable situations. We knew this was going to be something different.

We got to the quarter-finals of Euro 2004, then in the game against Portugal we lost Rooney, who had been a revelation, to injury in the first half. I was still yet to play a minute. We were 1–0 up when Scholes came off injured after an hour and I thought this had to be my chance. I could tell Sven was looking at me and asking himself whether he should put me on. We were not playing well. In the other dugout, Big Phil – Luiz Felipe Scolari – was just going for it. Portugal were throwing caution to the wind. Big Phil was trying to win the game. Portugal flooded the midfield: Rui Costa, Hélder Postiga. They already had Cristiano Ronaldo in there – and they were so attack-heavy that Deco, their creative midfielder, went to play right-back. I knew that I could blitz Deco. He could not defend and I wanted to get straight at him. Sven's choice was me or Phil Neville. He went for Phil Neville. I was dumbfounded. It seemed such an obvious counter to Scolari's changes. It made me wonder why I was ever there. But Scolari was ready to be brave. To risk a little to get the equaliser and then to win. It also stifled us because their attacking mindset meant we could not get our game going. We needed to puff our chests out and hurt them a little bit. I was smart enough to play in that 4-4-2, defensively as well as in attack. Deco wouldn't have been able to run past me. When we had the ball, I could take him the other way. Something like that might just change the course of the game. But Sven was not a risk-taker. He put Phil Neville on to stop Luís Figo or Ronaldo or whoever he was up against. We had a great team. We just did not have a manager prepared to risk something. As for Euro 2004 . . . we all know how it ends. Postiga equalised. That game ended 2–2 after extra-time and we went to penalties. But we didn't just lose it on penalties. We limped to penalties and lost deservedly.

In those days we did not do much more than practise penalties. And, of course, in training no one misses. But the Gareth Southgate years proved you needed something different. It helps to have, for instance, a goalkeeper who can affect the confidence of penalty-takers, as Jordan Pickford has for England. Portugal had Ricardo that night in 2004 and he had a bit of a swagger about him. I wouldn't have had Darius Vassell taking a penalty knowing his character. A lovely lad but he just didn't have the confidence. I would rule myself out for similar reasons. Even I can admit I am a bit too emotional. I took three penalties in my career and missed two. As a manager you have to take responsibility. You have to know your players. You have to believe in their mindset.

I just couldn't get my head around it. I had gone to Euro 2004 having played at the highest level. I had reached the semi-final of the Champions League and Claudio was picking me to start for Chelsea even with the range of players he had. Sven should have had no worries with me dealing with the magnitude of tournament football. In the end I didn't even play a minute at Euro 2004. I already had my doubts about Sven and it would not really get any better. But I did resolve that I would not let this happen again. Next time I would be in that XI. I knew I was good enough to be the kind of player an England manager could not leave out.

The highlight of the summer turned out to be Martin Keown's testimonial. I played in it with a few of the England lads at Highbury after the season finished and while I was happy to support Martin I did have an ulterior motive. I wanted to meet Paul Gascoigne. He had agreed to play and it meant that I would be on the pitch with my football hero. Gazza was so nice to me. He said he had been looking forward to playing with me. He was only thirty-six but he was pretty much finished with football and about to sign for Boston United. The affection in which he was held by the best players in the country was something else. We were all in awe of him. Martin made a nice speech thanking everyone for coming. He went round the room and thanked us all individually, noting those who had come a long way. Robbie Fowler had come down from Liverpool. David Beckham had delayed his return to Madrid. Then Gazza said, with perfect comic timing, 'And I've come straight from the Priory.' We all laughed but looking back, maybe he wasn't joking.

As that year developed with England, Sven tried everyone ahead of me on the left side of midfield. He was on a quest to have a left-footed player on that side. Kieron Dyer, Alan Thompson, Stewart Downing, they all came and went. He tried full-backs there – Ashley Cole and Bridgey – just because they had a left foot. But anyone could have told him that playing as a winger requires completely different strengths to what was being asked of a 1990s or 2000s full-back when their job was all about defending. You had to be able to receive the ball with your back to goal, to rotate into the central pockets of space. You needed to have a range of passing. I knew I had all of those things, but the fixation was with my mistakes. That bad pass to James Beattie for Chelsea in August 2004 was chucked around like a piece of incriminating evidence.

I had to take risks otherwise I would just become a normal player. All the things people loved about me – they came at a price. But it was not that steep. My pass completion rate was as high as anyone else's. The bottom line is that you cannot play a game without losing the ball. If I stopped taking risks with the ball, then I wouldn't be the player that I was. But even so I was not losing it any more than the next guy. At the back of my mind was whether I could hold down a place in a Chelsea team that was winning trophies. I was sure that I could, but I needed to prove it. Unless I could prove it then it would not mean anything. With England I stuck to my guns.

Finally, I began to start matches for England in 2005. The problem was that José's public criticism of me seemed to become Sven's thinking as well. In March 2005 I started for

England against Northern Ireland in a 2006 World Cup qualifier at Old Trafford. It was 0–0 at half-time and the crowd were getting restless. A couple of minutes into the second half the ball dropped to me and I banged it in. We won 4–0. Afterwards I was having a drink in the players' bar with my mum and dad and Sven came over. He said, 'Joe, you defended really well tonight. You are now the complete player.' Of course, I was polite and said thank you, especially as my parents were there. But really I was wondering: have you even been watching me? Because that was the way I played every week, for Chelsea and – when I got the chance – for England.

After Sven left, Kieron Dyer, who was sitting with us, told a different story. He had been on the bench at that moment. Sammy Lee, one of Sven's assistants, had then told Kieron that he was coming on for me. I was dumbfounded. So much so that I said to Kieron that I was one of the best players on the pitch at that point. Kieron didn't disagree. He also pointed out that Sven was not going to take off Beckham, Lampard or Gerrard when he could take me off and cause much less of a fuss. If I hadn't scored the goal I would have been hooked. At that point it might have taken me three or four more games to get back in the team. With England, what can seem like relatively small details of a comfortable World Cup qualifier win can be a pivotal moment in your career. That, unfortunately, was Sven's weakness. He struggled with managing the bigger players.

We lost against Denmark in a friendly in August 2005. It turned into an embarrassing 4–1 defeat. Sven called me out after the game in his interviews as being at fault for their first goal. He said about me: 'Maybe you have to expect that Joe will lose the ball and that is the price you pay for having him in the team.' When I was told about it by reporters afterwards it knocked the wind out of my sails. Yes, I did lose it, but I was high up the pitch when it happened. A lot had to happen after that. David James came out and failed to get the ball. Ashley Cole had a chance to win it back and slipped over. It was not like I had lost it on the goal-line. My issue with Sven was that I felt I had to be perfect. While I certainly was not that, I was by no means careless.

The worst of it was about to come. In September 2005 we played a World Cup qualifier against Wales in Cardiff. They had a good team that day, with Ryan Giggs and John Hartson, and they made it hard for us. I scored the only goal of the game and although we had not played well I felt we had got through it. I was playing well for Chelsea at the time, by then a Premier League winner. I felt I was one of the best English players in the Premier League. We were already very close to qualification for 2006 by that point and the next game was at Windsor Park against Northern Ireland four days later. Sven dropped me. We were training in Belfast the night before and he came up to me and said he was leaving me out because he wanted the pace of Shaun Wright-Phillips in the team. That was not the real reason. The real reason, as we all knew, was that Michael Owen was back from injury and so Sven immediately felt that he had to put Michael in the team. That meant Sven had to change the shape.

I was stunned. I asked: 'You're dropping me?'

Sven responded: 'I am not dropping you, I am just doing what is right for the team.'

I told him that I thought he was wrong. I went out to train, but my head was not in it. Not much gets past the attention of a group of footballers and the rest of them had noticed the awkward nature of my conversation with Sven. John Terry just came out and asked me straight: 'Has he dropped you, Coley?' These are miserable occasions in the life of a footballer, but you can never put yourself above the team. I had to get over my own discomfort. I always felt embarrassed telling my family that I was not starting. Carly and my mum and dad had come over to watch. It was a filthy night in Belfast and a terrible game – and we played poorly. I ended up coming on for Shaun after fifty-odd minutes. Anyway, we lost.

The issue had been playing on my mind so much that I went to see Sven in his office. That was common practice at a club where you might pop in to see the manager after training for a private chat, but with the England manager, outside of international breaks, it presented more of a challenge. My friends had whipped me up a bit. They said: 'Well, if you don't like it then go and see him. Ask him straight what it is you have to do to get in the team.' So I did. I went to the FA's headquarters, which then was in Soho Square in central London. I just turned up. Everyone was a bit surprised and the people on reception asked me if I had an appointment, which of course I didn't. Sven did eventually see me in his office. I suppose I wanted to put him on the spot and see if I could get him to say what he really felt about me or admit that maybe he was just parroting a lot of what José had been saying. In the end I didn't feel like I got the kind of honest chat I was looking for. He just fobbed me off. But, after the Northern Ireland game, I did start to see a change in his attitude towards me. I became a starter for England, and by the time the World Cup began the following June, I was established in the team. Something had changed.

16

England: Why Did It Go Wrong?

The 2006 World Cup in Germany was the greatest tournament of my England career, and its biggest disappointment. A raucous, joyous affair; a s—show; and for most of our families, a bit of a piss-up. A very weird event, like a wild family holiday played out in the public gaze. All of it stalked by a despicable breed of paparazzi photographer who followed the young girlfriends and wives of the England players everywhere. On the pitch a non-stop drama of injuries, ever-changing lineups, missed penalties and tearful departures. It came before social media – one last hurrah for the tabloid newspapers who probably couldn't believe their luck. Somewhere in the middle of it I should point out that I scored what was maybe the best goal of my life. One that I had practised for hours on the old training pitches at Chadwell Heath and then, when the moment came, I did it at a World Cup.

But let's not get ahead of ourselves.

Into the squad came Theo Walcott, aged seventeen and at the time still yet to play a Premier League game for Arsenal who he had joined from Southampton the previous January. We couldn't believe it. For Sven it was totally out of character. Very risky, very un-Sven. By then, though, it was clear he was on his way out. The Football Association had decided enough was enough after an unfortunate episode with the *News of the World* undercover reporter known as the Fake Sheikh. Sven was to step down after the tournament. Most people can remember Theo coming into the squad, but I always think about the man who missed out. That was Jermain Defoe, who I'd known since my days at Lilleshall where he was in the intake just after mine. I had played with Jermain at West Ham. I rated him. I thought he should be in the squad, and I wasn't wrong.

When Theo was announced in the squad, I had a look for some videos of him playing. There was barely any footage. When he had signed for Arsenal, he hadn't even attended his own introductory press conference. That was a bit different to me at seventeen when West Ham cheerfully pushed me out there to take on Fleet Street's finest. They treated me about as gently as the opposing team's centre-midfielders. But the world had moved on. Theo wandered into the England camp like a little kid. I couldn't really blame him, he wasn't even an adult yet. He didn't know anyone in the squad. He brought a video camera and just filmed people – something which most of the players could see the funny side of. He was confident, though, and he could hold a conversation. A nice polite boy. Everyone gave him a chance, but the real picture gradually emerged fairly swiftly.

In the first session you could see little glimpses of talent, but this was not a teenager like Wayne Rooney who was ready-made for international football at sixteen. After the second session, I was growing more sceptical that Theo could play at the level required. By the third and fourth I was trying to find reasons to believe in him. Maybe, I told myself, when we moved to the full-size pitch Theo could have an influence. By the fifth session we knew: he was not ready yet. Not that he would never be ready. He did go on to have a very good career at Arsenal and almost fifty caps for England, but back in the summer of 2006 I knew it was a mistake before we left for Germany. Wayne Rooney was trying to come back from the broken metatarsal he had done at Stamford Bridge. Michael Owen had been injured for a long part of the season. Peter Crouch was only just starting out as an international.

I was in the team and playing well. I scored the winner in a friendly against Uruguay at Anfield in March. Crouchy was becoming a regular in the squad too, having made his debut the previous summer. In the build-up to the World Cup, he went on a goalscoring hot streak and when he launched his robot celebration the whole thing went up a level. Football fans love a player who doesn't take himself too seriously. It had started when Crouchy was caught by the cameras doing the dance on his own on the dancefloor in the documentary that featured David Beckham's pre-tournament party. From there it was only a matter of time before he did it after a goal. When he scored at Old Trafford on the way to scoring a hat-trick against Jamaica, I happened to be the guy next to him when he did it. I had gone over to celebrate with him but in that moment Crouchy was concentrating on the robot and so I was left hanging. My raised hand went unnoticed. I was doomed for eternity to be the spare man in one of England's most famous goal celebrations.

The robot went so big that when Prince William, the FA president, came to visit us at our training camp, he even mentioned it. We egged Crouchy on and in front of the cameras, on the training ground, he danced for the future king. We went back to the hotel and were told that William was going to do a walkabout after lunch and pop into a few rooms, followed by some cameras. The instruction was to leave the door open and be aware that it might be you. I did as I was told, put the telly on and soon forgot what was happening. I have always found hotel rooms a bit too warm for my liking and after a while I had stripped off. England tracksuit, then my T-shirt, shorts and socks until I was in just my FA-issue white Y-fronts. I was watching TV when I heard someone come into my room. In the few seconds it took to realise who it might be, I could see my clothes on a chair in the corner. Like the split-second calculation you make to hit a through ball, or lunge for a cross, it was obvious Prince William was going to be in the middle of my room before I could get a leg in my tracksuit.

Suddenly he was standing there, saying hello to me. People were piling in behind with cameras. I could see the cameras focusing on me and then, when they realised what it was they were filming, the camera lens being manoeuvred cautiously away from me. Even they seemed unsure whether you were allowed to shake the hand of royalty while wearing so little. I was relieved to see a smile on William's face. I mumbled an apology and grabbed my tracksuit bottoms. As I got into them William quietly said to me: 'Those pants are terrible.' I said I couldn't disagree but this was what the FA had given us to wear. I didn't see William again until the FA Cup final the next year. He was introduced to the teams on the pitch as per the convention and when he got to me a smile played across his lips. He stopped in front of me. 'I hope,' he said, 'you're not wearing those ghastly pants.'

In Germany we stayed in splendid isolation in the Schloss Bühlerhöhe hotel in the Black Forest. Down in the nearby spa town of Baden-Baden life was a bit different. The FA had suggested that all the families stay in the same hotel. Carly was there along with my parents George and Susan. It was a good idea in principle. In many respects they had a great time but it just became a feeding frenzy for the media. A small town with nowhere that was not within sight of the packs of paparazzi roaming around. A lot of drinking and late nights, and then all the pictures in the newspapers and on the websites. You could see that some of the WAGs enjoyed the attention, but the bottom line was that they were just young women out on the town having fun.

My friends were calling me from home asking if it was all as mad as it looked in the papers. In the quiet of the schloss, built before the First World War on a rocky ridge deep in the forest, I was mystified by these calls. What the hell was going on down in Baden-Baden? During one of our trips into town between games it became obvious what sort of place it was. Carly would go out for a run in the morning and have four paparazzi following her. But it was a lot scarier than that. I don't know who these people were, but they had nothing to do with the agency and newspaper photographers I saw every week shooting the action pictures of our matches and the occasional training session. The paparazzi tried to take pictures of the girls when they climbed out of taxis – the up-skirt violations that were part of that creed of photographers. For Carly it was her first real experience of that part of the media and she hated it.

Looking back, the Baden-Baden experience was wrong. It was organised with the best intention but someone might have spotted the likely problems when they scoped out a town which was so small. It has never happened since and the FA was very sensitive to a repetition of the same thing in 2010 in South Africa, which was part of the reason we ended up in the middle of nowhere that time. The hotel in Baden-Baden where the families spent the tournament was also where most of the football reporters covering England were staying. That was not such a bad thing. I think it was good for both sides. It humanised us as players – because the journalists saw what our partners and our parents went through – and it meant that the families could get to know the journalists a bit better. My mum had a good chat with Oliver Holt, then at the *Daily Mirror*. My dad knocked around with the Bridges and the Crouch family. My mates came out to Germany and slept on the floor of my parents' hotel rooms. Those poor hotel staff must have been delighted when we all went home.

I played well in our first group game against Paraguay but it was obvious we had problems as a team. Rooney wasn't yet ready to play and Owen came off in that game. He wasn't fit. If Sven had taken Defoe he would have been starting. Walcott wasn't an option. Owen tried to get his full sharpness back in the games against Paraguay and Trinidad and Tobago and then early on against Sweden he ruptured his cruciate and was out for the long haul. Rooney was back but not fully fit. Crouchy had scored the first goal in a 2–0 win against Trinidad but two games in we were so short of options. We really needed Jermain. Michael had won eighty caps in just a shade over eight years in what had been a brilliant England career up to that point. Yet at twenty-six, he would play only nine more games for England. He will tell you himself he was not the same player. He was still a great finisher but playing alongside him that year, I could tell he had lost the pace that allowed him to sprint away from defenders and score. Playing off Crouchy, Michael would score goals because he had an instinct for goalscoring, but he was not the same. We – Sven – had made it hard for ourselves. In the heat of a summer tournament, you cannot carry players who are not fit. I felt as good as I ever had and yet the games were draining. You would lose kilos in the heat. Dehydration was an issue.

Michael's injury came four minutes into the Sweden game.

We had six points and we were through already, but we wanted to finish top of the group. Crouchy came on for Michael. I had one of my best games in an England shirt playing with Ashley off the left, which is where I had always thought I should play. Sweden played a midfield diamond which was a mistake because our best asset was our crossing. I was enjoying the game. I felt free. Those moments are rare in big games but when you get that flow it feels wonderful. You should never shoot from as far out as I did on that angle. A terrible decision, in theory. I was barely in the final third of the pitch. The only time you do that is just before half-time. It ends up in the stands and the team resets to defend. It's considered reckless in these days of patient passing sequences and gradual territorial accumulation. But I just thought: eff it, I'm going to have a pop. If I could trouble the keeper, we had players around him to pick up the scraps because we had just been attacking a corner. The original position I took was out on the left channel, to keep the attack alive if Sweden cleared. First thing is: don't lose the ball because then they are on the counterattack. But that was all I had to worry about.

A weak header from Niclas Alexandersson and with one bounce it was on me. First, I pushed it upwards with my chest so I could set myself and strike it with my right foot as it dropped. Where did that goal come from? It came from West Ham's training ground and we even had a name for that kind of strike: the paintbrush. We called it that because you strike upwards – like a brushstroke – against a falling ball to put topspin on it. Steve Lomas was brilliant at it. We would line up to practise them after training at Chadwell Heath: me, Steve, Frank, Jermain, Michael Carrick. I cut across the ball ever so slightly which added some fade but it was mostly about the dip. Goalkeepers will tell you they hate that shot. A straight hit, they can pick its trajectory. The dipping one is different. They know it is going in, but if their positioning is slightly off, as Andreas Isaksson's was this time, they cannot reach it. I never realised at the time how far out I had been when I hit it. When we were back in the dressing room about fifteen minutes later the priority was Michael and what sort of state he was in. A lot of pain was the answer. I didn't realise the distance I had hit the shot until John Terry came over and said, 'Coley, what an effing goal. Do you know how far out you were?'

In the second half, it was from my cross that Steven Gerrard scored our second. We drew the game and won the group. We were not playing well but we had moments. Stevie's goal against Trinidad and Tobago. Beckham's free-kick in the next round against Ecuador. But Michael was out, Rooney was not fit, Theo was obviously not ready. If Crouchy had been injured we wouldn't have had a striker. Maybe me as a false nine with Stevie playing off me. The team kept changing. Beckham was not really fit either but Sven just couldn't bring himself to drop his captain. Carrick was excellent against Ecuador. We played 4-5-1 with Owen Hargreaves at right-back. Then Carrick was left out in the quarter-final against Portugal because Gary Neville came back in and so Hargreaves moved from right-back to midfield. The tension was huge at times but there were always silly moments in the midst of this huge global event. We came out of the dressing room in Stuttgart for the Ecuador game and the music was blaring. No one could find the remote control to turn it off. We were standing in the tunnel, the cameras on us as we tried to look serious, and 'Get Up' by Byron Stingily was blasting. I could see a few of the lads' heads bopping along to the beat. I caught Crouchy's eye. He had the giggles.

We got to the quarter-finals of the World Cup and we had

not even played well. Privately I felt I had played as well as anyone, certainly in the Paraguay and Sweden games. Against Portugal, Ashley and I were up against Miguel and Luís Figo and first we fought each other to a standstill. I ran at Miguel once in the first half, jinked past him and had a half chance. I did it again. I thought: I have got him now. Figo was older and although he was a great player I was comfortable leaving Ashley with him. I started to feel like I was going to have my moment with Miguel. I felt confident. I felt we were going to win. Then Rooney got sent off. In the seconds after he kicked Ricky Carvalho I looked at Wayne's face and I knew immediately he was guilty. Wayne, don't ever rob a bank and try to get away with it.

As a footballer, as a human being, I would like to say my first thought was for Wayne – stupidly culpable for a red card at a World Cup. But my first thought was for myself. I knew the likelihood was that we would make a substitution because we were going to have to change shape. I also knew – based on my performance – it should not be me. I could hold the ball and take it up the pitch. But I also knew that Sven had form in this regard. Beckham, Lampard, Gerrard – he wasn't going to take them off. In the aftermath I said to Steve McClaren, Sven's assistant: 'Is he going to take me off?' Worryingly, Steve didn't give me a clear answer. When, eventually, Sven did take me off just a few minutes later, all my frustration came out. I shouted at Sven. I chuntered away on the bench. I should have taken my medicine, but I let my emotions get the better of me. It infuriated me. I knew I had got the better of Miguel. I knew I could do the job defensively. I was a double Premier League winner. An experienced Champions League player. I knew my job. I knew we were not going to have the ball. I played in Chelsea teams who were happy not to have the ball and who could play effectively without it. This was a critical moment when my reputation and my status behind the team's biggest names was going to take me out of one of the biggest games of my career. On the bench I just thought: please don't let this be the end. If we had survived, and won it on penalties, I think we would have won the World Cup. We had something. All of a sudden, the country would have been behind us. The lads did well. Owen Hargreaves was a man possessed. It was the best I have ever seen him play. Ashley was outstanding against Figo and Cristiano Ronaldo.

After we lost to Portugal, I went into the dressing room and saw Wayne. I just left him. I knew he would be feeling lower than anybody. There was nothing to say. I was angry at the world and although you say you don't want to blame any one person, I was angry at Sven. I was angry at the referee. As for Wayne – sometimes his genius for playing football pushed him over the edge. There is always someone who carries the can for England at tournaments. We knew that it could have been one of us too. The mood was of anger more than disappointment because the tournament was there to be won. The Italy team that did win it was not as good as us individually, in my opinion, but collectively they were a better team.

The next day, Beckham quit as captain at a press conference. I thought it was a strange thing to do. I did not see why it had to be announced on that day; the timing felt wrong. It must have been in his mind before the tournament. I couldn't see what he had to gain by doing it. Maybe he thought his days as captain were numbered and because he loved playing for England that stepping back as captain made it easier for him to say he would be in the background. The emergence of Shaun Wright-Phillips and Aaron Lennon on the right side – two very different players to Beckham – might have made him feel he was under pressure. It happens to us all: young lads come along and take your place. There were tears again at the announcement. The next England manager, Steve McClaren, cut Beckham from the squad completely and having seemingly ended Beckham's England career then brought him back the following summer. He did so because it was going so badly he felt he had no other choice, but that just about summed up Steve's time. It was just too early in his career for him to be England manager. You have to stick with a big decision like getting rid of Beckham. You have to show you have belief in the young players like Shaun and Lennon, who Steve had worked with for years as a coach with England. Beckham was playing in the United States by then, at a level a long way below the Premier League and the European game. Beckham probably did have a role to play with England and another manager would have handled it differently. He would have kept Beckham around and tried to get him onside, and then gradually managed him out. If you want to stamp your authority, you have to be sure. By getting rid of Beckham and then bringing him back, it made Steve look like he was dithering. Worst yet, it was like he didn't know his own mind.

There were lots of mistakes. In some of those massive Euro 2008 qualifiers in the autumn of 2007 we would come in at half-time and walk past Steve talking to Bill Beswick, a sports psychologist who was Steve's guru in many ways. It never felt right. Nothing wrong with discussing what your team-talk might be, but a manager needs to maintain at least the pretence of knowing his own mind. Those sorts of conversations needed to be out of sight of his players. At half-time of a critical game like that final defeat by Croatia at Wembley, it is all on the line. All eyes are on you as manager. He is the man who has to tell this group of top footballers what they need to do. It is natural to be nervous or insecure about how you deliver that message in the short time available but you have to put on a show of strength and confidence. The Manchester United players in the team had learnt from Sir Alex Ferguson. Those of us at Chelsea were used to José Mourinho – who could come up with any kind of performance to surprise us. Sometimes it was a b—king, sometimes it was a tactical change. On one occasion José just got his crucifix out, kissed it and said: 'We are not effing losing this game.' It might sound mad, but it was just what we needed in the moment. Other managers would send in an assistant for a few minutes to assess the mood and then go in and dish out the blame or the praise. Once that door opens and the manager walks in, everyone looks up and listens. But we had already seen Steve always chatting away to Bill as we went in.

My injury problems during the 2006–07 season meant that I played just three times for England. Once in November and then the two games in June 2007. The Euro 2008 qualifying campaign was not going smoothly. We had lost to Croatia in Zagreb and dropped points against Macedonia and Israel. The second of the games I played, a friendly against Brazil in June 2007, was Beckham's comeback. In the next, a qualifier a few days later against Estonia, I scored and we won 3–0, although I will admit I did not play that well. It was hard for Steve to adjust to the status of the job having been the friendly and accessible assistant during the Sven years. At John Terry's wedding later in the summer of 2007, a year into Steve's time as England manager, he sat with a few of us. A few drinks had been had. Steve said to me: 'How bad were you against Estonia?'

I shot back: 'You would've got the sack if I hadn't got that first goal.'

ENGLAND: WHY DID IT GO WRONG?

I would never have said that to José, but then it would be hard to imagine being in a similar situation with José.

We seemed to have turned a corner until the defeat to Russia in October 2007 put our qualification in the balance ahead of the last game. The game in Moscow had been an eye-opener. I felt much the same way about the Russian team as I had about the South Korea team in the warm-up to the 2002 World Cup. Their energy was astonishing. We expected them to tire but they just never did. It was remarkable. They chased us down for ninety long minutes and, having beaten them 3–0 at Wembley the previous month, we lost 2–1. It was like we were playing a different team. Russia then lost to Israel the next month and only beat Andorra 1–0 in their final game. It meant that we only needed a draw against Croatia at Wembley to qualify. It looked like we were off the hook.

Steve had all these ideas. He brought back Terry Venables as a coach. He had played a back three for the first of the two Croatia qualifiers in Zagreb in October 2006. But in that game our goalkeeper Paul Robinson had been at fault for both the goals and then when Croatia came to Wembley the following year for that fateful last qualifier, Scott Carson threw in the first. We would play them a third time in September 2008 in a World Cup qualifier and win 4–1 in Zagreb. I would argue if you look at the three England performances there was not much that was different. But the goalkeepers' performances cost Steve. That factor, as well as the injuries, and the inevitable, irresistible sense that we were sliding into a disaster.

We had a lot of injuries ahead of that last Euro 2008 qualifier: Wazza, John Terry, Michael Owen, Rio Ferdinand, Ashley Cole. Wayne Bridge was really ill. Flu, sweating, feeling like death. He never said anything at the time because he didn't want to let anyone down. There were not any alternatives but under normal circumstances he wouldn't have played. But that's football – once you're on the pitch everyone assumes you're fit and ready. Even so we only needed a draw on the basis that Russia would beat Andorra and we would nick second place on goal difference. McClaren decided to start with Carson – a big call. He was twenty-two and had only just made his debut less than a week earlier in a friendly against Austria. We didn't know who was playing in goal until the morning of the game when someone spotted Paul Robinson with his golf clubs heading out to the course that adjoined our hotel. It was pretty obvious then that Robinson was not in the team. An hour before the game I glanced at Carson in the changing room and there was something in his eyes that prompted me instinctively to say something. Not much more than: 'Come on, Scotty. You're ready.'

But I was not convinced. He looked really nervous. As I got older, I realised that it was important to project confidence however you might be feeling inside. You need to mask those feelings of uncertainty and try to carry people with you. But I was thinking: I hope he doesn't make a mistake. Croatia seemed to have the same notion. Everything they did in the early stages suggested they didn't think Carson was up to it. That first goal from Niko Kranjčar that went straight through Carson was a case in point.

Beckham had been dropped again for the game and then came on at half-time when we were 2–0 down. We got it back to 2–2 and Carson did make some saves. But the winner from the substitute Mladen Petrić was along the same theme. Croatia just kept hitting shots at Carson and eventually one went in. The rain came down. I never saw McClaren unfurl his infamous brolly. But missing Euro 2008 was a massive hole in many of our careers. I felt that from 2005 up to my injury in January 2009 I was among the best players for the England team. Euro 2008 would have been my fourth tournament. At twenty-six I would have been at my peak and it was the classic sixteen-team Euros – high quality from the start. I am not saying we would have been better than that Spain team that won it, but we had a great side when we were all fit.

Perhaps there was a weakness in us too. I remember one of the England players of that era coming in at half-time and telling me out of a mix of fear, frustration and embarrassment that he was worried about the individual mark out of ten he was going to get in the newspapers the next day. I was stunned that it was the first thing on his mind. He wasn't one of the big hitters in the team but he was a talented lad. The marks out of ten were a bit of a preoccupation for players in the days before social media. Nowadays all you need to do is turn on your social media mentions to find out what the world thought of your personal performance. Back then, players would read the ratings. It was the one part of the reporting where each player was guaranteed a mention. I won't name the player. That wouldn't be fair. For lots of the big players like Wazza, Frank, Stevie, the criticism was part of the job. They could handle it. There was lots of it after the Croatia game in November 2007. Opposing teams' fans chanting, 'You let your country down.' That happens in crowds when people feel the anonymity of being part of a large group. No one ever said that to my face. The following May I would line up for Chelsea against Manchester United in the first all-English Champions League final, in Moscow, one of ten Englishmen to start the game. Yet our national team had not made the best sixteen sides in Europe.

I do believe it comes down to handling the pressure in key moments. That goes back to my days in the youth team at

West Ham and those who could make the step up to the first team and those who just could not handle it. The issue was the same at all levels up to and including the big games for England. You have to accept that there are games when it is all on the line and that if you lose you are going to face a lot of ridicule and recrimination. That twenty years on you are going to be recounting it with regret to your ghostwriter. That's life. You have to swallow the pressure and perform anyway. Never more so than with England when the eyes of the whole country are on you, and for decades there has been heartbreak after heartbreak. Some can handle it and some cannot. You only find out who they are in the moment.

17

England:
Fabio's War on Snacking

There was one training session early on in the Fabio Capello era, when I swear Capello thought I was Wayne Bridge. I wasn't the only one who suspected Capello was still figuring out who was who in the squad. His main man, chief lieutenant and general manager Franco Baldini, who could speak English, was doing most of the talking. Capello and his coaches set up a session where we doubled up in every position. It was principally a drill to coach an attacking team shape. We would have two defensive teams who would swap in and out. He sent me over to stand with Ashley Cole, which could only mean one thing. He thought I was the back-up left-back. Ashley watched me trot over and said: 'What the effing hell are you doing over here?'

'I don't know,' I said. 'But I think he just called me Wayne.'

I threw myself into the role of an attacking left-back. I whipped in crosses with my right foot. I have to say Bridgey played well in that session. I wonder if something clicked among the coaches because when Capello announced his first England team to play Switzerland the next day I was in the team, albeit back in my favoured position of left midfield.

It had been a rocky start. My first experience of Capello

was him shouting at me for sitting on a football. I was excited about working under a manager who had coached one of my favourite teams, the AC Milan of the 1990s. As he divided us into groups, I decided to rest my legs and keep my backside dry by sitting on a ball – and Capello lost it with me. I had been around enough tyrannical managers to know it was nothing personal. He was just trying to assert his authority. Eight years on from wearing the wrong shorts under Kevin Keegan, I was once again doing the wrong thing. I don't mind a telling-off. It would just have helped to know the rules beforehand so as not to break them. As he let rip at me, my first impression was: he is quite hard to understand. Capello could not speak good English. It felt like the reverse of my attempts to speak Italian on holiday. At least, in my case, even if I was unsure exactly which pizza I had ordered, I could be sure that whatever was coming out of the oven would be tasty. It was not quite so simple for Capello.

Early on I got the impression from Baldini that he and Capello and the Italian staff were surprised at how technically accomplished we were. That was what we heard anyway. We got the impression that they came with this notion that England players were lazy and undisciplined. I can understand that in part. None of them knew the Premier League and Capello had been appointed because England had failed to qualify for a major international tournament. They thought it had been too easy for us under Sven and Steve McClaren, but that was not the reason we had underperformed. We were crying out for better tactical ideas. Instead Capello did much the same as we had done before. Perhaps he thought we needed iron discipline to ensure we worked hard in training – but generally speaking British players give everything in training. We may have our shortcomings but those would never include a lack of effort.

Yet Capello never understood until it was too late. What might have worked in Italy in the 1970s when he was a player, or later as a club manager, just did not work with us. To play for England is enough pressure without lots of unnecessary shouting. The years that Gareth Southgate was in charge showed that England teams perform best when they have a manager trying to take the pressure off the players, or find effective ways of managing it. Capello only really had one way and that was to control everything. In many ways that felt petty and meaningless. If he had sat us all down and explained his rationale, then maybe it would have been easier. I would have understood where he was coming from, even if I didn't agree. But he never did.

By now the stories of the Capello ban on tomato ketchup and various other foods are legendary. He didn't just ban ketchup. He banned fun. And for the long hours in the hotel, we needed that. I hated the fact that he stopped the masseurs' room being the hub of the squad in the hotel. I loved going there to talk and drink tea with my teammates. I wasn't interested in gaming and I didn't want to sit in my room gambling on horses. I wanted to see my friends. At the Grove Hotel, our base in Hertfordshire, we would gather in the masseurs' room and gossip about the game. It was silly and harmless. I would hide under a pile of towels and when the waiter came in the masseur would ask him to pass a towel. Then I would grab their arm from beneath the pile. There was no meanness about it. Just silly footballer stuff. The staff at the hotel joined in the fun and we trusted them.

The worst was the food restrictions. By three o'clock in the afternoon after training in the morning and lunch a distant memory, my stomach would be rumbling and I would head off for a sandwich, some fruit and a little bit of chocolate. Under

Capello all those snacks were removed. Just a few nuts and a coffee machine. As a twenty-something professional footballer your metabolism burns pretty quickly. We just wanted some food, and in a five-star hotel that didn't seem too much to ask. In fact, food became such an obsession under Capello that we would contrive ways to get our hands on it even when we were not that hungry. It became a point of principle. The meals were fine. Mounds of pasta. But it was the long hours between that gnawed away. There were takeaway McDonald's smuggled into the hotel in the empty box that the FA staff brought their printer in when they set up a temporary office. Security guards were given a few quid to look the other way. If Baldini and Capello had checked our luggage, they would have found enough junk food to fill a picnic hamper. It was contraband. We didn't really want to eat it. We just wanted it there in case we needed it. I remember trying to wind up Jermaine Jenas as we jogged around at the start of a training session. 'What have you got in your room?' I asked. No need for me to say what it was I was referring to.

'Biscuits,' Jermaine said.

I tried to get him worried: 'Have you heard that Baldini is doing a sweep of our rooms while we are out to check for food?'

'I'm not bothered,' said Jermaine. 'The biscuits are in my safe with my passport and my watch.'

That summed it up really. It was less about the food and more about the control. If Capello had regaled us with stories about how Franco Baresi and Ruud Gullit had gone without butter on their toast and how it had made all the difference for AC Milan, then maybe I could have got on board with butterless toast. But he never tried to sell it to us. He just demanded we did what he said. I went up to the chef at breakfast and pleaded for some butter for my toast but the chef said it could cost him his job if he did. 'Fabio thinks English people eat too much butter.'

'That might be right,' I said. 'But I feel pretty confident my football career has gone quite well so far with butter on my toast.'

As the captain, John Terry was endlessly lobbied by the rest of us to go to see Capello and sort it out. John was used to managers listening to him. Even José and Luiz Felipe Scolari, big names who had won a lot, would take John's view into account when he was talking on behalf of the players. But this time he came back and said: 'Sorry, lads, the boss is not budging.' It was pointless. We spent no more than fifty days a year in the England bubble. The rest of the time we were free to live without the Capello restrictions on our lives. By the time we got to the World Cup in 2010, Capello realised he had made a mistake, but it was all a bit too late.

It was likely that Capello will never have met anyone like Jimmy Bullard, before or after his brief spell as a member of one of Capello's England squads. I knew Jimmy, an east London boy, from my West Ham days where he was a young professional who had joined the club from non-league. I once made the mistake of picking up a fire extinguisher and giving Jimmy a little squirt with it. He never forgot. For the next year he would lie in wait around the training ground emptying fire extinguishers all over me. Had there been a fire at Chadwell Heath between 1999 and 2001 we would surely all have perished. There probably wasn't a functioning fire extinguisher left in the place.

I had been on nights out with Jimmy. They were big nights. I had a feeling he wasn't going to play by Capello's rules. Jimmy asked me to come over to his room to introduce him to life at the England squad. When I got there he wasn't in. As I made my way back through the hotel I spotted him. He was on the first tee of the hotel golf course, swinging a club and wearing his England tracksuit. He was being his usual loud self and chatting to a group of golfers. From that moment, I could tell it was probably not going to be a fifty-cap England career for Jimmy. Our part of the hotel was out of bounds to the rest of the guests, which Jimmy found hard to understand.

'Facking hell,' he told me at the first lunch, 'this is like a facking prison camp.'

A character like that will always look for the chance to rebel. For Jimmy it was his nickname for Capello: Postman Pat. He started whispering to me as we jogged round the pitch at the start of the training. When we stood to listen to Capello's instructions at the start of the session, Jimmy was repeating it incessantly in my ear. I was fighting the urge to laugh. I felt like Capello was looking straight at me. I wondered if he could hear. I wondered if he knew who Postman Pat was. All I could hear was Jimmy who was by now singing the *Postman Pat* theme tune.

Capello was under pressure from the start. Performances were not great. We had no qualifiers until the autumn of 2008. Come the new season we were 2–1 down to the Czech Republic in a friendly at Wembley with full-time looming and, as a second-half substitute, I got an equaliser in the 92nd minute against my Chelsea teammate Petr Čech. As a pundit on Setanta Sports, my old manager Harry Redknapp was unequivocal: Capello had got it wrong. The second half was, Harry said, diabolical. They didn't play like the same players who perform week in week out in the Premier League, Harry said. What are we doing to them? The pressure continued to build. A couple of weeks later I came on as a substitute again at half-time of our first World Cup qualifier, against Andorra with the score 0–0 and the travelling fans in Barcelona booing us. I scored twice and we won 2–0. A few days later in Zagreb we had lift-off. A 4–1 win over our old enemies Croatia and a hat-trick from Theo Walcott. After that I wouldn't play again for England for another twenty months as injury changed my life.

By the time I returned in 2010, I was in the last weeks of my seven years at Chelsea and my mind was whirling as to where I might be going next. There was a list of thirty players shortlisted for the World Cup, although I had been told that I was in the twenty-three definitely going when we set off for the training camp in Austria. I wondered if Capello had perhaps mellowed a little bit but come the first training session he was screaming at Joe Hart, then a 23-year-old who had one cap from two years previous. Capello was still not sure who he wanted to play in goal in the first game, so his idea seemed to be to put Joe under pressure to find out how he reacted.

We went to the tournament in South Africa still not knowing who our goalkeeper would be for that first game against USA. It was ridiculous. A team has to know who its goalkeeper is before the day of the game. For the media it naturally became an obsession. We were asked about it all the time and, when it was my turn, I had to pretend that the uncertainty of not knowing was a strength for the squad, not a matter of bemusement to us all. In private I could not see what it was Capello was offering England that other managers had not done in the past. He called up players who had retired, including Jamie Carragher. Ledley King came back for the first time in three years. Paul Scholes was asked to return but declined. Capello did not seem to know what to do. He was hanging on to this notion that England players were poorly disciplined when that was not the case. We wanted some guidance and preparation for games from this famous Italian manager, but we went into the first game of the 2010 World Cup in the same formation we had used in the first game – and every game after – of the 2006 World Cup. Good old 4-4-2.

Ledley lasted until half-time of the USA game and came off injured, never to play again for England. It was obvious to me that this was a player who had to manage his game time with the utmost care and yet he was just being pushed to play before he was ready, especially once Rio Ferdinand was injured in training just before the tournament began. Rob Green, the goalkeeper preferred to David James, fumbled Clint Dempsey's shot for the equaliser and didn't play again at the tournament. It was a shambles. As a team we had not looked settled.

We were tucked away in the middle of nowhere, more than two hours' drive outside Johannesburg, near the town of Rustenburg. Nothing on the horizon but the great waste piles from nearby mines and nothing to do but hang around the Royal Marang hotel. The FA were desperate to avoid a repeat of the circus in Baden-Baden four years earlier and as usual went too far in the opposite direction. I was happy to spend my days knocking around the hotel and watching the rest of the World Cup on television although I could tell lots of the lads were going stir-crazy. Capello and his staff watched the games and in particular their native Italy. They cheered every Italy goal like a bunch of fans. I could not tell whether it was done ironically or not. Either way it reminded us that this was not an Englishman managing the team. I had never felt that with Sven, even though we played against Sweden in the previous World Cup. I just found it a strange way to behave in front of their own players who were all on edge about the tournament. The funny part of that was – as bad as we were,

Italy were even worse. They were the holders and they went out bottom of their group behind Paraguay, Slovakia and New Zealand. Italy didn't even win a game.

We were a stressed-out group of players. Rio had been injured in the first training session. David Beckham had long since been ruled out with an Achilles problem and was there as a coach. Ledley was obviously overtrained and broke down. Rob Green had lost his confidence. Rooney shouted something critical of the fans into the television camera after we drew 0–0 with Algeria in our second game. One night in the Royal Marang I was so bored that I asked our chef Tim discreetly to pass me a bottle of red wine. I just needed a couple of glasses to relax and unwind. We would both have been in trouble if Capello had found out, but Tim understood. It had got too much for everyone. That said, Capello became so desperate to change the mood that suddenly we went from not being allowed butter on our toast to being offered a few beers after games. That came after the Algeria match when John Terry went to see Baldini and asked whether it was time to relax the alcohol ban and just let the players unwind with a few beers. John had the captaincy taken off him before the World Cup, but he still felt like he had something to say. Then in a press conference after the game John also said that I should be in the team before the last group game, which we had to win, against Slovenia in Port Elizabeth. I hadn't played a single minute by that point. I was behind just about every other attacking midfielder in the squad and a few who were not – Aaron Lennon, Shaun Wright-Phillips, James Milner. As soon as John said it, I was pretty sure that Capello would go the other way. I wasn't picked for the Slovenia game, which we won 1–0, although I did finally get twenty minutes as a substitute in the second half. John was used to dialogue with Chelsea managers, but Capello didn't want a dialogue. Baldini was more accessible, although he was mainly just a go-between by virtue of the fact he could speak English. The other coaches on Capello's staff – Italo Galbiati, Massimo Neri – didn't speak English either. There was no connection between the players and the staff. It was not a happy camp.

The last 16 game against Germany was a disaster. I came on when we were 2–1 down and chasing the game and we conceded two goals from Thomas Müller very quickly. We had been denied the goal from Frank Lampard which would have made it 2–2 and perhaps we would have seen a different story. There were other mistakes too. Gareth Barry was exposed one-on-one against Mesut Özil for the fourth Germany goal, but then Gareth wasn't fit at the time. It is very hard to play in those games when you are not at your best. Just look at the way that Özil sprinted away from him – and it was not like Özil was particularly swift himself.

After we lost that game in Bloemfontein I was the only one who said much to the media afterwards. I agreed there were a lot of issues with the team and a lot that had gone wrong. I wasn't picked by Capello for the next game in August. It cannot have been my performance at the World Cup because I only played about forty minutes in total. But that was that. I had won my fifty-sixth and final cap in that defeat in Bloemfontein. I would never play for England again although there was a time when I thought that I might.

It was towards the end of the 2012 season when I was playing some of my best football in two years on loan at Lille in the French Ligue 1. I was back in England at a restaurant in Essex and Harry Redknapp walked in. He had been over to watch Lille because Tottenham had some hopes at the time that they might be able to sign my young teammate

Eden Hazard, although they soon had to accept defeat in that respect. I poured Harry a glass of wine and he drew a chair up to our table. He told us he was going to be England manager. Capello had walked out in February after a row over whether John – who he had reinstated as captain – could skipper the side at Euro 2012. The same day as Capello had quit, 8 February 2012, Harry had himself been acquitted of two tax evasion charges at Southwark Crown Court. The way was clear, or so he thought, to be Capello's successor. Harry was convinced that he had the job. 'I'm telling you,' he said, 'I have got it. Joe, I will get you back in.'

We discussed the young Swansea City coach Brendan Rodgers. Harry wanted to play that style of possession-heavy football and control the ball, which I agreed would be suited to international football. Harry discussed appointing Brendan as a coach with England. Harry thought the Pep Guardiola revolution at Barcelona – which had laid the foundation for Spain's Euro 2008 and World Cup 2010 wins – could be replicated by England. Harry was smart. I was delighted by this news and went back to France awaiting the announcement of Harry as the new England manager. On 29 April we beat Paris Saint-Germain at home. A couple of days later I parked the car and looked down at my phone. My news alert told me that Roy Hodgson was the shock choice of the FA to be the new England manager. And with that I knew it was over for good.

18

Right Club, Wrong Time

I had joined Chelsea at the best time in the club's history. I joined Liverpool at the club's lowest point in years and from the first moment things looked like they were going to be difficult. Roy Hodgson was immediately under pressure. I liked Roy but it was obvious that we had different ideas about how the game should be played. I was used to playing in teams that went after opponents and dominated them. Roy wanted us to keep our shape, mostly a 4-4-2, and be in position to spring forward when we won possession and hit teams quickly. But that was not the way the supporters wanted it either. They had been used to seeing their team dominate the ball and control games. It did not take long for things to go wrong.

First of all, my body was starting to break. I would come to learn to manage it but at this stage I was still consumed with being the player I had always been. There is something so debilitating about the kind of muscle injuries that stop you playing for four to six weeks. In the span of a career that does not seem like much, but everything gets reset. You have to regain your fitness, your rhythm and your place in the team. I might do something as simple as check a run or cut inside and feel something go in my leg. It got to the stage where I barely needed the MRI scan. I could tell just from the pain what grade of muscle tear it was. Then I started to doubt my body. Could I still do this?

It started badly for me in my first game at Anfield against Arsenal. Perhaps that was an understatement. I missed a penalty and was then sent off. I had made what I thought was a perfectly decent tackle on Laurent Koscielny as he clipped it down the line and I tried to block it. Our legs got tangled. This big centre-half went down on the floor like I had ended his career. The referee Martin Atkinson saw it as reckless and could not get his red card out quick enough. I had never been sent off before in the course of a game. I looked down at Koscielny, who had done more rolls than Greggs and remembered my old friend, the great Arsenal captain Tony Adams. I don't think Tony would have made such a fuss. Koscielny was fine to finish the game. My Anfield debut had been inauspicious to say the least.

We had the basis of a good squad: Steven Gerrard, Javier Mascherano, Glen Johnson. Fernando Torres was still there although he had a problem with his knee. He would leave to join Chelsea in January. Training was very structured, and I could see why Roy had such success in his career. He knew how to establish a good shape and he was clear about what each player had to do. He was precise about our positioning and the pressing distances he wanted. All that was perfectly solid, but at Chelsea we had played differently. We passed through the lines, we took risks and we backed ourselves. That was the way the Liverpool fans were accustomed to seeing their team playing too and the two approaches were just so far apart.

In Roy's defence, he had a squad that had finished a long way off the pace the previous season. The George Gillett and Tom Hicks ownership that appointed him had known what kind of manager he was – his career had been long enough.

In October 2010, Fenway Sports Group (FSG) bought the club, which hardly did much to stop the doubts around Roy. We played Utrecht in the Europa League in December and in the build-up work on team shape there had been a lot of instruction from Roy about the defensive position he wanted me in. It was another reminder that even at the age of twenty-nine there were plenty of people who thought I had not spent my whole career tracking my man and covering my full-back. I cannot say that I agreed with the approach Roy adopted. Utrecht at home should not have been a game to play it safe. But, I thought, I would be a good soldier and follow his instructions to the letter and we got the game that we played for. The crowd at Anfield were not happy at how cautious we played, and Roy was angry. He wanted to know why we had just never got going. I bit my tongue in that moment. We had played exactly as he had asked us to do.

It got worse. We lost to Wolverhampton Wanderers in our next game when I came on for the last twenty minutes. Roy singled me out at a team meeting the next day. He accused me of being wasteful or, in his words, flicking the ball. At that point I had heard enough. I told him he had got it wrong. I had watched the game back immediately afterwards and I had touched the ball fourteen times and lost it once. That time I had tried to turn it around the corner and get an attack going – because we were losing. Roy was conciliatory after that, but we all knew the writing was on the wall. In the October, we had lost 2–0 to Everton at Goodison Park. I had played there many times and the general rule of thumb was that you have to dominate Everton in all the basics and that keeps the crowd quiet. But we were never able to do that in this derby and it was just so hectic from start to finish – which was how Everton liked it.

RIGHT CLUB, WRONG TIME

As soon as FSG took over my agent David Geiss started hearing whispers that they wanted me out of the club. My wages, as a free agent, were just short of £100,000 per week. This is football. Nine months earlier, they had been moving mountains to persuade me to come to the club. Now they were desperate for me to leave. Over the course of the contract, and the twists and turns that lay ahead, I have to say FSG were always decent with me. I have no complaints. But at the time I told them I needed ten games in the team to get my rhythm and manage my training so I could avoid injury. Once I had that I knew I would have been able to contribute. I had come from a double-winning Chelsea side. I might not have been the player I was pre-January 2009, but I certainly had enough to play in a Liverpool team that was not troubling the title race. That chance never came.

Roy was sacked by FSG on 8 January 2011 after winning 13 of 31 games. Hard not to feel sorry for a man who had worked so hard to get a chance at one of English football's great clubs. He was replaced by the Liverpool legend Kenny Dalglish, who was also of the view that I should leave. He told me that there was the possibility of a move to Turkey. I told him I wasn't interested. I also told him what I had said from the start: that if I could manage my body and get a run of ten games in the team, I would be an asset to them. It was clear that it would never happen.

When Torres left in January, Liverpool immediately spent £35 million on Andy Carroll, a lovely lad it never worked out for at the club. Much lower profile at the time was the other striker who arrived, Luis Suárez, from Ajax. He would go on to become one of the best signings Liverpool had ever made. I was fascinated by Suárez. I never doubted he had the potential to be a great player but not everyone was convinced in the early days. In training, I saw a player who did things very differently to a lot of strikers. His style was messy in its execution, but it was so effective. There were lots of intricate touches, lots of chops and feints but it was his reaction to the unexpected movements of the ball – the ricochets, the bobbles – that made him so good. Suárez was cat-like in the swiftness of his reactions. He had a signature move where he would basically play it off a defender's shins and then react first when the ball broke loose. In that moment of chaos, he would just snare control of the ball and run away from the defender. He was as strong as a bull so once he was on the run no defender could squeeze him off the ball. The feeling from some was that he was too rash, but I could see he was getting better and better as he adapted to the English game. He was hyper-aggressive in training – he trained as he played. I would have loved to have played more with him. Off the pitch he was a friendly, cheerful soul. On it he was completely focused.

By the summer, Liverpool were telling me that I had to go and that there was no chance of me playing. At times like that you just have to remember that it is all just a game. The club is managing budgets. They want to redeploy wages. The recruitment department wants to look good to the ownership. The key thing is not to take it personally. But we both knew the problem. For the salary I was on, relative to the number of games I had played, and the perception that I could not survive physically over a long period, there was no one prepared to take me on loan, let alone sign me. I started pre-season with Kenny now in charge on a permanent basis. At first we had focused on a Premier League move but when nothing solid came through I told my agent David to test the interest in Europe and the response was immediate. Lille, Bordeaux and Marseille in France immediately said they felt they could do a deal with Liverpool on my wages. Dave said that Lille had been first and had invited me to meet them. I went to Euston that day and got on the Eurostar to see them. By the time I had got off at Lille, word was out that Liverpool were prepared to do a deal on my salary and suddenly Aston Villa and Newcastle United were interested. But I felt a sense of loyalty to Lille. They had been so decisive. I was intrigued.

In terms of how to pitch to a prospective player, I learnt a lot from Lille. They were so well prepared. The owners came in first and very quickly we mapped out a financial deal. Then Rudi Garcia, the manager, arrived at 8 p.m. Lille had won the French title the year before, and they were in the Champions League, but it had all happened quickly. They were trying to adapt to their new status. Paris Saint-Germain were spending a fortune on players and Lille did not have that kind of money – but they wanted to do something. In his excellent English, Rudi took me through the team's situation with clarity. They had two fantastic young talents: Eden Hazard and Dimitri Payet. I was to come in with experience of the Champions League to help those two adapt to a new level – and Lille had no doubt that they would. They wanted to play out from the back and, it would turn out, Mickaël Landreau, their goalkeeper, was as good with the ball at his feet as fifty per cent of the midfielders I had played with. Rudi also knew about my injury problems. He said they would manage my games and ease me in at the start. I wouldn't be expected to train every time the first team trained. There would be days when we would have to work through team shape, but the club would listen to my concerns about my body and act accordingly. After more than two years of injury, and a couple of rejections at Chelsea and Liverpool, I felt like I had found a club and a manager who understood me. It turned into one of the best seasons of my career.

Lille were in an old stadium while their new home was being built in time for Euro 2016. The Stade Lille-Métropole was a great place and so was the city. We rented an apartment with high ceilings on the Boulevard Carnot near to the Eurostar terminal. A place was found at a nursery for Ruby. On the evening we arrived, it was the start of the university term and the cobbled streets were filled with students in fancy dress. As we got out of the taxi dozens of Batmans and Spider-Mans were out drinking and enjoying themselves. It was like we had walked into a strange dream but it was great. I loved it from the start.

Rudi was a talented manager and very good at handling players. He told me that he would always speak French to the team but he would also take me aside quietly and explain the plan in English. Before the first game against Saint-Étienne, he came to my hotel room and explained he was going to start me on the bench and ease me into it. I was immediately impressed. When the moment finally came and I walked to the touchline I glanced over at the Saint-Étienne manager and thought: I recognise that bloke. It was Christophe Galtier, who has gone on to manage Nice and PSG. Back in 2011, I remembered him as the bloke I used to chat about football with at a hotel bar during a holiday a few years earlier.

'What are you doing here?' I said. 'I'm the Saint-Étienne manager,' he said, 'what are you doing here?'

I felt at home out there. I got the rhythm immediately. Towards the end I wriggled out of a few challenges, just like the old days, and squared it to Ludovic Obraniak for the third goal. It felt good. I played forty-two games that season. I would never play more again in a single season. As a thirty-year-old, and an old one at that who had been a first team player from the age of seventeen, I didn't pick up a single injury. Rudi had been a player and he knew what it was like to suffer from injuries that wouldn't go away. He laid it out like this: you play Saturday; you have Sunday off; you take it easy Monday; we train hard on Tuesday; you take Wednesday off; and Thursday is à la carte day. That meant some players would do head tennis, some would do finishing, some were in the gym. Whatever you wanted. If you wanted to come in and have a coffee and go home, that was fine, he said. Friday was tactical work. Of course, some weeks we had to adjust for midweek Champions League games, but Rudi was good to his word.

I scored nine goals that season, four in the league and five in the cups. I scored a good one against Lorient. I scored against Lyon in a televised Sunday game and ran into the crowd. From somewhere I got my hands on a Union Jack and waved that around. I was so full of the joys that I even attempted to give an interview in French. The television crews in France don't wait until the end of the game, so when I came off with ten minutes left I found them sitting next to me on the bench with the microphone under my nose. My French was so bad I would rather you didn't look for the interview on YouTube. Just let me assure you that my attempts caused great amusement among my teammates. I had tried to speak a bit of French from the start with mixed results. I had introduced myself with a line given to me by the club masseur, Cyril, which turned out to be unrepeatable in polite company. Luckily, I was not in polite company – I was in a football dressing room. The boys fell about laughing. It did the trick in breaking the ice.

I scored the first and only hat-trick of my career against Chantilly in the cup. It included an overhead kick that was so bad I felt I couldn't possibly celebrate. The goalkeeper's attempt to save it reminds me of playing with my kids in the garden when they were very little and I let them score. There were other unexpected benefits: for the first time in my adult life, I had Christmas off. My Lille teammates were a lovely bunch and I enjoyed all the new French traditions. If we won a game, everyone would stand around the table slapping it. If we lost our captain would speak to us – Rio Mavuba was one of the best captains I played with. They played 'Hey Jude' when I scored – I'm not really sure why but I loved it. It was much less formal than the English way. The France manager at the time, Laurent Blanc, would come into the changing room after games and chat to the French players. We could probably have won the league, but the club had to sell and that meant our striker Moussa Sow went to Fenerbahçe in January having got ten goals for us before Christmas. It was a blow and we finished third. The president came into the dressing room and said that he was proud of us – we had made the Champions League qualifiers and the team would get to the group stage.

When I arrived at Lille they told me again and again: we have this kid who is really good. I had watched Eden Hazard play in the Europa League the season before. He had made his Lille debut at the age of sixteen. He was only twenty years old when I arrived on loan, but Eden had already played three full seasons as a pro at Lille. The coaches told me he was very special, so I took particular interest in him in training. At first I didn't quite get it. The kid barely moved. I could see he was skilful, but I felt like perhaps I was missing something. I thought I had seen better in Damien Duff and then later Arjen Robben. But I was wrong. Eden was the best player I ever played with. About three months in, Eden scored the greatest goal I have ever seen in a training session. Someone said at the time Rudi had dropped Eden and for one of the only times in the season I played with him – and the years I watched him at Chelsea – I sensed that he was annoyed. He was such a happy chap most of the time. He was unburdened by any of the worries of the world but this day it was a different mood. I could see it in the snap of his movements and the sharpness of his acceleration. He won the ball somewhere in his own half, dribbled around four of his teammates and then launched a shot from about thirty yards out. There was a beat of silence at the training ground as we all contemplated our own inferiority. There was that realisation that this was the real Eden. That he had just been going easy on us all that time. I think someone broke the silence by applauding.

It turned out Rudi hadn't even dropped Eden, he had just told him he was being rested. But it could be easy to miss it with Eden. He trained at fifty per cent because most of the time his fifty per cent was better than everyone else's one hundred per cent. He is the closest player I have seen to Lionel Messi. Eden could turn so quickly it could feel on the pitch like he had just vaporised and reappeared heading in the opposite direction. Like Messi he had incredible strength, which some underestimated. He had an elite-level technical ability allied with great explosiveness. You could see it best close-up. Eden was impossible to stop in small-sided training games where the goal was always in range, because it was impossible to stop him finding space for the shot. Every few minutes he would get the ball, drop a shoulder, make room for the shot and lash it past the goalkeeper. He would do it again and again and again. Another interesting part was that there appeared to be no ego to him. Or at least not one I could detect – which was why it was so surprising to find him out of sorts. Win, lose or draw, he would just shrug and get on with it. The talent was extraordinary.

If Messi had played in the Premier League he would have

had a few more injuries from being kicked. It was Eden's misfortune that although he had some protection from referees it was not as much as you would get today. It was never as much as José Mourinho asked for in that famous post-match press conference when he talked about the treatment dished out to Eden. I only wish José had made the same speech about me. Eden played at a more enlightened time in the English game, but he still got kicked and that must have taken a toll by the end of his career.

The season I played with Eden was to be his last at Lille and there was not a big club in Europe who didn't want to sign him. One of the two Manchester clubs – I forget which – sent a private jet to take him to one of the Manchester derbies that season. I could see the attraction for him in both clubs and he came back really excited about the passion of the English game – and the atmosphere created by the presence of away fans in grounds. But he was also a huge fan of my old team-mate Didier Drogba so I started to talk to him about Chelsea. I advised him that he should at least have a look at my old club. I extolled the virtues of the Eurostar for a boy brought up near Brussels. I said that there was a big difference in terms of distance to living in the north-west of England to London, however close they looked on the map. I knew the Chelsea fans would love him, and I told him that. I knew the club would always challenge for trophies too. I cannot claim any credit for Eden choosing Chelsea. I don't know whether what I said resonated with him. It will have helped a great deal that at the end of the 2011–12 season the club won the Champions League in such a great final in Munich. Eden announced his choice shortly after that.

19

Mitchell Cole, 1985–2012

My brother-in-law Mitchell Cole was twenty-seven years old when he died suddenly and unexpectedly on 30 November 2012. My sister Charly, his wife, was eight months pregnant with their third child. She would give birth to Leni, their second daughter, seven days later with our mum Susan by her side – where Charly's husband should have been. For her oldest daughter Rhys and son Georgie, growing up without Mitchell has been the challenge of their lives. Charly has brought up three children – now four, with the arrival of Sadie with her new partner Ray – in exceptional circumstances. Our pride as a family at what she has been through and survived is huge. This is primarily her story, and I tell it with her permission, but it also serves as something else. What football can give you, and also what it can take away.

Mitchell was a professional footballer. He came from Islington and shared our surname. I first met him when I was a teenager having broken into West Ham's first team. Mitchell was four years my junior, a very talented teenager in the West Ham youth team and soon to be, like me, an England schoolboy international. I recognised in him the traits of kids from my part of north London. Energy, confidence, a cheekiness and those skills honed on the streets and in the cages of the neighbourhood. He walked straight up to me at Chadwell Heath and introduced himself with a certain self-belief. Within six months he was dating my little sister. Safe to say that when Charly discovered, aged seventeen, that she was pregnant with Rhys it counted as something of a surprise. There was an emergency family meeting convened at the flat at Donnington Court to discuss the development. Like all strong families we took it in our stride and pulled together.

Mitchell became part of the family from there on. But the chirpy teen that I had first met had the wind taken out of his sails. He was diagnosed with hypertrophic cardiomyopathy, a heart condition that asked serious questions as to whether he could have a professional career. More immediately it meant he was dropped by West Ham from their youth programme which was very hard for him to take. Only one year earlier, the club had witnessed the death of their former player Marc-Vivien Foé, who collapsed during a game for Cameroon, due to the same condition as Mitchell. West Ham did not want the same thing to happen on their watch and so released Mitchell who felt he had been jettisoned by them. For quite some time you could see the difference in him. Mitchell's shoulders were down. He was lost.

Football had been his life, as it was mine, and I suppose I could see something of the path not taken in the way Mitchell's life developed. That was how arbitrary it could be for any player. I might have cruised through my schoolboy years from West Ham to Lilleshall and then into the first team, but I realised I was only one injury away from a very different outcome. Mitchell had a lovely left foot and great pace. I would compare him to Stewart Downing in terms of the player he could have been – at his peak an England international and a good Premier League winger. Yet all that was taken away from Mitchell in an instant.

MITCHELL COLE, 1985-2012

By 2003 I had joined Chelsea, and I was in the England squad. My career was taking off. Meanwhile, my parents George and Susan concentrated on helping Mitchell get back on his feet. George called his old buddy Ronnie Joyce, who got Mitchell into Grays Athletic, then in the Conference South. The doctors were of the opinion that Mitchell's condition should not stop him playing football. At Grays he was just too good for the level and he was soon back in the Football League with Southend and then Northampton. He even briefly played in the Championship with Southend, but he eventually ended up at Stevenage in the Conference and became a really important player for them.

Having played at Wembley and racked up scores of games, at the age of twenty-six Mitchell found himself struggling again. He just could not cover the ground in the way he needed to, so he went for a heart scan. This time the doctor was unequivocal. Mitchell had to stop playing football. He needed to stay fit but not to the extent that he was pushing himself in the way that competitive football requires. He had the option of having a cardiac defibrillator implanted. In the US that measure is standard. The advice to Mitchell was that he did not need one and there were other factors that influenced that decision. The implanted device that was proposed to correct Mitchell's condition would have meant he could not drive. He was now the father of two children and he wanted to build a career for himself. He and my sister were living in Hertfordshire and Mitchell was working with my dad and my agent David which meant he needed to be able to get around. We all look back on that decision not to get the device fitted and wish we could change it. Mitchell was his own man. Like all of us he was just trying to make the best decisions he could for his family.

On the night in question, he was back in Islington playing five-a-side with his friends. I can remember the evening very clearly. Carly and I were back in our house in Formby on Merseyside. We had put Ruby to bed and I was thinking about Liverpool's game against Southampton the next day and whether I had a chance of playing any part in it. When I picked up the phone to my mum, I knew straight away that something terrible had happened. My immediate assumption was that it was my dad, who had already suffered one heart attack. Susan Cole is the person you would want on your side in any crisis. She has taught us all never to panic. She coped when she had three young kids and we were flat broke and Dad was in prison, and she coped now.

'Joe,' she said, 'I don't want you to come down.' Those were her first words. 'There is nothing you can do. Mitchell has collapsed and died and your brother is with Charly. Dad and me are driving down to London to be with them. Please stay where you are and play the game tomorrow.' Suddenly, our family were in a hell that many others who have lost a partner or a parent unexpectedly will recognise. Charly was a widow, pregnant, and in the morning she would have to tell her two children that their daddy had passed away. Mum's argument was that I would only get there in the early hours even if I left then. It was a sound point. But there is a part of me that will forever regret not just driving down south and hugging my sister there and then. What was it that stopped me doing that? Part of it is the ingrained routine of the footballer. I had to report to Melwood, the Liverpool training base, the following morning. I probably had no chance of playing but that was my life and even in that moment I seemed unable to break it. You learn that in these moments nothing else should matter. The Coles are, like a lot of families, at times a bit mad

279

and a bit chaotic. But we always show up for one another. I should have gone.

The next morning at Melwood, the squad list went up and I was 19th man – only required if someone from the matchday squad withdrew. It was not much more than I expected and after the meeting I took Brendan Rodgers aside and explained to him what had happened. He looked at me in utter disbelief and then I think he recognised what I needed to be told. 'Joe,' he said, 'you just have to go to your family.' Brendan and I did not have a good relationship at that point, but he is a good person.

Mitchell's story is not really my own, but I tell it because it is part of that of our family. Mitchell was closer to my brother Nicky than he was to me, but we were good friends. Nicky and I went on his stag do. I would like to think I supported his career. I love my sister and what she went through in the years that followed Mitchell's death was not easy. Charly is very much my dad's daughter in her character – good and bad. Like my dad she suffered from addiction. Charly went into rehab and she beat it. She is an open book about that, even more open than this book. She is a wonderful mother to her four children and I am very proud of Rhys, Georgie and Leni for what they have made of their lives without a dad to guide them. My parents kept Charly going in the worst times. My mum was there with her when she gave birth to Leni after Mitchell's death. It gives me great pride in what a family can do in the bleakest circumstances.

20

Big Sam:
We Don't Play like That Here

I first met Brendan Rodgers when he was coach of the Under-18s at Chelsea, a figure around the Cobham training ground different to any of the homegrown coaches I had encountered before. He was confident and knowledgeable about the game and, at lunch in the canteen, he would discuss the game with famous first team players who were not easily impressed. Yet he held their attention. Brendan could chat in English or Spanish. He was at ease in the company of the young players he coached or the senior pros on the first team pitches across the road. I liked him. I could tell that he was going places.

In the summer of 2012, I had just left Lille and the club were clear with me that they would not be able to justify taking on my whole salary for another season. I was weighing up whether to take a pay cut to sign for them permanently. My life by then was managing the problems that afflicted my body. I was slowly, but surely, coming apart at the seams. The year in France had shown what I could do with a sympathetic manager, like Rudi Garcia, who valued my qualities but acknowledged that I could not train like a 21-year-old. I just needed to find one in England.

Carly and I – with our daughter Ruby – had lived between

the apartment in Lille and another in Marylebone at the other end of the Eurostar line – a short walk from St Pancras Station. We were on holiday in Marbella that summer and into the restaurant walked Brendan, newly appointed as the Liverpool manager. He greeted me like an old friend, drew up a chair and told me that he wanted me back at Liverpool. I was taken aback. I was so certain that it was over at Liverpool that I had bought a house in Chigwell, Essex, near to the old West Ham training ground at Chadwell Heath. I felt sure we were coming back to London as a family. Yet here was Brendan, knowledgeable about my season in France, talking about playing the kind of football that valued a player of my qualities. As he departed to join his family for a meal, I turned to Carly and said: 'I guess I'm a Liverpool player again.'

I had a good pre-season. In the heat of our tour to the US it felt possible we might have a decent season, and Liverpool would do so the following year – just without me. In the summer of 2012, I looked around the team and saw some promise. There was Luis Suárez, Daniel Sturridge, Stewart Downing as well as the great Steven Gerrard, my old mate from the England teams. I was also asked by Ray Haughan to keep an eye on two teenage signings from London the club had a great deal of faith in. Ray ran the first team operations – the logistics of getting everyone where they needed to be, with the minimum of fuss, while keeping everyone happy and content. Ray was brilliant at it. You may not recognise the name, but you will have seen him in the stadium or in the background on television. He was someone who had an emotional intelligence that the most ruthless football teams need. By way of example, in my first spell at the club in 2010–11 when I was struggling with injury and form, we were away for a game in a hotel on my birthday. I would never expect anyone to make a fuss. I'm not nine years old. Ray organised a cake for me, as he did for every player, and in that moment just the thought and the care meant a lot to me. That was how he worked.

Ray asked me to look out for Raheem Sterling, then seventeen, and Jordon Ibe, sixteen, who Liverpool had signed from Queens Park Rangers and Wycombe Wanderers respectively. He felt my London background would mean I had more in common with them than others. I enjoyed chatting to them and seeing the world of football again through the eyes of a hopeful teenager, as I had once been. They were nice kids. In training I felt their ability meant they were both potential England internationals. They had skill, speed and strength, but with a crucial difference. In Raheem I could see pure hunger. It was there when he played and when he listened to Brendan. With Jordon I felt that his mind was elsewhere. Brendan might be talking but Jordon was thinking about something else. Easy to say now, with both their careers having taken the paths they did, but it is a story as old as football. Some have that focus and the competitive spirit. Others, through no fault of their own, do not.

My body was creaking, but I was playing well enough that I thought I had a chance of starting the first game of the season. Brendan seemed to have convinced the owners, Fenway Sports Group, that I was worth another try. The sort of game that he was trying to play – passing between the lines, keeping the ball, all felt very hopeful to me. I was in the team for the first competitive game, a Europa League qualifier against the Belarusian club Gomel. On my first run in behind with around twenty minutes played I felt my hamstring go. The game was over for me. I held onto the positive aspects. It was only a four-week injury. I had shown what I could do in pre-season.

Our first Premier League game of the season against West

Bromwich Albion was just sixteen days away. Two days before it, when I was working with the physio, Brendan asked me to join first team training the following day. I was delighted to be considered so important, but I was also anxious. After training on Friday, Brendan asked me if I could go on the bench the following day. Usually, it would be five or six days working up to fitness in training before you might be considered for matchday. I said: 'I've only had a few days' training. I have barely opened up yet.'

Brendan replied: 'I will only use you if I have no other option.'

'I'm not confident that my hamstring can take it.'

I will never understand why I came on at 2–0 down. Our defender Daniel Agger had been sent off. I understood that it was a terrible start for Brendan and he was under pressure, but the game had already been lost. I had eleven minutes on the pitch before the hamstring went again and I had to be substituted. I left the Hawthorns furious – furious at my situation and also at Brendan for what I regarded as needlessly bringing me on in a game we had already lost. Now the hamstring tear was much worse. It would be two months in rehab. The bigger picture had changed again. Brendan seemed to have lost almost all faith in my ability to play for Liverpool from that point on. It would not be my last game, but something had changed in my relationship with Brendan. It felt like he was not going to pursue the project of my rehabilitation.

I understand now that it was difficult for him too. Brendan was a young manager at a famous club that was not doing as well as their fans demanded and he had to manage his relationship with the American owners. He had used up some of his capital persuading them to take another chance on me and it had gone badly. But I had warned him about the delicacy of my injury. Now I could feel Brendan distancing himself from me. It was about seven weeks before I played again as a substitute and then, at the end of October, I was in the side for a League Cup game against Brendan's former club Swansea City at Anfield.

I played as a number 10 behind an eighteen-year-old German kid who Brendan had pulled out of the Under-21s. We had never played alongside one another in these roles before. I wish Samed Yeşil no ill, but he was nowhere near the level required. I remember thinking after twenty minutes: why had Brendan not just picked someone else? Anyone else. Swansea were popping the ball around. We were one goal behind at half-time and Brendan subbed me and Yeşil. We lost the game 3–1, but what came afterwards really stung me. In a press conference, Brendan said that he expected more from me and then he referenced what he said was the astronomical investment in me. He was talking about my wages.

> The best team won. It shows the size of the job here. I know how much work is required. We have a small, thin squad and when you give players opportunities and they do not take them, there are even less to choose from. You look at Joe Cole, he is a talented player the club paid an astronomical amount for and this was an opportunity for him, but we were too slow and it just wasn't what I expected from a team set up to be dynamic.

I can accept criticism for a bad performance. Even when there are mitigating factors: my injury problems, the weakened team selection, my lack of game time. But the point on the salary hurt me more than anything. Liverpool had offered me that contract. They had pursued me relentlessly in the summer of 2010. I had done everything I could to get fit. I had gone on loan when the previous manager had not wanted me at the club, and I had made a success of that loan. I had been prepared to leave again in the summer of 2012 until Brendan ushered me back into the fold. Now he was focusing on my salary – which was big, and big by the standards of Liverpool in that era – but anyone in football knows that talking money risks turning supporters against an individual player. Especially as to answer back would be to invite all sorts of fresh problems. Brendan was under pressure, which he was trying to deflect.

Even worse, the following week Brendan sent over one of his assistants to review the game with me. It put the coach, who was younger than me, in an impossible position. He was relatively inexperienced and realised that this was a sensitive subject. I was angry but I knew that it was not the fault of the assistant in question – Chris Davies, who is now a manager in his own right, at the time of writing at Birmingham City. Chris was a nice kid and he came over dutifully with his laptop to go through the collection of clips of my involvement. I tried to make it easier for him and as we started watching it became clear to us both that I was not giving the ball away or failing to press. It was simply that the team was a mess. The whole structure of the side was missing. We got to about thirty-four minutes and Chris said: 'Look, Joe, I'm embarrassed. It's obvious you're just not getting the ball.' I chewed over what Brendan had said about me. I never challenged him on it. By that stage of my career, I'd seen these things play out before and I didn't have to be told twice if I thought I was being used as a human shield by a manager who was under pressure. I accepted any hope of resurrecting my Liverpool career was over and I asked David, my agent, to look for alternatives in January.

I played six more games for Liverpool. I scored a couple of

goals. If you look at the sides I was playing in, especially a 1–0 defeat in the Europa League away to Anzhi Makhachkala, they hardly look like Liverpool teams. There are names in there that all but the most devoted Liverpool fans would struggle to remember. I played a few minutes in the league against Swansea towards the end of November, my second game in three days after scoring against Young Boys of Berne in the Europa. Three days later we were away at Spurs and Brendan wanted me to play. I had to explain that, as I had pointed out to him from the start, my games had to be managed. My hamstrings were screaming. But when I said I was struggling, I don't think Brendan believed me and there were lots of accusations about me not wanting to play. The truth was I wanted to play – I just knew I couldn't. I scored against West Ham on 9 December and the next month I was back there on loan, a West Ham player for the second time in my career.

Ahead of joining, I spoke to the man who would be my new manager, Sam Allardyce, on New Year's Day 2013. I was keen to come back to live in Essex for my family's sake and perhaps that meant that I did not listen to my instincts about the kind of team I would be playing for at West Ham.

In my first training session back at Chadwell Heath with Big Sam, almost ten years after I left for Chelsea, I took a pass from the right-back on the back foot and pinged it to the left-back with the outside of my left foot. Immediately, Sam's whistle went somewhere behind me. A gruff northern voice said: 'We don't do that here, son. When you get the ball, you spin it in behind, into the channels.' I had stepped back into the football of my childhood. Long balls into the channels for runners to chase. Percentage football. Winning the second balls. We would be doing it the way Big Sam had done it for years.

Like my first West Ham debut in January 1999, my second

in January 2013 was at Upton Park in the FA Cup third round. I got to the stadium so early the steward was still unlocking the gate. As I wandered about later it was like an episode of *Cheers*. The same faces at the bar, a little older, a little more tired, but basically just as they had been fourteen years earlier. The day itself, a 2–2 draw with one of the last great Manchester United teams, was one of the most enjoyable days of my career. I got both assists for two identical James Collins goals. The welcome from the fans was moving.

In the years that had passed since 2003, I had been back there as a Chelsea player and scored against them. I had left as a kid, albeit as the club captain, with the team in the Championship. I had won those trophies at Chelsea, super-charged by Roman Abramovich's money. In the meantime at West Ham they had been through more of the same – and now I was back. Nonetheless, they gave me so much love and it meant a lot. I don't know what many of them felt. In my head I was like an ex who had moved on and then came back into their life after a marriage to someone else they would rather not think about. Although, to continue this tortured analogy, perhaps I was not as good-looking as they remembered.

Against United we were leading 2–1 when I came off on 75 minutes. I shut my eyes and imagined I was seventeen again, with Upton Park at fever pitch and the possibility of something extraordinary. And then, as it so often did, the dream faded and died. A brilliant pass from Ryan Giggs, a goal from Robin van Persie. United, naturally, won the replay. That day I felt like life was going to be fine. I was a slave to the weaknesses in my body but I still had some games in my legs even if I was allergic to the style of football under Sam. I scored against Queens Park Rangers and Tottenham. There were a few assists. The hamstring went again. I tried to manage my way through the season.

I also had to manage my relationship with a new manager who saw the world very differently from me. Sam Allardyce, I recognised, had a genius for taking a club in the middle or lower half of the table and drilling them to achieve a certain goal. There was a ceiling to this approach but Sam did not mind. He had got West Ham promoted to the Premier League the previous season and he intended to keep them there. Central to that were his principles, chief of which was there were no risks taken in the middle third of the pitch. His theory was that if we got the ball into certain areas a certain number of times, we would score a certain number of goals. I felt that was an archaic approach when I was introduced to it at Lilleshall in the mid-1990s and now we were almost twenty years on. The English game had been through several different tactical awakenings since then, but Sam was staying with his tried and tested.

Playing on the wing in that West Ham team, my job was to wait to see if the second ball dropped from our centre forward – Andy Carroll or Carlton Cole – and then play from there. We had to get it wide, clip it into our big striker and get around him for the second ball. It was all so arbitrary. Some games I would see loads of second balls come my way, some games there were none. If I got it in a wide position, my only job was to sling the ball into the box – even if I felt there was a better option, or that our striker had no real prospect of getting there first. I was inclined to preserve possession. To wait for the right moment. But under Sam, if I didn't cross the ball as soon as I got it, I soon learnt I would be coming off. When we lost the ball we would drop into a midfield of five. If we couldn't get the press on the opposition we would concede possession and just track our runners. If the team lost possession, we all ran back. It did not suit my physical condition. Playing that wide position you have to keep checking to make runs.

Despite all this, bouts of good football did sporadically break out. But it wasn't by design. Generally speaking, and I take no pleasure in saying this, the style of football was abysmal. There was nothing I could do about that. Sam was a manager with a track record of success. I was not the player I had once been and everyone knew that. In my second season, 2013–14, we accidentally got to the semi-final of the League Cup. We lost 9–0 on aggregate to Manchester City. We lost the first leg in Manchester, 6–0. I marked Pablo Zabaleta and after about an hour I experienced something new on the pitch. During a break in play, Pablo looked at me with a genuine sorrow in his eyes. I would like to think he knew a little bit of what I had done in the past and the kind of player I had been.

'Why,' he asked, 'do you play football like this?'

I was knackered. I could barely get a word out in reply. I said between gasps: 'Pablo, I don't know.' Then we were back into our battle.

There was always pressure on Sam. The West Ham fans didn't much like what they saw but to be around him you would never know that pressure existed. I had never known a manager so adept at hiding any sense he felt pressure, if indeed he did. He had charisma and he knew how to motivate a certain type of player. He did lose his rag a few times with the players. I have no problem with that, it's something I've seen plenty of great managers do. But he never betrayed any sense of uncertainty to us as players, and there is an art to that.

During the pre-season I had with Sam, the team went to Germany. I found myself in the hotel room at our base just above where Sam and his staff were drinking every night. They were having a great time just under my window: booze, food, some tunes on. There was no air conditioning and so my window was wide open. I lay in bed listening to them and thinking about being up for breakfast at 8 a.m. Purely for my own entertainment I rang down to reception and explained that I was one of the West Ham players – I didn't say which one – and could they please tell the party outside to keep the noise down. Then I settled down to listen. This would be interesting.

'Excuse me, sir,' I heard a few minutes later; halting English, strong German accent. 'Excuse me, sir. One of the West Ham players has asked me to tell you to keep the noise down.'

There was a pause. Then Sam's reply. 'Which fookin' one?'

'I don't know, sir,' the member of staff replied.

'Well, tell 'im I'm fookin' turning the music up,' Sam said – and he did that. You just had to laugh.

West Ham had finished tenth that first season back in the Premier League. The second season was more difficult. After a game at home to Norwich in mid-February 2014 we had eleven days until our next match. Sam organised a mid-season break in Dubai. It was supposed to be warm weather training but essentially it unfolded along the lines of a stag do. It had started with me and Sam having a row. I had stayed with the squad the evening before the Norwich game at the hotel, spent the whole day there and then at the meeting ahead of the evening kick-off, my name was not even among the substitutes. I waited for the rest of my teammates to leave. 'Gaffer,' I said, 'did you need to bring me here?'

Sam turned to me: 'Fook off, you.'

By now I had bitten. 'Who you telling to eff off?' I said. 'You eff off.'

If he had said to me, 'Joe, I'm sorry, I just wanted you around the squad', I would have accepted it. But because he came at me, I went at him. The mistake was to do it in front of his staff, who really worshipped him. He couldn't lose face.

I got on the bus to the Norwich game. I didn't want to make a drama. The team had to win a game and that was more important. I turned up the next day at the airport for the trip to Dubai. By then I knew I was leaving anyway. I was happy to play some football in the sun but the lads who had been on these before with Sam said that there wouldn't be much training. On our first day we went straight out on the booze. The second day everyone was told to meet in the hotel in training kit. We were hungover and the staff and all the squad went for a walk down on the beach. I assumed we might do a run, or something to build up a sweat. We got to the end of the beach. Sam said: 'Right lads, meet you in the bar in two hours. We are just getting you in your kit, in case there are any pictures of us. Then we can at least say we did some training.'

We did two football sessions in the seven days. At least I went to the gym every day and trained. Although there was a part of me worried to let Sam know I was training. It was perhaps the only mid-season training trip where you might be disciplined for training. Many of the foreign players couldn't really understand what was going on. I have to say I did have a good time. I was out with the lads most nights. We went on a boat trip that was just another excuse to drink. Sometimes I wonder if I had my time again as a footballer, knowing what I do now, whether I would be teetotal. The other side of that is looking back at some of the best times in my life out celebrating with my teammates. There is, of course, a price to pay for all that. In a strange way, Sam's Dubai trip worked. At that time at West Ham, the football was not great, but we had a real spirit. The kind of spirit that was absent at my next club, Aston Villa.

That was probably what kept us up that season and Sam will have known that. The team bonded.

On the last night, I wanted to go to bed so much but I was determined to stay out longer than Sam who was a few tables across from me. I was drunk and tired and I had to be up early the next morning for the flight. When he finally went to bed, I felt triumphant. God knows why. 'NIGHT SAM,' I called across the bar. We hadn't spoken since the row. It was a ridiculous way for me to behave. All I can say is that perhaps the West Ham drinking culture had me in its grip at last.

My last game for West Ham the second time around was at Manchester City, another defeat, on the day in May 2014 they won the Premier League title for the second time. I played the last ten minutes which was mostly what I did when I was fit. Just six Premier League starts that season. I scored three goals in twenty Premier League games which was remarkable given the state of my body at the time. The injuries were overwhelming me. The style of football was just so far from how I wanted to play the game. At that time, I was seeing anyone who had said they had a new strategy to keep me fit. With the rips and tears that beset my muscles, my body felt like it was out of control. For some it might have seemed like an inauspicious way to go out at a club that I had once captained as a young man. Looking back, it was something of a miracle that I managed twenty-five games that season. On a good day I was still capable of scoring in the Premier League. On a bad day I could hardly get out of my car in the stadium car park.

I almost missed the team coach to the airport that day. At full-time I went straight up to the hospitality boxes to see a friend, and Liam Gallagher was there. He is the lead singer in my favourite band. I had been to see Oasis play Knebworth in 1996 as a fourteen-year-old, walking back with tens of thousands of people over the A1 motorway in the early hours to try to get a lift home. 'The squad is going to leave without you,' our team chef, Tim De'Ath, informed me. I did eventually make the West Ham coach, although I considered missing it. It would have been an interesting challenge to make my way back to London alone in my West Ham kit and a pair of sliders. Although as far as my career was concerned, without a club – and my body an unholy mess of fragile muscles and intense pain – it would have been symbolic of where I found myself aged thirty-two.

21

Time's Up, Joe

The decline and fall of a professional footballer is not a pretty sight. You don't get carried out on your shield. There is no Hollywood ending. You're either peering out from the back of the bench, hoping the manager might just ask you to warm up, or you're touring the ranks of the medical professions, from the professors of the knee to the specialists of the hip, the great and the good, the weird and the wonderful. In my case it was both.

Most of us are chasing what we know we can never have – that durable body of our past. In my more rational moments I knew mine was gone forever, but as long as there was someone out there who would tell me otherwise, I was prepared to live in denial. I saw them all: celebrity sports doctors, reiki masters, even a faith healer. Most of the time, I only needed a few minutes sitting opposite them to realise I had heard it all before. Some told me that my body was salvageable. Others contemplated my creaking hips and hamstrings like I would be best broken up and sold for parts.

At Aston Villa, who I joined in the summer of 2014, I was at my lowest. I arrived at the club for one game and my hip was so bad I struggled to get out of my car. Stranded in the players' car park, I had to lift my leg up and out of the open door. For the first time in my career, I felt insecure about my ability. The pain was so bad that I worried about competing in training sessions and there were days when I barely could. It was one of those sessions at Villa where we were going two-against-two and I heard my partner in that exercise, Charles N'Zogbia, joking with his mate Leandro Bacuna that he could not be held responsible for a goal that had been scored against us. He said that being partnered with Joe was like playing on his own. It took me back to that moment when a young John Obi Mikel had got frustrated with Andriy Shevchenko.

I told N'Zogbia myself: 'When you have played in the games I have, and won what I have won – then you can say what you want about me.' I had never uttered that kind of thing before, or since for that matter. It still makes me cringe now at the memory. In the moment I was struggling for self-esteem and, in a squad that was plummeting, I needed to assert myself. As for N'Zogbia, I don't bear any grudges. He retired early – not long after I left Villa. I hope he found his way.

I was injured almost as soon as I arrived at Villa and never really recovered. I wanted to do well for Paul Lambert, a lovely guy who took a chance on me. Roy Keane was briefly his assistant, and Roy must have known that I was just a shadow of the player I had been. He had played against me many times over my career. Roy's standards were high. Lambert had brought him in to try to teach those to the group, but they never had the spirit required. Saying that, Villa definitely had more quality than my previous club, West Ham, in the likes of Ashley Westwood, Gabby Agbonlahor, Kieran Richardson and a very young Jack Grealish. In February 2015, Lambert was sacked and Tim Sherwood took over. We beat Liverpool in the FA Cup semi-final. I came on to man-mark Steven Gerrard for the last fifteen minutes. However, the final was much too easy for Arsenal. I was on the bench. My body was so unreliable by then that I was indifferent to coming on. I had won FA Cups in the past. I felt that if anyone was to come on, then it should be one of the young lads, so he could at least say he had played in an FA Cup final.

I had tried managing the pain with anti-inflammatories but my wrecked stomach lining from all those painkillers meant that there was a limit. I went over to New York to be screened by a specialist who worked with the NBA franchise, the New York Knicks. I went to Holland where I saw chiropractors and osteopaths. I went to see a hip surgeon who told me I would need a double hip replacement before I was forty years old. He said I had the worst hips he had seen in football with the honourable exception of Bobby Zamora. I was tempted to ask how bad Bobby's were. This surgeon said I needed an operation immediately that would take me out of the game for six months. I said: 'Mate, I'm not trying to win the Ballon d'Or. I'm just trying to play another season or two in the Premier League.' I'm well past forty now and I've still got the original hips.

I went to Germany to see Dr Hans Müller-Wohlfahrt, the famous sports specialist who worked with the German national team and with Bayern Munich for many years. His office in the centre of Munich was like stepping into the stately home of a celebrated scientist of the nineteenth century. There were huge rooms with artwork on the walls. You waited for hours, occasionally glimpsing in a corridor, or through an open door, other famous people who were there for treatment. I saw Usain Bolt, Bastian Schweinsteiger, Toni Kroos. Bolt had dedicated an Olympic gold medal to Müller-Wohlfahrt. The treatment cost a lot of money. But the clinic had an internationally recognised expertise for sports injuries and particularly knee problems. I was desperate to get fit.

Müller-Wohlfahrt cut an interesting figure. He was already in his seventies then. There was a touch of flamboyance, to say the least. He had long hair. The man himself reminded me of Emmett Brown. He welcomed me like an old friend. There were pictures of him around the place, skiing and snowboarding. There were nurses in attendance. It was very different to what I had encountered thus far. He said: 'I'll have you two yards faster by Thursday.' No chance, I thought, I've got a grade two hamstring tear. They injected the affected muscle with stuff. They injected my back. They scanned me. They injected me again. There were lots of add-ons you could opt into – for an additional payment. One of his personal trainers wired me up to something and got me doing lunges. I'm sure it all worked for others. It just didn't work for me. Maybe I was too sceptical. I caught a glimpse of myself in the mirror. I thought, what am I doing here?

Through sheer perseverance, and following every lead I could, I finally found the man who could help me. Ronan McCarthy is an Irishman who trained as a physiotherapist and then travelled the world seeking different approaches to treatment. He subjected me to the most painful manipulation of my muscles I had ever endured. Going to see him was an ordeal. His hands, made superhuman by all those years of deep tissue exploration, grabbed my muscles. I had to stop myself from yelping like a trapped animal. Sometimes I could not. Ronan was counterintuitive. The first thing he said was I should not do anything in the gym. The problem, as Ronan saw it, was less the hip joint, and more the muscles around it. He said the nerves were entrapped. That was making me feel pain. It has been the complete opposite to what everyone had been saying to me. The treatment was agony. But after four weeks of sessions my hip started to improve. I had previously felt no improvement in a year. There had been times when my hip was so painful I couldn't strike the ball for weeks on end. Nowadays, my hips feel better than they did in my early thirties. Every now and again I feel the pain come and I go to see Ronan for a session. He resets it all. I call him The Muscle Whisperer. He shuts his eyes and lets his hands feel their way. It feels like he reaches into me and grabs a tendon or muscle. The pain is exquisite. The results are more than worth it.

In the summer of 2015, my hip had improved and I felt if I could manage my training I might have a better chance in my second season at Villa. I went to see Tim and told him that two training sessions a day were just not suited to my physical state. If I could tailor my training, then I knew I could be much more available to my manager than I had been in my first season at Villa. I felt as good as I had done in three years. Tim saw it differently. We were in Portugal doing double sessions. Tim put it bluntly: 'If you can't do the double session, you can't play for me.'

It was obvious to me then that I could not stay any longer, but after all those injuries at West Ham and Villa, the perception of me was that I represented too much of a risk. I felt good, but it was clear that others needed persuading. I was thirty-three years old. I just really wanted to play professional football for as long as I could. There had been some good offers from the United States but by the start of the season in August 2015, those had gone away. I was earning somewhere between £20,000 and £25,000 a week at Villa. My agent David told me, not for the first time in my career, I could not simply walk away from all that money. I even played a League Cup tie for Villa in August but otherwise I was out of Tim's plans. My third child Max was born in October of that year, around the time Tim was sacked with the team bottom of the Premier

League. There was a slim chance that the new manager might want me, but I knew that I would be free to leave. I told David to ask anyone out there if they wanted an old England international with some limits on his mobility but none on his enthusiasm.

Tony Mowbray, the manager of Coventry City called me. He said: 'Is it true you want to play in League One?'

'Tony,' I said, 'I just want to play some football.'

I liked Tony immediately. When you meet him, you recognise a man with some depth. I used to catch a glimpse of him sometimes and think he reminded me of a stoical farmer out there alone in his fields contemplating the land and the sky and the meaning of life. He certainly liked to play good football. I asked if he would mind me adding a few conditions. First, that I would train when I could and that when I couldn't no one would insist that I did. Second, I could commute from Essex. I did so with my dad George at the wheel doing what he did best: getting me places on time. Tony said I could play when I wanted. He also told me that he had some great young players. He wasn't wrong. There was James Maddison, Adam Armstrong, Ryan Kent, Jacob Murphy. Villa did a deal with Coventry and saved a bit of money and, having initially joined on loan, I then went on to my last pro contract in English football at Coventry. About £2,500 a week.

There were a couple of times where Tony called me into his office and said, 'This game is not for you.' It might be a tough away trip when he needed some young legs in midfield. I was only too happy to bow to his experience. I played twenty-two games in my last run in English football, which was something of a miracle given my body. I loved it. My debut was at Rochdale, away on a Tuesday night. I played at Crewe and Shrewsbury and Peterborough. I had never even played in the

Championship, so League One was all new to me. On the first day I came into the changing room and looked around for the bottled water. Someone pointed out that I needed to bring my own bottle in and then I needed to walk over to the tap and fill it up.

Tony liked to play football the right way. I admired his enthusiasm and I loved being around the players, especially the young lads at the start of their careers. I am pleased they have gone on to do so well. When I first arrived I got a lot of calls from friends and former teammates asking me, slightly aghast, whether I was okay. They would enquire discreetly: was I in debt? Was I desperate? No, I replied, I just loved playing football. I wanted to retire on my feet, not on the subs' bench.

We didn't quite make the play-offs. The end was coming. I was either going to retire, or maybe eke out one more season locally nearer to home lower down the leagues. But in February 2016, we got an approach from the Tampa Bay Rowdies, a famous old name from American soccer who were trying to get back into the big-time. They played in the second tier of US football, and the Rowdies had designs on a place in MLS – Major League Soccer. To do so they needed some faded old star from the European game to give them a bit of profile – and the faded old star they had in mind was me. I said to Carly it was her call. She had followed me up to Liverpool and down to France and back again. If she liked this corner of Florida, we would go as a family. If she didn't like it, we would stay in England. She flew over in February with our three little ones and just her parents to help her decide. She got off the plane in Orlando, tired and fed up. She says that she got half way down the main street of St Petersburg, Florida – St Pete to the locals, home to the Rowdies – and had already decided. She called me: 'I want to live here. It's beautiful.'

TIME'S UP, JOE

All I knew about the Rowdies was that Rodney Marsh had once played for them and that Rodney had been a favourite of my QPR-supporting grandad John Holloway, my mum's dad. They had been a team in the golden era of the 1970s when Pelé, Franz Beckenbauer, George Best and Rodney had played in the United States. Their home was a beautiful old baseball stadium in St Pete where Babe Ruth had once played. They were owned by a remarkable local businessman, Bill Edwards. He had served in Vietnam and worked as a plumber and an electrician, making his money late in life selling insurance to military veterans just like himself. He did not know football – soccer – but he knew St Pete. He owned a lot of property and he liked being the owner of the local football team. Tampa Bay had the NFL franchise, the Buccaneers, owned by the Glazers. It had the National Hockey League franchise, the Bolts and the Major League Baseball team, Tampa Bay Rays. But Tampa was twenty minutes away over a bridge. St Pete was a different world.

The second tier of US football was an unusual convergence of careers on the way up and careers on the way down. I was told by those who knew it that I should take it seriously. Strong, fit, young American college athletes. Ambitious players from Central America. Some old-timers from Europe and South America like me. You might be playing in the tropical heat of Puerto Rico one week or well below freezing in Canada the next. The Rowdies had a lush green pitch, although there were some pitches that were like concrete, others that were artificial, and one where a surging midfield run could take you up and down the remains of a baseball mound.

There was no drug testing in the league which meant that there was a fair bit of weed smoked by some of my teammates. It made me wonder about the kind of drugs that were being taken to enhance one's performance. Most of the players were in the league as a lifestyle choice. My American teammates had college degrees and were about to embark on professional careers in the real world. Others could have played MLS but liked the Florida life. In England, even in League One, everyone is hanging onto that dream of making the Premier League one day. These lads in the US were the ultimate journeymen, moving around after better pay or waiting for the moment to exit for another career. A different culture. It fascinated me.

I was paid around $850,000 a year – between £500,000 and £600,000 – which was average Championship money at the time to play in this beautiful city. As the warm weather eased the aches and pains of my body, and my performances got better, there was a part of me too that thought: maybe I should go back to England and give it another go in the Championship. Then I would look around me at the pool, the beach, my contented family, the glass of wine in my hand. This was me now as a footballer. It was a great life. It wasn't the worst way to end my career.

Training started at 7 a.m. After that it was too hot to run around. At 6 a.m. I would be walking along the beachfront to the stadium in my flip-flops. I would stop on the way for a coffee and a chat with the local cycling club whose stop-off coincided with mine. None of them had a clue who I was or wanted to ask questions about José or Sven. They were just a friendly bunch, slightly mystified as to why an Englishman would come all this way to play soccer. We were off the pitch at 8 a.m. and I would be back with Carly and the children by 10.30. We would spend the day by the pool. We had season tickets for Disney World and Universal Studios.

Travelling around America for away games, we flew on budget airlines. After years of chartered jets as a player I finally got to sit next to people on flights who were not also footballers. I got to meet many fascinating people. My favourite was a man whose job it was to dredge the water hazards of Florida's golf courses for lost balls. Clearly the main difference between doing this in Florida or, say, Essex was the small detail of the alligators. By the end of the flight, he was showing me the scars the bites had left. It was an adventure. In Puerto Rico we got a pre-match team meal from an enchilada shack. There were no posh bars or roped-off VIP areas. No five-star hotels. Sometimes after a game we ended up in a nightclub alongside a crowd of young people who were living parallel lives to us – travelling, working, studying. We weren't famous. No one knew who we were – or cared. It was wonderful.

You never knew what was coming up. We played in front of about 800 fans in Toronto and then 25,000 in Cincinnati. At one away ground I slid into a tackle and finished up just off the pitch, entangled in a giant octopus inflatable that was advertising something. The Rowdies stadium itself was simple. There was a grass bank behind one of the goals. My children would play there during games and after the final whistle they could come on the pitch.

When we lost a few games, Bill would call me and another player to his office and demand answers. He would say to me: 'Why aren't you scoring more goals?' I didn't know how to explain to him I was playing holding midfield. On one occasion, in Bill's office, he paused mid-rant and handed me and the goalkeeper Nerf guns. What had been a debate about the team's performances ended with three grown men running around his office and shooting each other from behind the furniture. I don't think Roman Abramovich ever did that.

As a family we could go to the beach to watch the sunset. We could walk everywhere. For the first time it was just the five of us. No one wanted anything from me other than my obligations as a footballer. It was blissful. It made me think that for a lot of my life, I had been giving my time to people and to things I didn't really want to. There had been people I knew asking me for favours, or for cash, and I felt I was constantly fending that off. Of course, I liked to treat people when I could. When it came to my parents, and Carly's too, and our siblings, we always want to be there, but your time and energy does get monopolised by other people. St Pete was an escape from that.

I was lucky with the British lads in the team who became good mates. Neill Collins was a big tough Scottish defender who had played at a good level all over England and Scotland including Wolverhampton Wanderers and Sheffield United. Tam Mkandawire was a talented defender who played for Hereford United, Leyton Orient and Shrewsbury Town. I organised a deal with the players' union in England, the Professional Footballers' Association, to send over a couple of coaches who oversaw us for our UEFA A and B coaching licences. In my first full season, 2017, we came third in the Eastern Conference and got to the last eight of the play-offs. The next season, the wheels started to come off for the Rowdies. Bill had not managed to get the MLS expansion place for Tampa Bay. The manager at the time, Stuart Campbell, a Scot who had played in England, seemed worried that I was after his job. Privately, Bill confided that he wanted me to take the job, but I certainly had no interest in managing the Rowdies and I told them so. I was quite happy living my last few months as a footballer. I didn't want any extra responsibility. Managing or coaching is hard, and when the time comes I will be ready. But the time was not then.

Things came to a head with Stuart when we were on a five-hour bus journey to a cup game against a Florida club even smaller than us. Stuart was not with us and the bus, which had no air conditioning, broke down. We managed to get a lift to a local casino, which happened to be owned by Bill. It was not the sort of thing one would expect on a Chelsea Champions League away trip but these are the misadventures that can happen in lower league football. We eventually got to the game in Jacksonville and lost. There was an inquest and Stuart was sacked. I told our chief executive Lee Cohen that he should give the job to Neill, and he duly did.

Neill will have an excellent management career, and to date he has managed Barnsley, Raith Rovers and, at the time of writing, Sacramento Republic back in the US. He asked me to be his assistant and while this was not how I saw my role, Neill was my friend and I wanted to help him. It was only a temporary measure while he appointed some staff. I made it a condition that I would be a player first. So began my move to the other side – and I saw football from a whole new perspective. Our star player was a talented Jamaica inter-national, Junior Flemmings. I am sure Junior would also admit he was, at times, high-maintenance. On one occasion he put in a transfer request five minutes before kick-off. He had just finished telling a stunned Neill that he'd had an offer from Colorado Rapids when the buzzer went to call the teams into the tunnel to go out for kick-off.

We were dumbfounded. Junior was central to everything we had prepared that week. Now he was telling us he wanted to leave. There is no coaching course in the world that teaches you how to deal with that. But that is the way with footballers. They will let you down. They will do selfish things. I could see from the expression on his face that Neill was about to go full Alex Ferguson. Neill loved Fergie and had that same quality of what you might describe as open and direct communication.

We managed to get the players out to play a game that they would inevitably lose. When they came back in, Junior made a bit of a show of being in a bad mood and kicked a bin over. At which point Neill chased him into the shower. I was not far behind them intending to play the role of peacemaker. Mainly because I didn't want to have to be a bystander while a naked Jamaican and a naked Scotsman had a fight. Neill bellowed at Junior: 'PICK THAT EFFING BIN UP.' I think Junior assessed his chances against Neill and didn't fancy it. He picked the bin up and went off in a sulk. Neill had won that battle, but we worried we had lost Junior's commitment.

On Monday, Neill asked me to sit in on his meeting with Junior. Mainly, I suspect, because he didn't trust himself not to go full Fergie again and come over the desk at the lad. What followed amazed me. Junior opened up a bit about his life and it ended with him and Neill hugging each other. After he left Neill and I just looked at each other, emotionally drained. I said to Neill: 'Big man, that was not the outcome I was expecting.'

This was management. A lot more complicated than playing. It wasn't the last incident. Two of our players – they all lived in the same block – had a huge fight over a girl and the police were called. When I looked at the pictures of the aftermath, it was quite gruesome. One in hospital, one in jail. We managed to resolve it but they both had to leave the club a few days before a big game. Another player moved out of his club apartment when we got rid of him and his landlord called to tell us he had left two unlicensed guns behind. I even did my first bit of recruitment. I was on a romantic weekend away with Carly in Miami and Neill called. Could I just speak to a Ghanaian lad we wanted to sign and persuade him to come to the Rowdies? I sighed, okay. He came to the hotel and I sat chatting to him about football, all the while a little concerned that Carly might have packed her bag and headed back to St Pete.

I knew my career as a professional footballer was over on 14 April 2018 in the fifth league game of the season. We got pumped 5–0 by the New York Red Bulls II. What alarmed me this time were my own limitations. In the past, whatever my physical pain, or my dodgy hips, I still had the old tricks to fall back on. The legacy of the Camden cages stood me in good stead – even in my late thirties. The opponents might be much younger, but I knew how to use their momentum against them, how to deceive and how to draw the foul. All those occasions in games when fulfilment had swept over me, when the tune would play in my head as a sign of my contentment. Suddenly, none of it was working. It was like I had been denied my super-power. I was being pressed in possession and I just didn't seem to be able to find an escape route. For the first time on a football pitch, I felt helpless. However many games you have in your legs, when that moment comes it is a shock. It is incredible just how clear the message rings in your ears. I can't remember the names of those young lads playing for the Red Bulls that day. I doubt they remember mine either. In my imagination it was as if they had been sent to tell me something. And they were telling me: time's up, Joe.

22

Love of My Life

I met Carly Zucker in the summer of 2002 and, for the first time in my life, I fell in love. Where did I meet the love of my life and the mother of my three precious children? Exactly where the captain of West Ham United should meet his future wife. On the dancefloor of Faces nightclub in Ilford, on a student night.

I appreciate you coming this far with me. I hope you have enjoyed the stories about the great characters like José and Sven and all the thrills of playing professional football. Please allow me to take you, briefly, on a different route, on the subject of getting married and having children and the joy of doing that, all against the backdrop of the weirdness of the kind of fame that football brings.

When I look back at that evening, I wonder at my sheer good fortune. I was only there because an old mate of mine from Camden was having a tough time and he needed a night out. I was, as they say, not even planning a big one. With pre-season training still a week away, I settled down for my first drink with Paul Ellis when I first spotted Carly. She was dressed all in white – and she was beautiful. She was also on a date. But I was besotted, and I am told by Ellis that I did utter the immortal line: 'One day I'm going to marry that woman.' As anyone who has seen my punditry will know, I'm capable of making a bold statement one moment and retracting it the next. This was one that I had no intention of going back on.

As the night wore on and I got a little worse for wear, I guess I behaved more like the stereotypical footballer. Not quite as obnoxious as some of my profession can be when drunk but my status had introduced me to a new reality. That being a footballer can potentially make you more interesting to women than you might be if you were not a footballer. I don't mean that in a way that might be disrespectful to any women. I am simply being disrespectful to the looks of footballers in general. Or just realistic. No one would argue that the Premier League is full of male models. Fit, conditioned athletes? Yes, certainly. But we are by no means all George Clooney. Yet in every players' bar, in every stadium, you will see wives and girlfriends who score much more highly than their footballer partners. That, as Rafael Benítez would say, is a fact.

Perhaps it was that knowledge which gave me the confidence to approach Carly, who would in any other circumstances have been out of my league. She listened patiently to what I had to say and told me politely that she wasn't interested. She did know I was the captain of West Ham. She just wasn't at that time interested in football, or me. Of course, that only made her more intriguing. I chatted to her friends. I chatted to everyone else, and later I tried again. I did finally secure a telephone number. And so, tentatively, began the romance.

Naturally, she had blown me away with her looks. I can't pretend that I expected to meet an astrophysicist in Faces nightclub, but as I got to know Carly I recognised that she was incredibly bright and I was struck by her confidence and sense of independence. I couldn't stop thinking about her. I'd had girlfriends before. The tabloid newspapers – or at least the photographers they did business with – had occasionally pursued me on holidays and nights out. But at the age of twenty, I had previously only had one relationship that'd lasted more than six months. I called Carly the next day, and the day after that, but got no response. My suggestions over text message that we go out for dinner were politely declined. My urgency was heightened by the knowledge that she was about to embark on a gap year, travelling around the world, and I felt the clock was ticking on any chance I might have to impress her. Eventually, Carly did agree to dinner. It was shortly before she was about to depart.

Carly was eighteen and heading off for a trip to Thailand and then Australia. I turned up at her parents' house in Leytonstone, in east London. Noting that there was a black cab outside I applied the old rules of social mobility learnt on the Clarence Way estate in Camden and assumed Carly must be posh. Of course, this wasn't the case, but Carly's family were a world away from life in Donnington Court. They had good jobs. Her dad Nigel was a black cab driver. Her mum Dawn worked in the NHS. Her brother and sister were then just kids but they were good at school. Maddie became a physiotherapist after graduating from Loughborough University. Jamie was at Edinburgh University and went on to work for the Department for Education.

Living in Essex was very different to my old life in Camden. Essex people are often east London people who have moved out in previous generations. Although, east London was where they saw themselves as belonging – and football was a big part of that. Not everyone who moved out to Essex had a Chigwell mansion – lots of Essex folk were ordinary hardworking types. Along with my mates, who would come to see me in Essex and stay for the nightlife, I noticed that people in Essex made a major effort when it came to their appearance. Sometimes the boys took longer to get ready for a night out than the girls. This was not the sticky floors and worn tables of pubs in Kentish Town and Somers Town. We quickly realised that we had to raise our game.

On my drive over to pick up Carly for our first date, I felt something new: nerves. I had booked the best restaurant I knew, Il Bordello, an Italian in Wapping, east London, where I could be sure I could park my black Mercedes without fear of making myself look stupid. Nevertheless, I managed to anyway. In my haste to get out and open the car door for Carly outside her parents' house, I hooked my foot in my seatbelt and fell out of the car. It would be hard to replicate if I tried but in the circumstances it was a pretty spectacular fall. Carly had to ask me if I was okay.

The date, which ended with me dropping Carly back in Leytonstone and a kiss on the cheek, must have been successful. Carly went off backpacking to Thailand for a couple of weeks and we spoke on the phone when she could. Her plan was that she would come back to Leytonstone for a couple of weeks and then she was going to Australia and South America. She had wanderlust. I wasn't certain whether she was about to head off again, or stay and make a go of our relationship.

At the end of pre-season in 2002, I came back into the West Ham team for a friendly at Roots Hall – the ground at which my career would change for the worse seven and a half years later. At this stage of my career a low-key friendly would have been an afterthought. But this was different. For reasons that I still don't understand, I had agreed to have my head shaved, save for a strip of hair on the top of the right side of my head that the barber suggested he dye red. Why did I do this? No good reason. I had been with my West Ham teammate Izzy

Iriekpen, hanging around his barber shop in east London. The barber had suggested it and after a couple of drinks I agreed. Once it was done, I was mortified but in my usual people-pleasing mode I decided that I could not just shave off the red strip. That would be too upsetting for the barber. So working on this paper-thin train of logic, I decided to play the Southend friendly with that hairstyle. In a bar in Thailand, a friend with Carly looked up at a screen and asked, 'Isn't that Joe?' Carly was polite about it but not that impressed with my new style. Within forty-eight hours of it being done I had shaved off the red strip, but the damage was done. The photographers had recorded it for posterity and the pictures are still there on the internet, which never forgets anything.

Carly had met my family shortly before then when she came to our new house in Romford, where we had moved from the council flat in Donnington Court. Carly may have felt she had walked into an episode of *EastEnders* when she came through the front door. As well as my parents there was my nan Pat, my mum's mum, who had moved in with us from her home in Lisson Grove in north London. Not that Nan ever accepted it was Lisson Grove. She always told people that she lived in St John's Wood. There was also my teenage brother and sister as well as Binny, our bulldog. On top of that it was the summer, so it was Dad's tendency in the heat to wear just his underpants around the house. Everyone popped their head out to have a look at Joe's new girlfriend. Carly took it all in her stride.

We became an item, she put her further travelling on hold to be with me, and we have been together ever since. One year later when I signed for Chelsea the club put me up in one of their hotels at Stamford Bridge and Carly spent a lot of time with me. She would come to stay in the first flat I lived in away from my parents, in Esher, Surrey, a well-heeled commuter town near the new training ground in Cobham. Even then Carly was still doing shifts at the Toby Carvery in Snaresbrook while I was playing Champions League for Chelsea. I would pick her up after work on a Sunday.

Carly found that she enjoyed watching football, but she was also determined to work herself. She also studied, first a leisure and tourism course, and then she became a personal trainer at a gym in Kensington, west London. With my parents she would watch me play all over the country when work allowed it. Carly never needed the validation that some seek in being famous – which is why she never wanted to be a public person. It was that assuredness that made her the person she is and another reason that I fell in love with her.

She worked hard. She would leave for work at the gym in Kensington before I was off to the training ground. She did long shifts that included all the jobs you would expect to do on a gym floor and got home late, but she enjoyed being with her colleagues. I found it harder at home on my own. Without her I probably spent a bit too much time in the bookies. I would play some bad golf. I would drive back to Camden to see my friends or to the gym where Ellis worked. I would burn things on my George Foreman grill trying to make dinner. Which is not to say I thought Carly should cook for me. Just that on my own there seemed to be no food item I couldn't carbonise while trying to follow George's instructions to turn it a delicious golden brown. I feel guilty that I didn't encourage Carly's career more – obsessed as I was with my own. My view was that she did not need to work if she didn't want to. I earnt good money. Really it was my own restlessness that I needed to address rather than asking Carly to fill my time away from football.

At the 2006 World Cup in Baden-Baden, the attention on

Carly went to another level. The paparazzi came to photo-graph the likes of Victoria Beckham, Cheryl Cole, as she was then Ashley's wife, and Coleen Rooney. But they also took an interest in Carly. Carly had some good nights out with the girls but she never became giddy with it. She wasn't even in Baden-Baden for the duration of the tournament – going back home for a while. Even at the World Cup, my agent David was getting calls about Carly. Would she like to front a fitness DVD – the cutting edge of mid-2000s technology? Would she put her name to a column in a magazine? No, Carly just wanted to go back to her job at the gym.

Instead, after 2006 she found herself propelled into a new world. New clients signing up for PT sessions would turn out to be journalists who wanted to ask her questions about my teammates and their wives and girlfriends. Then there were men trying to book a session who were just plain creepy. It was nothing that Carly could not handle. I found it more difficult to deal with than she did. Eventually, she had to stop doing the job that she loved and that hurt her. I don't wish to complain. As a family we have been very fortunate. In 2007, we had moved into Chelsea from Surrey for my last three years at the club so that Carly could be closer to her job, but I acknowledge now that just about everything has revolved around my career. I didn't always realise that at the time.

In the end, Carly agreed to go on the show *I'm A Celebrity . . . Get Me Out Of Here!* in 2008. As soon as she touched down in Australia she knew it was a mistake. We had discussed it and thought it might be an adventure. A chance to go and do the exploring she had put on hold six years earlier when we had got together as a couple. It was not a decision Carly took alone. I made it with her too and I misjudged what the experience would be like. She never did anything else like that again. She gave up her column in a women's magazine.

Admittedly, when we got married in June 2009 we did sell the rights to our wedding to *Hello!* magazine. I hear you ask: why would a couple seeking privacy choose to do that? We reasoned the paparazzi were going to find a way to get those pictures somehow. They were relentless. We were concerned they might even get jobs undercover as catering staff at the wedding. We wanted to protect our privacy and the privacy of our guests. By selling the rights, that side of it – the security – would be taken care of. We had originally agreed a deal with the rivals of *Hello!* magazine, *OK!* – the magazine equivalent of Spurs to *Hello!*'s Chelsea. The *OK!* deal was £1.2 million which I thought was an astonishing amount for a footballer's wedding. It was not like they were getting David Beckham. We agreed a deal but crucially did not sign a contract. Then *OK!* said it would have to renegotiate the price in the light of the financial crash of 2008. So, George Cole and I went off to see the owner of *OK!*, Richard Desmond, to tell him that was not right. I sternly asked George to please let me do the talking. I knew my dad's reputation would precede him. Desmond was a bit nervous. Still, he held his ground. The price was now half what we had agreed, he explained. I told him a deal was a deal. He told me I wouldn't get that money elsewhere. And he was right. But I said I didn't want his money and that was the end of it.

We got married at the Royal Hospital in Chelsea, and the photographers from *Hello!* were so discreet I forgot they were there. Most of my England teammates had their weddings in the glossy magazines. We were on the cusp of a social media age and the Instagram generation. These days famous people seem to take all the pictures themselves. Our reception was at the Hempel Hotel. These occasions were always stressful for my dad who felt responsible for keeping things in order. It had been the same at my twenty-first birthday party, and would be the same at my thirtieth party and my fortieth. Unusually for my dad he would never drink at any of these parties so he could react to any trouble. At the Hempel, Dad and one of his brothers had to carry out one of my cousins who had passed out with a skinful. But he proved too heavy. So they famously had to drag him by his ankles out through reception. At some point in the night our wedding cake went missing. We had done the ceremonial cutting and then it was taken away and after that we never saw it again. I suppose there is a market for everything – even second-hand wedding cakes.

As a couple, Carly and I did not want to be famous. I never wanted to be famous, I just wanted to be a footballer. The fame came as a mandatory bolt-on. I understand why people chase fame, but you feel different once you live it. It changes everything. Every human interaction is different. Everyone who recognises you knows something about you or has a view of you which you can find yourself trying to second-guess. On the other hand, you know nothing about them. It is a strange imbalance. I admire Carly for recognising that life was not for her. Some people don't work that out. They cling to fame. But it doesn't make you happy. If I could click my fingers and make my fame disappear, I would do so. I love all the memories from playing professional football, but I don't need the fame.

We discovered that Carly had briefly been pregnant and that she had miscarried when she was in the show in Australia. Carly did not feel herself when she was on the show. She had been tearful and unhappy. She had done a test beforehand which had come back negative. As is the case for many couples, that was hard news to take. But we did at least know that we could conceive. At the time I had football and the relentless nature of it, even though I was badly injured, meant that there was always something to focus on. I was lucky to have that. Again, I don't know that I ever realised the effect it had on Carly. She had not enjoyed the experience of being on television. Carly was strong enough to see it for what it was and to walk away.

I would like to say something about my three wonderful children.

Our daughter Ruby was born in March 2010. I desperately wanted a daughter. Ruby always says to me that I must have been hoping for a son first but that was not the case. Ruby was exactly the little girl that I imagined I would have. It was a long and difficult labour and when at the end Ruby's heart rate dropped, I have never felt fear like it. Our excellent doctor Jeffrey Braithwaite told me to put the scrubs on and said later that he could not believe that when he turned around five seconds later, I was changed and ready to go. All those times coming on as an impact sub at short notice had served me well. Ruby was tiny and when they put her on Carly's chest she lifted up her head, looked us both in the eye, as well as Carly's mum, Dawn, who was also there, and, satisfied with what she saw, she settled down. I cried and cried. I found the emotion in this new life and the love that I felt totally overwhelming. It just rolled through me. Carly wondered if I have some kind of abandonment issue because my own biological father never showed up. I disagree strongly. The basic truth is that I'm just a soppy bloke.

I call Ruby 'Sunshine Face', Carly calls her 'Tats', after her middle name, Tatiana. She is like me in many of her mannerisms. She is adventurous and has a good sense of humour.

Ruby has a great resilience. She can be spontaneous. She is full of life and wants to travel the world and explore different cultures – the same dream as her mum. She loves seeking out challenges and she is at her happiest when she is swimming in the ocean. I am very proud of her.

Harry's birth in October 2012 was the opposite. He was out quickly. Jeffrey remarked that this was one of the easiest births he had overseen. As I, again, cried uncontrollably, Harry calmly surveyed it all with his blue eyes – eyes that have stayed blue – before dozing off. Like me, he loves football and sport and he is a really good athlete. Unlike me, a hyperactive toddler who would sprint to nursery, Harry spent much of his first four years sitting in his buggy watching the other kids play. He seemed to be figuring it all out. Now he has turned into a great footballer and plays all the time. He also has Carly's eyes and cheekbones, and he is measured and thoughtful. He loves football and he cooks really well. He is certainly a lot more competent in the kitchen than me.

By the time Max was ready to come in October 2015, Carly had decided on a water birth and did so without any pain-killers. I had lodged my objections. I had on my mind the difficulties of Ruby's birth. I wanted to keep it simple. Don't overplay. Stick to the basics. Play the percentages. I had become the Sam Allardyce of the delivery suite. Max came out kicking and screaming. He had giant hands and feet. Carly once again stayed calm and collected. I sobbed for the third time.

We all say the spirit of my dad is in Max. He is full of life. Max is an old soul – kind and sensitive and he has a cheeky side. He loves to make people laugh. He loves animals and that's another aspect where his protective and loyal qualities come out. He is also a really talented footballer, just like his older brother.

Like many marriages we have had our ups and downs. Carly has supported me through the rise and fall of my career. She has moved with me to Merseyside, Lille, back to Merseyside, then on to Essex, Birmingham, Florida. We have moved about fifteen times and although we know how fortunate we are to have the rewards that football provides, it can be unsettling for families. The world changes in an instant – a loan, a transfer and suddenly everything has to be rethought. We had seven years at Chelsea and then a few months after Ruby was born I was on the move – seven times in eight years. Carly has been a fabulous mother to our children. We are settled now, our children established with schools and friends and a lovely home in west London. We have our challenges and we work them out. I love Carly very much. I am grateful for the kindness she has shown me, always trying to understand my problems – whether they were injuries or issues with managers. My career has become hers, too. I know a lot of footballers' marriages do not survive the hard landing of retirement, but she has been there every step of the way. Carly has given up her own freedom at times to support me and care for our children. Now I am retired from playing I want to support her in whatever she wants to do next.

23

Families like Mine

When George Cole called a family meeting in 2016, I knew something serious was afoot. The last one had been in 2003 when we convened to discuss my sister's teenage pregnancy. It's a high bar. This time when we all sat down, Dad just said: 'Well, I'm dying. Nothing I can do about it. Don't want anyone to feel sad. I love you all. Let's enjoy what I've got left.'

It was lung cancer, which in itself was not a great surprise, but the news itself? I had a moment. A flash of white light across my brain. Dad had been ill before. There had been a heart attack. No one would argue that he lived a life of moderation, but he burst through life's challenges. He always had. How else to describe a man who had grown up poor and neglected, declared a lost cause by the education system? He had survived on his wits, but his wits could not save him now.

I said: 'I am not going to Tampa.'

He said: 'You are.'

I said: 'I'm not, Dad.'

He said: 'You effin' are, you [redacted].'

It was his go-to word. He would drop it without warning or remorse. This man had saved me and my mum. I was his son. He had adopted me as his own when he had no obligation to do so and he had loved me unconditionally. He had protected me and guided me in the only way he could. Then when football had got really serious, he had found me David Geiss, my agent, and Malcolm Webber, my accountant, and told them to take care of me – and Dad's instincts being what they were, he had found two great men. I was thirty-four years old, but I was not ready for life without George Cole.

His old life was, by then, a long way behind him. There had been one last tangle with the police in 2011. Dad had an argument with my brother Nicky during a family meal at a pub near where they lived in Hertfordshire. Dad had stormed out of the pub and then driven away. Mum rang me very worried. I told her to ring the police for his own safety. As it turned out Dad just drove a short distance to a petrol station and had a nap in his car. When the police turned up there was a bit of a row. Dad was likely not in the best frame of mind and the police officers were naturally a bit annoyed by his lack of co-operation. He got arrested and the judge gave him a ban for dangerous driving and refusing to take a breath test. He also got community service at a charity shop in Stevenage. He loved it. The routine was great for him. Mum would take him his lunch every day and find him ironing the clothes donations – ironing being another one of his unlikely life skills. The boss of the charity shop was a good guy, a Leeds United fan, and so they bonded over football.

By 2016, Mum and Dad were living happily in Upminster in east London. Dad was going to turn sixty-two in July that year. We had spent a lot of time together in the months before when Dad had been my driver from Essex up to Coventry while I lay in the back trying to nurse my back and my hips through the last stage. I could see from the smoke coming past my window that, having pledged to quit smoking, Dad was still having the occasional crafty cigarette. It was something of a miracle when he switched from chocolate bars to granola bars, although I pointed out that he didn't need to eat four in one go. 'But they've got effin' nuts and seeds in them,' he would protest.

Then his cancer was discovered. The local hospital had already mapped out his treatment and Mum and Dad were quite stoic about it. I felt there was more we could do. Dad didn't want to cause a fuss, but he did want to stay alive long enough to see Nicky married to his partner Elisha, with the wedding due to take place in July. We wanted Dad to live as long as possible and for it to be comfortable for him, but he was going downhill fast.

I love the NHS. For families like mine, who had very little at first, we owed it everything. But I knew that I would spend the last pound I had to make my dad comfortable. My mum was struggling, and when I asked her if she would allow me to take charge I could see she was relieved. At this point it wasn't really me who took over, it was Carly. She called everyone she knew. She researched treatment options and eventually it was a doctor recommended by Jeffrey Braithwaite that my dad went to see. That was Justin Stebbing, a great man and a brilliant cancer specialist. Justin kept my dad alive to see Nicky get married and tie up all the loose ends of his life. Not just that, but to celebrate the end of his days with his family and his friends.

I like to think Dad was an interesting experience for Justin too. Mum said that when they first went to see him, Dad just cut through the early chat. 'Doc, how long have I got?'

Justin said that he could not pretend otherwise: Dad was a very sick man. 'Well, George, you could live another three months, or you could walk across this room now, sit down in that chair and die.'

'Well,' Dad said, 'I ain't gonna effin' well sit in that chair then.'

That broke the ice. Justin treated Dad intensively.

Dad spent most of those last few months in a hospital in St John's Wood, which was also symbolic. He was back in north London, not far from his old Camden territory, for one last time, like the elephant going to his sacred place to die. There was not a day he did not have a visitor. His sisters, Pammy and Carol; his old friends like Ronnie Joyce; my friends from Camden who had known him since childhood; Carly's dad Nigel who had become a friend; and then all of us. Many of those who have palliative care develop depression, for obvious reasons, but Dad never felt down. Nevertheless, he did manage to talk the hospital pharmacist into giving him some of his happy pills. When I went to see him that day, I have never heard the old boy talk so much nonsense.

Being in hospital so much changed all our lives. People don't have time for small talk when they are dying. I was asked by other families to speak to patients who were football fans and there were some very profound chats. All the other stuff just gets put aside and people speak directly about their emotions. We saw families leave when their father or mother had passed away and it made us think about the time that was running out for us too.

On my mind was one thing above all: I had to say something to Dad. I had to say to him what I felt about him. I didn't know how to do it. Our relationship was so close, so uncomplicated. We had not spoken about the fact that I had another biological father since that day in Hertfordshire – long ago in my childhood. That day had changed nothing for either of us, just as my dad had promised. He had been a parent to me in his actions more than in his words. He had demonstrated his love for me in the things that he had done. So, I wrote my dad a letter. I wanted to get it right, and also I didn't want to see him upset. I asked my mum to read it to him when the two of them were together on their own. Above all I wanted to tell my dad that I had never ever felt for one second that I was not his son. I never felt that I wasn't his. That I loved him. I know he wasn't perfect. Who is? He did some things he shouldn't have done but when it came to being a father to me, he was perfect. When I came in to see him after Mum had read it, we embraced. Mum said later that as she had read it, Dad had got emotional, and he didn't often show his emotions.

I came back and forth from Tampa to see him. As he spent longer on the ward we noticed that when a patient was taken up a floor, and they put the mask on, they never came back. One day, Justin told us that the end was close. He said to Dad then that it was time for him to go up a floor. That evening Mum went to sleep in Dad's room and I went to a hotel nearby. I was due back at 7 a.m., but I got a call from Mum around 5 a.m. to say Dad had gone. Knowing my dad as I do, I think he wanted to slip away without anyone there.

He did get to see Nicky married. He got to see Charly recover from her problems. He met some of his grandchildren. But he had had an enormous influence on many others too. One of my closest Camden friends is married to a lovely woman who lost her first husband to a brain aneurysm. My friend is now father to her son and while he knows he can never replace the father who has been lost, my pal says to me that he follows my dad's lead. To be a father is a wonderful thing, and it comes in many different varieties. The beauty of George Cole's and my mum's parenting is that they just kept it simple. They loved their kids. George never overthought it. I was his son and that was that.

Before he died, Dad asked me to do something for him. When Dad was much younger one of his friends who had worked for him on one of the market stalls – we will call him Eric – was convicted of a very serious crime. Dad, and three of his mates, knew that Eric was innocent. They were with Eric on the night in question, but none were ever asked to give evidence because all of them, Dad included, had criminal records. This was the late 1980s in Camden. Eric was a young black man. He was found guilty. But there was another problem too. All his life, Eric had certain challenges – he had special educational needs and since then his time institutionalised has only made it more difficult. He lives his life now but there are limitations on what he can do. The doctors treating Eric had told Dad that Eric's mental condition was so serious there was no way he could have concealed the truth of the crime had he committed it. They were just as sure as Dad that Eric was innocent. Dad had always stayed in touch with Eric. At least one phone call a week. Visits when he could. That responsibility is now mine. Some people get a house in the will. Or an antiquarian book collection. I got something very different.

As well as Eric, Dad also asked me to keep an eye on Nicky and Charly. Both of them have made so much of their lives. Nicky set a first for the Cole family: he went to university. He is a financial advisor. Charly has come through the great challenges of Mitchell's death and raised her children. I am very proud of my brother and sister, and of course, my wonderful mum Susan. From being a single mum to the life we lead now and the experiences we have been through and her ten grandchildren – it all started with her. She was just twenty-four when I was born, on her own but determined to make a life for me.

I don't think I would have fared very well with an overbearing football dad – or an overbearing football mum for that matter. The sort who shouts from the touchline and then analyses your performance on the drive home. I know many of my most successful teammates had dads who could be fierce critics. Whatever works, I guess. But I like to think of the Coles as a family blissfully unaware of where I was headed. That was our superpower. No one got hung up on it. We were just a family from a council flat in Camden and if football had never worked out for me, that would have been fine too.

24

Life After

When a football career ends, so the world begins. Like a delayed adolescence or young adulthood, or somewhere between a student gap year and a full-blown identity crisis. What was I now? I knew what I wasn't, and I knew lots of other former teammates who also weren't footballers any longer. All of us going through the same thing, much of our life dictated by our previous career. What we had won, who we had played for. Our status as former players now sealed.

First, I started doing other stuff. Physical challenges undertaken for charity because the physical was what I knew best. Plus, I wanted to experience new things. Like the hyperactive young kid I had once been, I needed to stay occupied. I climbed Mont Blanc. Or rather I scrambled up Mont Blanc behind Wayne Bridge who seemed to find the whole thing easy. I cycled from London to Amsterdam. I kayaked across the Channel with a friend for another important charity. I climbed Ben Nevis, Snowdon and Scafell Pike – the Three Peaks Challenge. I had an amateur boxing bout, getting into the ring more terrified than I had ever been in my life. Then, during the first Covid lockdown, Carly and I started a charity.

I have always tried to step outside my comfort zone. You realise that playing football gives you a chance to do that every week and also that at that point in your life you're young, strong and ambitious. The games keep coming and take on a momentum of their own. Pushed into the real world in your late thirties, you have to go looking for the opportunities.

On Mont Blanc, two hundred metres from the summit, the guide told Bridgey and me that he was duty-bound to warn us. The windspeed was reaching a level where it might be officially dangerous to continue. We rolled the dice and – like the couple of real-life action heroes we are – we went for it. Bridgey strolled up there with me behind sucking the air in. We had a quick look at the view, took a picture, gloried in the achievement and went straight back down.

I completed the Three Peaks Challenge with Carly, my niece Rhys, daughter of my sister Charly and Mitchell Cole, and my cousin Peter. We did so to raise money for the cardiomyopathy charity that treats those with the same condition as Mitchell. I felt I owed Mitchell's memory that. But most of all I owed it to Rhys who has turned into a wonderful young woman. She wanted to do something in her father's memory.

On the Channel crossing, out there in the blue, a seal popped his head up beside my kayak and looked me dead in the eye. A stroke of pure good fortune. A beautiful moment. As a former professional footballer, I do like to perform in front of a crowd. This single spectator watched me struggle onwards for a few seconds and then dipped beneath the surface again.

I boxed three two-minute rounds against a fine young opponent, Max Thraves, in my one fight experience. I loved the training at the gym in Buckhurst Hill, Essex, run by the only Chelsea fan in the area – known to everyone as 'Chelsea Noel'. I loved the mix of people there. I met City boys, local lads, duckers and divers and those just trying to put their lives back together. The boxing ring is very democratic. Once the gloves are on you can't help but bare your soul. I only wanted to fight once. I am worried about the brain trauma that many footballers have suffered heading the ball. Although never renowned for my prowess in the air, I didn't want to make anything that I might develop any worse with too many punches. In the gym, I enjoyed learning a new skill. Essentially, I came to see boxing as high-level problem solving with dire physical consequences.

In the minutes before the fight itself, I battled the temptation to walk out and get the train home. An opponent who a friend had defeated walked past me with a broken nose. I just needed the fight to start so I could stop worrying and lose myself in the focus that I had for most of the time on the football pitch. In the first two rounds, I gave Max two standing counts and then, in the third, my wandering mind and general sense of empathy started to take hold. I began to worry whether Max was okay. I would never make a fighter. But I did just sneak the win on points.

In all respects I was a beginner. It was the same in my first steps as a coach. I had completed my UEFA A Licence qualification in Tampa and we moved back from the United States to Chigwell, Essex, which is prime West Ham footballer territory. But someone at the club decided they did not want me back. It was a minor inconvenience. Instead, I had a longer commute around the M25 motorway to Cobham and the home of Chelsea's famed academy. The club's great academy director of the time, Neil Bath, invited me to discuss what I wanted to achieve. Neil has produced so many great players and then, at the end of their careers, given opportunities to so many former players. I am very grateful to him.

At Chelsea, on a part-time basis, I helped coach a great new generation that the club had developed. I am proud to have played the smallest part in their progress – even if it was little more than a few sessions and a couple of chats. These were superb young players. Reece James, Mason Mount, Conor Gallagher, Jamal Musiala and Armando Broja were all teenagers then. Much younger were Tino Livramento and Lewis Hall. I have since gone back to part-time coaching at Brentford where my old friend Stephen Torpey is now running the academy.

The television punditry came gradually and I was encouraged that people thought I was good at it. BT Sport, as it was then, now TNT Sports, offered me a few games and so I had another new skill to learn. I declined the media training. I felt that I would be more comfortable as myself, a little unpolished at times but at least the person that I recognised when I watched myself back. I had one thing in mind above all – that I did not see myself as a football guru with all the answers. I had played the game professionally for the best part of two decades and I could bring that experience to bear. I was also conscious that we are all fallible. That the game changes from the one we knew as players.

Some pundits establish themselves as educators. For others it is about the showmanship. I feel that I have a bit of both to offer. I know the game instinctively. I can see how its challenges unfold for the players and interpret the ways in which those players try to navigate it. I want to speak to the viewers in the way they would talk to each other about the game in the pub or at home. As well as all the serious bits, I hope I do see the daft things in the game that make people laugh. I would also like to think I am explaining it in simple terms to someone like my ten-year-old self. A kid eager to learn everything he could about football. I feel I am talking to the fans, not the players. As a player I would pay no heed to the pundits. Well, most of the time. Back then, I was just doing my thing. Trying to play well. Trying to stay in the team. And I would say the same to the current generation. You can safely ignore us for now. Get on with your own careers and come back to it when you're nearing the end of your time playing. I am trying hard to master the skill of talking cogently and concisely. I enjoy the way it takes me out of my comfort zone. Some games are easier to pick apart than others but at the heart of what I do is my enthusiasm for the game. I like working with my friends too – Crouchy, Rio, Ashley Cole, Carlton Cole, Bridgey. The views they have, and the memories they prompt, help my thought processes. It feels surreal that my generation are now on the other side of the looking glass, and it is we who are passing judgement.

As well as the television pundit career, I have invested in restaurants, including one with the Michelin-starred chef Tom Sellers who has become a great friend, and watching the business develop has been a real thrill.

Since I was a little boy, I have loved to roam. Even now, in our family home in Chelsea, I find it hard to settle for long and then I am out of the door and on my bike around London. During lockdown, as we all had those freedoms removed, I found it hard. To keep busy, Carly and I did what we could to raise money. We set up with friends a charity called Help Them Help Us, to generate funds for the NHS. We pulled in favours from contacts and it did well. Then post-lockdown I was introduced to the OnSide Youth Zones charity which runs youth centres in areas that have been deprived of those services.

I visited one in Dagenham to do some coaching, as a favour. Once I got there, it all came back to me. Growing up in Camden I had taken the youth clubs and the football pitches for granted but now these places are under real threat. This centre in Dagenham had it all. Not just football, but rock climbing, boxing, theatre, and arts and crafts. The kids could get food if they needed it. And, when they were in there, it meant that they were not on the streets and possibly getting into trouble. I know what it is like for single parents who have to work and worry about their children left alone on the estate. My mum was sometimes alone but she always had my dad, even if he was occasionally in prison.

Since then, I have seen what the charity can achieve. In Dagenham, I met Owen who had been in a few scrapes but had found OnSide Youth Zones and the centre. He went on to university. He also kept coming back to help out. My brother Nicky got him some work experience and Owen is now working in the City, near Liverpool Street. It reminded me of my mates and their experiences and how most people do not need much help – just a little hand up. The rest they can take care of with their own qualities. Whatever I get paid from this book will go to OnSide Youth Zones and also to the charity It's Never You, which supports the parents of children suffering from cancer. Thanks for buying it. And thanks for reading it.

As for my long-term future, I know that I want to be a manager one day. It nags away at me. Retirement has its challenges, but I am fortunate to have been able to spend so much time with my children while they are still young enough to want me around. Yet football is never far from my mind. Now I ask myself whether I could meet all the challenges a manager faces. Setting the style of play, handling the preparation, the organisation, the staff, the media, the art of managing young men in a high-pressure situation. Why would I not want to try that? I am not under any illusion that a playing career qualifies you automatically as a manager. It confers some benefits, but the challenge of coaching is immense. It requires you to excel in so many different aspects.

I will never stop playing football. I like the occasional charity game for former pros but mainly it is with my mates back in Essex. Often on a Sunday morning I will put my boots in the car and drive back to Chigwell to play with Nicky and friends. It is not a bad standard at Colebrook Royals FC and I guess I am always chasing something when I go back there. The familiarity of what I know best. The ball at my feet. The nonsense of the chat in the changing rooms. The comfort of being among friends. Although all of us can be a bit too blokey to admit it, we turn up because we know that two hours later we will feel so much better for it. Football earnt me a living and now it does great service to my sense of wellbeing and that of my friends.

I look around at them, some of whom I have known since our days in Camden as kids. Here we are, a little heavier, a bit less hair on our heads, a few more quid in our pockets. Growing up in London, the prospect of success, for a working-class boy of my generation, felt very close. You just had to walk out of the estate and into Camden Town or Primrose Hill to see those who had cracked it. But how to get there was always the question. I have no doubt that even some of the more dangerous characters I knew in those days could have had very different lives had they been given the opportunity. By now I have met enough CEOs to know that with a different school and a different context some of those from Camden, who went the wrong way, could instead have run the kind of companies that submit accounts and pay taxes.

What do we tell our children? It was where I started when I first considered writing this book and I thought about Ruby, Harry and Max, and also their children to come in the future. I have learnt that we all have an opportunity, and for some that can be less obvious than it is for others. That we should do our best, when we can, to help those around us. That life is not the same for everyone, and it can feel unfair. I suppose some might have assessed the start of my life and considered me unlucky. But I had a mum – and then a dad – who just encouraged me to see the best in life. The world is tough. There will be competition. Your success can be many different things relative to where you start: your own market stall, a place at university, a job in the City, a contract to play professional football. It doesn't have to be about football – not everything is. But how lucky I am that, for me, it always was.

Acknowledgements

To my family, my wife Carly and our three children: Ruby, Harry and Max. I hope I have said clearly enough how much I love you all. To my children, and to my grandchildren of the future, I hope these pages stand as a record of what I did in football. And explain why my school grades aren't nearly as good as yours.

To my mum Susan, with love and admiration, as ever. I am so lucky to have a mum who is so strong and so kind (and found my dad, George).

My love to the Zuckers: Nigel, Dawn, Jamie and Maddie. To my brother Nicky, and his wife Elisha, and their children Cooper, Penelope and Annabel. To my sister Charly, who has her own part of this story too, and her partner Ray, and the children: Rhys, Georgie, Leni and Sadie.

To the whole Cole clan, too many to mention, all of whom can be found far and wide (within the London Borough of Camden) and to the Hayes family further afield. Thank you for all your support.

Now to the friends. A glass raised in the direction of the Camden boys: Paul Ellis, Ossie Hasan, Jason Richardson and also to Charlie Heim, Nicky's friend, who has joined us in the Premier League. To Ronnie Joyce, who could have been my dad's twin brother, thank you for being such a loyal friend to

ACKNOWLEDGEMENTS

Dad and to our family. So too Carol McElwee. We are lucky to have you in our lives.

To my teammates, and to my managers: thank you. For the good advice and the occasional ball to my toes in front of goal. I salute you all.

Thanks to Neil Blair and Rory Scarfe at The Blair Partnership for explaining the literary world to me with excellent football analogies. Thanks to Tierney Witty, and his team at Orion Publishing, who showed such enthusiasm for this book and read it with the eye of a football obsessive. Also, to John English, who weeded out the errors. Thanks to Georgia Goodall for managing the book through to completion. Thanks to Dr Gary Armstrong, reader in sociology and criminology at City St George's, University of London, who had an unerring perspective on the Camden in which I grew up.

Heartfelt thanks to my agent during my playing career, David Geiss, and my accountant, Malcolm Webber. They looked after me and my family. I was lucky to meet them.

To my current agent, Terry Ellis: thank you for everything. Not least for taking my calls multiple times a day.

Thanks to Sam Wallace for the hours and hours of talking. It has saved me a fortune on therapy.